The Labour Party, Housing and Urban Transformation

The Labour Party, Housing and Urban Transformation

In Place of Squalor

Phil Child

BLOOMSBURY ACADEMIC
LONDON • NEW YORK • OXFORD • NEW DELHI • SYDNEY

BLOOMSBURY ACADEMIC
Bloomsbury Publishing Plc, 50 Bedford Square, London, WC1B 3DP, UK
Bloomsbury Publishing Inc, 1359 Broadway, New York, NY 10018, USA
Bloomsbury Publishing Ireland, 29 Earlsfort Terrace, Dublin 2, D02 AY28, Ireland

BLOOMSBURY, BLOOMSBURY ACADEMIC and the Diana logo
are trademarks of Bloomsbury Publishing Plc

First published in Great Britain 2024
This paperback edition published in 2026

Copyright © Phil Child, 2024

Phil Child has asserted his right under the Copyright,
Designs and Patents Act, 1988, to be identified as Author of this work.

For legal purposes the Acknowledgements on p. viii constitute an
extension of this copyright page.

Cover image © Martell Brighten / Getty Images

All rights reserved. No part of this publication may be: i) reproduced or transmitted in any form, electronic or mechanical, including photocopying, recording or by means of any information storage or retrieval system without prior permission in writing from the publishers; or ii) used or reproduced in any way for the training, development or operation of artificial intelligence (AI) technologies, including generative AI technologies. The rights holders expressly reserve this publication from the text and data mining exception as per Article 4(3) of the Digital Single Market Directive (EU) 2019/790.

Bloomsbury Publishing Plc does not have any control over, or responsibility for, any third-party websites referred to or in this book. All internet addresses given in this book were correct at the time of going to press. The author and publisher regret any inconvenience caused if addresses have changed or sites have ceased to exist, but can accept no responsibility for any such changes.

A catalogue record for this book is available from the British Library.

A catalog record for this book is available from the Library of Congress.

ISBN:	HB:	978-1-3504-2343-5
	PB:	978-1-3504-2365-7
	ePDF:	978-1-3504-2363-3
	eBook:	978-1-3504-2364-0

Typeset by Integra Software Services Pvt. Ltd.

For product safety related questions contact productsafety@bloomsbury.com.

To find out more about our authors and books visit www.bloomsbury.com
and sign up for our newsletters.

Contents

List of Illustrations	vii
Acknowledgements	viii
Introduction	1

1 Abominations of squalor: Slum clearance in Labour thought   15
   Down with the slums: 1945–64   18
   Race and 'squalor'   25
   The move to improvement: 1964–70   30

2 Down with the old, up with the new: Labour and urban planning   39
   Towns for our times: Labour and the logic of urban planning   41
   'The practical application of socialist principles': The New Towns   45
   The heights of modernity: High-density housing and urban transformation   52
   Labouring the land: Labour and the politics of land control   62
   The power of ideal environments   71

3 'An elementary social need': Reconstructing housing for the twentieth century   73
   Housing as a social service: Labour and council housing   77
   Private property or public ownership: Labour and the private landlord   88
   Castles for all: Labour and owner-occupation   105
   'To stand still is to decline': The failure of housing as a social service   113

4 Workers' cottages and tall towns: Class, community and the modern home   117
   Getting rid of class barriers? Class, affluence and modern homes   122
   Designing modern communities: Labour and the social sciences   131
   The politics of progressive design: Modern architecture and socialism   140

'Our new homes are a model to the world'	149
Afterword	151
Notes	156
Select Bibliography	199
Index	212

Illustrations

Table

1	Permanent dwellings completed in Great Britain, 1945–70	75

Figure

1	Birmingham Borough Labour Party Recruitment Leaflet, *c.* 1955	76

Acknowledgements

Eight years ago in 2016, the doctoral thesis from which this book evolved was submitted, in the shadow of a very different Labour Party. With hindsight, we can see now how infused with radical potential that moment was, particularly in the context of housing and urban policy. Writing these acknowledgements in 2024, a comparatively poorer time for Labour political thought, I am nevertheless struck by the astonishing timidity of party policy at a time in which housing is unquestionably a significant electoral issue.

Thanks are due to a number of individuals who have helped this book come about. I cannot express enough my thanks to my doctoral examiners, Lawrence Black and Richard Toye, who have been a source of great encouragement throughout the lengthy writing process. My thanks too to Andrew Thorpe, my doctoral supervisor, for his support throughout.

I am eternally grateful to the editorial team at Bloomsbury, who have been professional, responsive and ever-helpful throughout the process.

My greatest thanks of all go to Isabel Galleymore, whose kindness, patience and constant enthusiasm for the project gave me the confidence to complete it.

In the course of writing this book, I have left academia but found a fitting home in the labour movement, serving as a trade union official with a major education union. It is from that vantage point that I have sought in my own small way to bring the ideas, insights and political commitment of Labour activists to the fore in this book.

Introduction

In 1967, the Labour Party-controlled Greater London Council (GLC) produced a documentary film account of London's housing issues, intended to promote the GLC's provision of new housing since its establishment in 1965.[1] As the film opens, new housing estates were contrasted with the worsening state of the rental market and still existing slum housing. Shots of dilapidated terraces and tenements are juxtaposed with shining low-rise and high-rise flats, as well as new semi-detached houses and bungalows. The film shifts to a dank, dark slum house with an outside toilet. One young mother expresses her frustration with the slow progress of local authority efforts to remove the slums: 'Of course the council say they're going to come down, they say they're slums, but they've been coming down since I was four!'[2] Her disappointment illustrates both the difficulties posed by 'all-out' slum clearance and, on another level, the desire for a 'modern' tomorrow in the late 1960s. The film's further juxtapositions of old and new housing are a reminder that comprehending the immense changes to the post-1945 urban environment requires a mental picture of the world that was.

The GLC film, which was exhibited in a special showing at County Hall in London, provides a useful example of the state-led (both local and national) 'mission' of creating a modern, urban Britain, as well as the reality of dreadful slum housing still in existence in the late 1960s. The common depiction of a seamless shift from the shivering slums of post-war austerity to soaring tower blocks against a pop soundtrack is rather misleading. In fact, the period 1945–70 was one of intense yet incomplete urban development. Whilst London's experience of post-1945 urban development may have differed from other British cities in some respects, all could be characterised by a desire to radically reshape the urban environment in a modern form, and to do away with an unwanted built past.

Crucially, the picture represented in the GLC film also challenges the historian to embrace the cultural, political and social complexity of change in Britain's built environment over the period. The legacy of urban transformation remains contested – in terms of both what was removed through slum clearance and 'comprehensive redevelopment' programmes, as well as the modern housing estates that served as replacements. Indeed, in the GLC film, tenants of modern flat blocks captured this paradox, variously describing their high-rise homes as 'jolly ugly' and '... when you come up here, you feel like you're a princess!'[3] Another challenge is presented by the tendency for scholars to overlook the intentions of those involved in the creation of housing and new urban spaces, or at the very least dismiss their convictions as secondary. Until relatively recently, histories of urban Britain have tended to see the advance of post-war urban modernism as a question of pragmatism over ideology. This is particularly true of one of the more influential works in this field: Patrick Dunleavy, *The Politics of Mass Housing in Britain, 1945–75: A Study of Corporate Power and Professional Influence in the Welfare State* (Oxford, 1981). Dunleavy asserted that the use of high-rise modern housing was guided less by ideology, and instead by central government directives and, especially, by corrupt councillors awarding building contracts to high-rise developers. He was later challenged by Brian Finnimore in *Houses from the Factory: System Building and the Welfare State 1942–74* (London, 1989), who suggested that corruption could not be treated as an uncomplicated explanation for the rise of the modern form, and that Dunleavy had overstated the role of the building industry in driving high-rise development. Likewise, Miles Glendinning and Stefan Muthesius in *Tower Block: Modern Public Housing in England, Scotland, Wales and Northern Ireland* (New Haven, 1994) assert that Dunleavy was too easily convinced by the 'anti-flat' atmosphere at the time that he wrote his study, and responded to the charge that ideology played little part by pointing to the political convictions of local councillors responsible for commissioning housing projects. This being said, Glendinning and Muthesius did not make full use of party politics as an avenue of investigation, their account being focused on architecture rather than the future-orientated trajectories proffered by the modern moment.

This book addresses a key element in the political rationale for post-war urban transformation, considering why and how the Labour Party utilised and interacted with modernism in their approach to the urban environment in the mid-twentieth century. In the title to this book – a nod to Aneurin Bevan's 1952 socialist tract *In Place of Fear*, published on the tenth anniversary of the Beveridge Report – I suggest that we should see the ways in which those within Labour thought collectively about an imagined socialist future and how they understood modernism within that representation as a part of a drive against the 'squalor' of the past. Doing so, I offer an alternate means of understanding mid-twentieth-century urban transformation in Britain, situating intensified slum clearance and the provision of good housing as explicitly political rather than paternalistic good sense. Understanding urban transformation in this manner enhances our approach to both urban and political history in the period, through avoiding an overtly bureaucratic conception of urban change by taking political conviction rather more seriously as a historical agent. 'At this moment we are between two worlds', wrote Bevan in a section that captured the potential velocity of the modern moment, 'we have lost the propulsions of one and we have not yet gained the forward thrust of the other. There is no place to halt'.[4] Concentrating on the thinking, deliberations and actions of Labour – in government from 1945 to 1951, again from 1964 to 1970 and dominant in the local governance of several major British cities throughout the period – allow for a focused study of the reasoning by which the modern reshaping of the urban environment was incorporated within the political culture of a major political party.

With some justification, Labour has been perceived as the primary agent of post-war urban transformation, in part due to the large increase in public housing.[5] Labour-led councils in Birmingham, Glasgow, London and Manchester, amongst others, were responsible for some of the most iconic (and infamous) monuments to the modern moment.[6] Whilst this is not to deny the Conservative involvement in the process – though it is certainly the case that 1960s Conservative advocacy for urban modernism has been largely obscured historiographically – it can be (freely) said that Labour adherents tended to be greater enthusiasts for modern schemes.[7] Why was this the case? And how did this enthusiasm relate to socialist aims?

Modernism and socialism

While there were differing visions of modernity, according to the philosopher Marshall Berman, all '… sprang from a largeness of vision and imagination, and from an ardent desire to seize the day'.[8] This universalising description aptly captures the modernist need to radically alter the environment within which its proponents existed. But what was modernity, exactly? Modernism (also 'modernity' and 'the modern') is a notoriously complex term to define, but it has been primarily utilised to refer to a temporal state of ceaseless movement towards the new, of revolutionary adaption to a shifting present.

There have been several 'moments' of modernity, to the extent that it is theoretically possible to take a long view of modernity dating back to 1500 (as Berman did).[9] But Berman was clear that his experiences of living in a 'modern building' in the Bronx area of New York City substantially informed his understanding of modernity, as did witnessing the urban transformation of the Bronx in the 1950s and 1960s.[10] It is the post-war 'modern moment' that this book is concerned with, although it is important to recognise the influence of past phases of modernity. Martin Daunton and Bernhard Rieger claimed that the form of 'modernity' that they dated as existing from 1870 to 1940 was first and foremost a means of 'locating the present' – a present which, as they acknowledged, varied considerably over their eighty-year period.[11] In his investigation into understandings of modernity by early British socialists, Thomas Linehan asserted that the Edwardian period was the 'utopian-modernist "moment"', whereby the future was perceived by many socialists as an exciting realm of possibility'.[12] Linehan's study of 'socialist modernism' was one of paradoxical progress. 'Utopian socialists' in his reading believed that through harking back to the mythical classlessness of pre-industrial 'Merrie England', they could bring into existence a new form of egalitarian paradise.[13] The philosopher Bruno Latour characterised the process of modernity, in the eyes of its adherents, as 'a veritable bulldozer operation behind which the past disappeared forever' – which we might read as an allusion to slum clearance as the most visible form of this disappearance.[14] Architectural modernism 'provided the visual language of urban reconstruction and renewal' in the post-war era in John Gold's reading.[15] Whilst it is important not to impose modernism as a rigid term to describe the post-war period within which this study sits, it is necessary to recognise that it is often how people at the time understood the circumstances of change. Modernity has increasingly been situated as a limited 'moment' in history, rather than simply a movement that ran out of energy. There exists a well-established literature on the distinct architectural and planning variants of modernism, but rather less on how it also represented a distinctly political phenomenon.[16]

In contrast to modernity, socialism has had a number of relatively well-defined meanings, but the variety practised by the Labour Party has frustrated simple explanation. Socialism could mean more than one thing for Labour members, and was, as Henry Drucker claimed, not a fixed doctrine.[17] This had important consequences for Labour's approach to the urban environment, with much of party debate on housing and urban policy focused on whether what was proposed was appropriate for a socialist party.

Labour's own difficulties of defining their 'socialism' were manifest. Martin Francis has rightly observed that Labour's socialism was 'not a methodical guide to action along the lines of Marxism-Leninism'.[18] Critiquing calls from the Labour left to go back to 'socialist first principles', Anthony Crosland pointed out in *The Future of Socialism* in 1956 that 'nothing is more traditional in the history of socialist thought than the violent rejection of past doctrines'.[19] Crosland's point was that socialism, especially the Labour variety, was capable of adaptation and evolution. It had originated as both a challenge to economic exploitation and as a moral purpose, and as Jeremy Nuttall has described, neither position was solely the preserve of the party left or right. He observed that the 1950s saw the roles of the Labour left and right reversed from their 1930s thinking – with the former becoming more concerned with ethics and the latter the use of power.[20] Ross McKibbin has demonstrated that during the inter-war period, Labour had moved from an ingrained distrust of the state to the belief 'that "bigness" and centralized control were synonymous with efficiency, and that the state could manage bigness more efficiently'.[21]

Whilst not decrying the use of the state to enact socialism, Ralph Miliband famously made the case in his 1961 text *Parliamentary Socialism* that Labour had diluted its radicalism in the cause of gaining parliamentary power.[22] For Miliband, there was no alternative form of socialism to a revolutionary Marxist one, but he noted that Labour's 'ambiguity of purpose' had been discussed since its inception as a political party.[23] The question of whether Labour should first seek to take control of the 'means of production', or to prioritise an egalitarian agenda of social justice, is a pertinent one, as the dominance of these outlooks at different times shaped Labour's socialism. Ben Jackson has made the case that the egalitarian agenda was pushed to the forefront during Hugh Gaitskell's period of Labour leadership from 1955 to 1963, as the 'revisionists' of Gaitskell's circle of friends and advisors believed that removing inequalities in British society would not be solved by further nationalisation.[24] Conversely, Lawrence Black argues that the left believed by the early 1950s that socialism was less likely to occur in the short-term, asserting '… the [economic and historical] forces that socialists imagined determined the course of politics, no longer seemed to presage socialism'.[25] However, if the socialist belief in radical change is considered alongside the advance of the modern to overcome an inadequate past, in terms of housing and the urban environment, Labour had the ability to 'create' socialism. Labour dominance of major British cities throughout the post-war period, as well as two spells of national government, ensured that party activists had plenty of opportunities to put a version of socialism into practice.

Writing in the early 1960s, Crosland stated that there was a clear, socialist form of housing policy, which '[reflected] social decisions and not solely market valuations – if necessary, at some cost to economic growth'.[26]

Whilst Crosland's socialism was not always the socialism of all Labour members, there were discernible common characteristics to the socialist vision when applied to the urban environment.[27] Collective state action to build council houses and demolish slums in favour of a modern form was viewed by Labour activists as the implementation of socialism. Discussing the municipalisation – or mass local authority takeover – of slum housing in Birmingham in 1953, Councillor J. S. Meadows gave a vivid description of his slum upbringing, noting that it was a 'small back-to-back house in a block of ten with one room down and two small bathrooms'.[28] He remarked that their 'garden' was a stone yard overlooked by all the houses, water was drawn by a standpipe and all the houses were gas-lit until electricity was installed 'at the tenants' expense'.[29] Labour's housing 'mission' was set against a laissez-faire Victorian past, with municipal schemes such as that in Birmingham serving, in Meadows' words, as 'a living monument to Labour'. On this basis, this book identifies socialism in Labour terms as first and foremost a case of ensuring all had decent homes regardless of income. Policies for housing and the urban environment, in spite of the multiplicity of priorities identified by Labour actors, were, therefore, consistently identified as a means of bringing socialism into being. Whilst socialism could appear a complex and uncertain concept, the provision of good homes and better cities was a relatively stable notion in the Labour belief structure.

What was 'modern', then, in Labour terms? We might for the purposes of this book start with Latour's contention that modernism was the belief that 'everything that [did] not march in step with progress [was] archaic, irrational or conservative'.[30] Labour rhetoric asserted that 'the modern', in the form of new housing and improved cities, symbolised ceaseless social progress. 'Labour has set out to build a new Britain', proclaimed a 1948 party pamphlet, 'socially, economically, and with bricks and mortar too'.[31] It is important to separate the theoretical sense of modernity generally discussed in academic discourse from the more 'colloquial' feeling of modernity used here. What Labour activists understood as 'modern' was connected more closely with discernible visions of the future and an ideal society. In a further 1948 party publication entitled *Science and Socialism*, the science journalist and socialist writer Ritchie Calder stated that 'today, we have to accept the fact that science is the pace-maker in politics'.[32] Calder went on to claim that science and socialism were 'mutually dependent and inseparable', arguing that the Labour government needed scientific ingenuity to realise utopia.[33] This echoed Fabian thinking in the earlier part of the twentieth century, which had anticipated an 'unambiguously modernist utopia involving science, technology, modern industrial methods and rational planning'.[34] Indeed, Calder himself would later be a fervent advocate of high-rise housing.[35] For Labour, 'modern' took on a distinct form: the process by which Britain would become a modern nation in architectural, mental and social terms was part of a journey towards socialism. The exact length of the journey in question was ambiguous. Jeremy Nuttall argues that this owed something to Labour's convoluted sense of time: socialism was seen as something not only 'relatively achievable', but also 'very long term'.[36] This broadly defined mission would, at least rhetorically, culminate in the 'White Heat' of Harold Wilson's famous vision of scientific socialism, before what Raphael Samuel characterises as 'the very essence of the socialist vision' – the belief in perpetual improvement – foundered in the late 1960s.[37]

Duelling narratives

Historiographical explorations of Labour's urban practice have tended to confine themselves to the architectural or to the grand plan, without interrogating why the party was perceived as the bearer of modernism and how modernism might have become entangled with the party's political aims at a particular moment in time. This could well be symptomatic of the myriad ways in which urban history is written. For example, discussions of public housing have often been spatially focused or linked to arguments about the rise and fall of the welfare state.[38] Others, focused on working-class slum areas, have concentrated on questions of what displacement via slum clearance and building new lives on council estates might have meant for class identity or gender experience.[39] Equally, those that do take Labour and urban change as a key subject tend to focus on local case studies to draw out a range of themes – whether racism in council housing allocations or the application of national policy more broadly – with critical interrogation of the link between Labour and urban modernism remaining absent.[40] Few studies have taken a broader view of the intersection between Labour, housing and the urban, with an equally thin field of study on Conservative political strategy in terms of housing and the urban environment.[41] The one partial exception to the rule, Peter Shapely's work *The Politics of Housing: The Politics of Housing: Power, Consumers and Urban Culture* (Manchester, 2007), focuses for the most part on local politics in Manchester and Salford, and devotes remarkably little space to analysing the influence of modernism on Labour in those cities.

Until relatively recently, there had been few studies taking a critical view on post-war urban transformation as a more ambitious means of understanding social and political change in Britain. A welcome shift has been marked by an emerging historiography which seeks to do precisely this.[42] In particular, we might look to four relatively recent works emerging from a certain scholarly milieu: James Greenhalgh's *Reconstructing Modernity: Space, Power and Governance in Mid-Twentieth Century British Cities* (Manchester, 2018); Otto Saumarez Smith's *Boom Cities: Architect Planners and the Politics of Radical Urban Renewal in 1960s Britain* (Oxford, 2019); Guy Ortalano's *Thatcher's Progress: From Social Democracy to Market Liberalism through an English New Town* (Cambridge, 2019); and Sam Wetherell's *Foundations: How the Built Environment Made Twentieth-Century Britain* (Princeton, 2020).[43] Through an examination of post-war municipal planning in Hull and Manchester, Greenhalgh contends that 'quietly radical, technocratic modernism' defined the efforts of urban municipalities to take control of their cities.[44] His interest is the role of the civic plan – especially the attempts by municipal corporations to condition urban subjects through the provision of amenities – and his study does not examine the political context of urban modernism. Taking the role of architect-planners such as Graeme Shankland as a means of exploring central urban redevelopment in 1960s Britain, in *Boom Cities* Saumarez Smith focuses in detail on architectural 'high politics' in city centre schemes, and, as such, does not investigate housing or how parties such as Labour might have understood urban modernism within a particular socialist context. *Thatcher's Progress* utilises a study of Milton Keynes to rehabilitate 'social democracy' – Ortalano's description roughly following Gøsta Esping-Andersen's universalistic welfare state model – against a post-1979 narrative that it was doomed to failure.[45] The assumption by Ortalano of 'consensus' surrounding urban policy – albeit with some allusion to the politics of council housing being rather less harmonious – means that *Thatcher's Progress* does not address the particularities of party thought as related to housing and the urban environment. *Foundations* takes a similar interest in social democracy (though Wetherell favours the term 'developmental social politics') to examine how post-war elites (administrators, businesspeople, planners) plotted out the ideal use of space to maximise the collective potential of the urban subject, before the focus flipped to building ideal individualised neoliberal subjects in the later twentieth century. Wetherell sees the earlier phase of urban forms as part of a 'directed programme of modernization', though follows Ortalano in seeing his 'developmental social politics' as consensus-based and explicitly distances himself from politics as a causal explanation in urban terms.

Building upon these studies and seeking to expand our knowledge of this period still further, *In Place of Squalor* goes beyond the elite architectural and planning cultures of post-war modernism and state collectivism, placing political cultures as an overlooked but nonetheless significant factor in the post-war urban transformation of British cities. It is important to note here, too, that I use 'Britain' in a relatively broad sense. There were certain distinctions between the post-war housing histories of England and Wales on the one hand, and Scotland and Northern Ireland on the other, that Glendinning and Muthesius have effectively laid out in their study. In brief, England and Wales shared a legislative system, with all the housing acts referred to in this book implemented within England and Wales with a separate but usually near-identical Scottish act in each case. As I will go on to describe, Scotland was especially distinctive in that modern flats were received in that nation with rather less controversy, given the history of tenement dwelling in Scottish towns and cities. Housing efforts in Northern Ireland existed within an entirely separate legislative framework as well as a complex web of political-religious divisions, although the province did manage consistently high levels of housing output in the 1960s.[46] I look to party publications and literature, both local and national, as well as published sociological material to understand the ways in which socialists perceived the modern moment. Given the fluid nature of the subject at hand, I show what the party rank and file thought about the process of urban change – rather than solely the 'great men' in the halls of power – to situate the urban transformations of the post-war period as occurring in an authentically 'modern' moment and being understood as such by Labour activists. In doing so, I call upon historians to take the ideological pretensions of political actors seriously as a factor in their decision-making and to approach their subjects with a rather less cynical eye: not in an attempt to dismiss real constraints on political choices, but to understand the sincerity with which those might have held those beliefs. Without understanding the relationship between a cultural phenomenon grounded in an optimistic sense of constant progress and the imagined, socialist future of a major British political party, the modernist legacy still standing in Britain is all too easily dismissed as folly.

Housing has become one of the most fraught topics of the early twenty-first century. Since the 2007–8 global financial crisis – one catalyst for which was dubious mortgage lending practices – housing crises have evolved across the developed world and have entered the political lexicon. In the British context, the 'housing crisis' has been characterised by shortages of both affordable and social housing, high house prices relative to income and rising private rents.[47] House building hit a post-war low of 135,500 homes built in 2012–13 and a combination of increasing house prices and steeply rising private rents ensured that all major political parties went into the 2015, 2017 and 2019 general elections promising an increase in house-building, as well as various measures for dealing with the housing crisis.[48] The return of housing to the centre of political discourse was perhaps most starkly illustrated by the surprising Conservative pledges from 2017 to build a 'new generation' of social housing and to take a tough line on 'rogue landlords'.[49] During the tenure of Jeremy Corbyn as an explicitly socialist Labour leader, the party renewed its commitment to council housing and promised robust rent regulation, appealing to 'Generation Rent' – those aged between eighteen and thirty-six (or even up to forty-five in some analyses) living in private rented housing – who appeared to have turned out in key marginal constituencies for Labour in 2017, if rather less so in 2019.[50] This brief radical turn was displaced with the succession of Keir Starmer to the Labour leadership in 2020, with the party indicating an apparent sympathy to the interests of private landlords over those of tenants.[51]

As this book will go on to explore, throughout the process of urban change in the immediate post-war period there remained a dissenting perception that modern buildings were inherently worse, in both physical and psychological terms, than the older constructs they replaced. I reflect on how this perception became dominant as enthusiasm for the modern project waned, and a broad reappraisal of Victorian architecture in particular took place from the 1970s onwards. Systematically negative readings of modernism have passed into popular culture, particularly in the case of the high-rise tower block, which has become a dystopian archetype in film, television and literature.[52] The development of social problems on some housing estates has combined with popular influences to create a wide-ranging cultural narrative that modern housing is for the most part aesthetically displeasing and socially undesirable. Writing on the subject of 1950s slum clearance in a 2006 volume, Peter Hennessy encapsulated this rather unsympathetic perspective, remarking that most of the public housing built at this time '… fifty years later, lacks a single defender'.[53]

Whilst Hennessy's attitude is by no means uncommon, an assertive counter-narrative has begun to form. The broadcaster and architectural writer Jonathan Meades was an early figure to reaffirm the value of modern housing, arguing of high-rise housing in one 1994 documentary that '… the ineptitude of so many of the system built blocks of those years [the sixties] somehow engendered the idea that it was *height itself* that was to blame [my emphasis]'.[54] Writers such as Owen Hatherley, John Grindrod and Lynsey Hanley have been joined by the geographer Danny Dorling in the muscular assertion that while modernist architecture was not always effective, there was nevertheless immense social merit to it.[55]

These duelling narratives present a historical obstacle, not least in that both are informed by a partially imagined past. The dominant perception – that the urban transformation of post-war Britain was a misguided if not malicious imposition of cruel slab blocks and other travesties on a captive population – assiduously overlooks both the parlous state of British cities in the period and the fact that new housing and redevelopment were supported by a large proportion of the citizenry, at least at first. Likewise, the opposing judgement – that, as Dorling puts it, the modernist output was expressive of the collective action of the period, but 'we so quickly forget those far more equitable times, as some of us return to older, outdated moralities' – is too sanguine a reading of the period.[56] In this regard, there is a danger of history slipping into polemic should the historian not be critically engaged with these opposing viewpoints. Moreover, as has been suggested, the focus on architecture may obscure the reasoning of those involved in the modern moment – for Labour, it was not always the precise architecture that mattered in urban transformation, but the spirit of modern, radical change.

In light of this debate, it is an auspicious moment to delve into the post-war 'politics of housing': the last great phase of far-ranging urban transformation. Labour were far from the sole actors in this process, but the contemporary appraisal of their contribution is distinct to that of the Conservative Party. The discordant nature of the discussion on what the urban transformation of Britain in the post-war period was – as well as how and why it occurred – indicates that a closer investigation of the motives and objectives of those involved in the political process of transformation is required. How did Labour understand urban modernism?

The forward march of Labour: Considering the politics of urban transformation

In Place of Squalor re-examines and complicates the 'modern moment' in post-war British history. It advances the claim that understanding the political appreciation of modernity is integral to a complete comprehension of urban change in this period. It challenges the dominant notion in urban history that the creation and re-creation of the urban environment is solely the outcome of rational, pragmatic decision-making or of bureaucratic incompetence. Whilst these elements are undoubtedly always there, ideology and sheer conviction do play a part, and this should not be overlooked. Labour's reading of the modern period within which they operated could be as complex and as contradictory as its own socialism.

A vista of highly modern, bright houses and low-rise flats was contrasted with old mining cottages in a 1962 film for the National Coal Board's cine-magazine *Mining Review*, showcasing the New Town of Peterlee in County Durham, built to house mining families. As the narrator comments, 'the master of painting at Durham University was appointed to collaborate with two architects of the corporation's staff. Together, they have produced homes of the future'.[57] It might be said that this was precisely the future that Labour hoped for, but Peterlee was far from typical. Built to house only 30,000 residents, Peterlee had been requested by the local miners and a development corporation was formed in 1948. Although the architect Berthold Lubetkin had been involved in the initial planning of the New Town, Lubetkin's ideas for high-rise flats were scrapped due to the geological instability of the mining area.[58] Whilst the result was generally well appreciated, in a 1979 BBC documentary on New Towns, the writer Colin Ward remarked that Peterlee was so bound up with the coal industry that unemployment had become rife as mining declined.[59]

The story of Peterlee encapsulates the complexity of the modern moment. Although it bears notice that New Towns, as much as high-rise blocks, only ever represented a limited proportion of the total amount of housing built after 1945, both have been given an iconic (if not infamous) status as the physical representation of urban modernism. The film of Peterlee demonstrates a point in time in which Labour in particular believed the modern was within reach, and were ambitious in their plans for Britain's urban environment. In the chapters that follow, I place this urban vision centre stage as a political phenomenon (as much as it was cultural or architectural) in order to understand further the formulation and consequences of urban change in Britain between 1945 and 1970. In doing so, I challenge the various notions that the Labour contribution to urban modernism was either wrong-headed, naïve or motivated by cynical electoralism, showing instead that a common belief that socialism could be quite literally constructed through the urban environment propelled party activists.

My inquiry into this imagined future spans four chapters, each analysing a different part of this vision as a means of demonstrating the extent to which urban modernism and socialism merged in Labour's imaginary. Chapter 1 considers the place of urban planning in Labour politics, drawing upon the influence of transportation and the importance of urban land in the development of Labour schemes. Chapter 2 goes beyond the plan to the bulldozer, discussing how the impact of ideas about urban squalor in 'Victorian' cities supported a turn to a thorough pattern of slum clearance, seeking to remove 'old' cities in favour of the 'modern'. Chapter 3 examines how Labour sought to re-imagine the housing system, determining what place public housing, owner-occupation and the private rented sector – including the council tenant, the owner-occupier, the private tenant and the landlord – had in the urban future. Chapter 4 assesses the fraught question of class – including the extent to which Labour actors viewed its housing plans as classless or for the working classes – as well as the importance of the murky concept of 'community' in party thought, and the aesthetic promise of modern housing. I close the book with an afterword considering what Labour's relationship with urban modernism reveals about the ways in which urban history is written and understood, as well as how thinking more deeply about Labour's rationale for reshaping the urban environment might influence future study. The four chapters make the claim that the bricks, mortar and bulldozers of urban transformation in post-war Britain represented for Labour a political vision of the future.

'[W]e think of the new housing estates, the new suburbs and the new towns as characteristic of the new Britain', wrote Raymond Williams in 1961.[60] This aspect of the 'new Britain' that Williams described – the urban built environment – is the part most visible in the present day, and perhaps the most fraught legacy. But less thought has been given to the reasoning behind the new housing estates, new suburbs and new towns of which Williams wrote. Indeed, as he stated, '… these communities were not planned by the people who live in them, but by others with their own versions of what these people needed and what a community is'.[61] Whilst these planners have often been thought of as malign, the political reasoning that ran parallel to this transformation has been far less considered. The purpose of *In Place of Squalor* is to challenge the notion that understanding the modern moment in twentieth-century Britain begins and ends with the tower block as an unwelcome imposition. A clear awareness of how Labour's political aims for the urban environment intersected with the modern urge to remove an unwanted past enhances our appreciation for the role of ideology in policy formation, as well as inviting us to consider in depth the problems that such radical solutions were intended to solve and the contemporary resonances of these urban topics. Without this, the modern moment will continue to appear as little more than a brutal misjudgement.

1

Abominations of squalor

Slum clearance in Labour thought

In a pamphlet on post-war housing published in 1945, the socialist journalist Douglas Brown portrayed the working-class districts of Glasgow, Leeds and South Wales that he had visited as panoramas of 'long dreary terraces of uniform cottages, soon blackened with grime, now decrepit, insanitary and overcrowded'.[1] Born in an 'ill-designed' Welsh mining cottage himself, Brown aimed to build support for a post-war effort to sweep away the 'dark places of the cities'. One such dark place was a Glasgow tenement flat in the Gorbals, home to a young woman and her eight children, with the mother compelled to sleep in the same bed as her youngest child to protect her from the depredations of rats.[2] Brown went on: 'There are hundreds of people in Glasgow who are paying anything between 25 [shillings] to 50 [shillings] a month for accommodation like this.'[3] When one considers that the Industrial Revolution had the greatest effect on the British urban landscape in the nineteenth century, through the mass migration of country workers to urban areas and the creation of often-inadequate housing to shelter those workers, then removing the slums had the same radical effect for the twentieth century. Slum clearance was, for those on the left, a fundamentally modern act and a phenomenon closely tied to the age of modernity. As the political scientist Henry Drucker put it, Labour was and is 'a party which exists, as a result of certain remembered past actions, to do a particular job now and in the future'.[4] The 'particular job' in housing terms for much of the twentieth century was to eliminate 'squalor': the preferred term for poor housing conditions, popularised by Beveridge as one of the 'Five Giant Evils' to be solved by the welfare state. Mass slum clearance was a global process, occurring as part of urban renewal strategies in all major cities worldwide.[5] Yet the mass state-sponsored removal of slum housing was by no means a teleological progression. Slum clearance can be divided chronologically into several phases, all of which represented different priorities and motives on the part of those ordering demolition. It should be remembered, too, that slum clearance directly addressed one of the preeminent political issues of the day: the failure of property owners – and private landlords especially – to deal with rundown houses in a satisfactory fashion amidst housing shortages. Housing was absolutely central to post-war British politics, and for Labour, it was the route to the socialist cities of the future.

Industrial slums had been a key concern for Labour throughout the history of the party. The First World War laid bare the astonishingly poor housing conditions suffered by many in working-class neighbourhoods of Britain, and the economic crash of the inter-war years gave rise to several polemics with a focus on housing, most notably George Orwell's account of the 'labyrinths of little brick houses, festering in planless chaos' that characterised much of the industrial North of England.[6] The 'jungles of tiny houses' aroused the anger of writers such as Walter Greenwood, who wrote bitterly of the indignity of '[paying] preposterous rents for the privilege of calling … grimy houses "home"' in his bestselling 1933 novel *Love on the Dole*, set in Salford.[7] Greenwood, who went on to become a Labour councillor, was fairly typical of Labour representatives hailing from such areas in his lack of sentimentality, seeing the replacement of 'grimy houses' by new (ideally council-owned) houses and flats as a mark of social justice. His point about private renting, again a focus of social commentators, was closely linked to the logic of slum clearance in Labour thought and is central to the third chapter of this book, which examines the housing system in detail. Salford went on to clear around a quarter of its 1955 housing stock between 1955 and 1985.[8] While there were dissenting voices, it was not until the end of the 1960s and the 1970s especially that a powerful left critique of slum clearance took hold, primarily focused around notions of community decline, which will be explored more in a later chapter. It should be noted, however, that the mid-twentieth-century notion of a slum was separate from its Victorian counterpart. Rather than referring solely to the unsanitary, cramped rookeries of the nineteenth century, the twentieth-century use of the term comprised any dwelling considered 'unfit for human habitation'.[9] J. B. Priestley's 'industrial England' informed the slum description, but what constituted a slum evolved over time. Setting aside the effects of wartime bomb damage, the worst housing stock in 1945 in absolute terms was in the 'industrial' Britain that mostly voted Labour: largely in the industrial North and Midlands of England, Central Belt of Scotland and mining areas of South Wales, but also in London and working-class areas of southern English cities. Brown's account described at the beginning of this chapter was far from exceptional. Even in Bristol, an area of relative prosperity during the 1930s, a survey estimated that 11,000 families in the survey area were impoverished, with a further 21,000 families 'whilst not in poverty, have a hard struggle, and whose lot is far from comfortable'.[10] In the view of those within Labour, the hard struggle of the working classes was worsened by decrepit, old housing, and it was this 'squalor' that the party sought to sweep away.

The legislation of slum clearance expresses the ideas and assumptions that governed the political thought surrounding urban renewal and notions of squalor. Although Labour were not responsible for every Housing Act, the elected representatives of the party nevertheless carried out at a local level the measures detailed, and upheld elements of previous statutes that suited the party agenda. Slum clearance procedures were at their core intended to remove housing 'unfit for human habitation' from the housing stock. The ambiguity of this term – as well as the term 'slum' itself – was indicative of a clinical and paternalistic attitude to housing issues, not unduly concerned with consulting the inhabitants of slum housing. Slum clearance originated in the Victorian era, but the first national slum clearance campaign began with the 1930 Housing Act of the 1929–31 Labour government, which allowed local authorities to acquire clearance areas of slum property and was better known as the Greenwood Act after the Labour housing minister responsible for bringing it to parliament. It was supplemented by the 1935 Housing Act, introduced by the Conservative-led National Government and focused on reducing overcrowding.[11] In the nineteenth and early twentieth centuries it was only the wealthy and influential districts of cities that could ensure properly paved and clean streets, parkland and observance of building or planning regulations.[12] Legislation like the Greenwood Act went some way towards changing this, as local authorities were required to produce estimates of slum housing and five-year plans for clearance.[13] However, the link between slum clearance and public housing of the 1935 Act – which had limited house building subsidies to homes constructed for persons cleared – made Labour initially wary of over-emphasising slum clearance.[14] Extensive destruction from bombing, damage and limited maintenance during the Second World War increased housing need still further. After 1945, the Attlee government prioritised house building, though Labour were clear that removing the slums remained a key aim. The issue was that the party did not wish for public house building to only proceed under the special conditions of slum clearance. In a time of limited finance, dealing with the housing shortage took precedence.

'The physical pattern of our cities was given to them by the early nineteenth century and all are at least 100 years old', stated the town planner Graeme

Shankland in a 1952 speech at Battersea Town Hall to the National Tuberculosis Conference, organised by the Socialist Medical Association. In the ensuing discussion, Dr Lewis of London Trades Council and the Medical Practitioners Union pointed out that while modern medicine could cure tuberculosis in patients, they had to return to the same unsanitary housing conditions that caused the disease, '[sending] them back to the sanatorium'.[15] Inadequate, old houses were seen by those within Labour to prevent the passage of progress, trapping much of the working-class population within a long nineteenth century. As the Labour MP Frank Allaun put it in a 1964 *Labour Woman* piece, there was 'not much of the press-button age' for those continuing to use 'zinc slipper baths' to cleanse themselves.[16] While Labour thinking would evolve on the subject over the post-war decades, slum clearance was inextricably linked to their understanding of modernity. Removing slum housing symbolised socialism in action.

Down with the slums: 1945–64

In March 1945, Birmingham Labour councillors refused to countenance repairs of 'back-to-back' houses, stating that it was wrong to ask returning servicemen to live in slum housing.[17] The back-to-back was quite literally a row of houses backed on to each other, sometimes with a court behind, or completely surrounded by streets.[18] Alongside the tenement block of flats, back-to-backs were considered the worst-built elements of the Industrial Revolution by reformers, the 'squalor' of the Beveridge Report incarnate.[19] Municipalisation would later be at the forefront of Labour attempts to manage the slums that were not scheduled to be demolished. In the absence of this as a key policy in the 1940s, Labour members were unwilling to pay slum landlords for the upkeep of their property. Yet the alternative, of letting tenants languish in squalid housing, was little better. The Labour MP Tom Braddock suggested in 1946 requisitioning hotels and boarding houses as temporary accommodation for slum dwellers whilst decrepit property was cleared away.[20] Indeed, housing shortages in that year had prompted a wave of squatting in abandoned army camps and unoccupied houses across the country.[21] Douglas Brown saw this as a measure of 'common justice', reporting a number of unused homes in Marylebone.[22] Given Orwell's infamous account of the foul conditions of inter-war boarding houses in *The Road to Wigan Pier*, it is hard to see how slum dwellers might have been persuaded that this would be acceptable.

The 1946 Housing Act directed resources towards house building and the vast task of reconstruction. Slum clearance and redevelopment became a longer-term goal, to be carried out when the housing shortage had been overcome. Labour's 1948 *Guide to Post-War Housing Policy* noted that over 1 million houses had been destroyed or damaged just through the V1 and V2 rocket campaign in the latter stages of the war, with some of those houses actually having been repaired before being destroyed.[23] Bevan was focused on providing public homes beyond the previous 'sanitary' policy and secured subsidies from the Treasury for this purpose, rather than slum clearance.[24] Overall, slum clearance was a haltingly slow process under the Attlee government.[25] Jim Yelling has argued that the 1949 Housing Act introduced a 'division of labour', in which local authorities would deal with redevelopment, but those private houses outside of redevelopment areas would be voluntarily improved by grants made out to private owners.[26] 'Improvement grants' were designed to be used on properties 'furthest removed' from those slated for slum clearance: structurally sound houses that could be made habitable for at least thirty years.[27] In spite of socialist visions of modern British cities unblemished by social squalor, inadequate housing had to be temporarily maintained.

The 1950s saw a clear change in government policy towards slum clearance. Prior to losing office in 1951, Labour had come under increasing attack from the Conservatives regarding their inaction on dealing with the slums. Labour responded by arguing that the 'slum problem' was a Conservative creation. In one January 1951 briefing, the party suggested that slum dwellers had been 'ignored by the Tories and Liberals. Between them these two parties had held power for all but two of the previous hundred or so years. They allowed the slums to grow. They did little to improve conditions'.[28] Though Labour were defeated at the general election of October that year, some of these points stuck as the Conservatives did not depart from house building as a priority. Nevertheless, Conservative policy did not directly address the 10 million households in England and Wales that by 1951 were either overcrowded, lacking basic amenities or living in conditions unfit for human habitation.[29]

Harold Macmillan, appointed Minister of Housing in the new Churchillian administration, pledged in his 'Grand Design for Housing' to build 300,000 houses annually by 1954.[30] As Labour had argued, Macmillan sought a return to the inter-war 'sanitary' policy, with subsidies for council house building limited to rehousing those cleared from the slums.[31] This was not an immediate development and Peter Weiler suggests the controversy of reducing housing subsidies meant a return to the 'sanitary' policy for slum clearance was not possible until well after the Conservative victory.[32] Though there is a case for political salience, this analysis downplays the impetus for action against the slums in the early 1950s. The Yelling contention that Macmillan intended to turn slum clearance into a separate concern from council house building entirely is more compelling when the scale of the slum issue is considered.[33] Clearing the slums was not solely a convenient excuse to pare back public housing: it was an end in itself. In the pages of the January 1954 edition of *Socialist Commentary*, the industrial relations academic Arthur Marsh made exactly this point, suggesting that '... what is required is a long-term policy for replacing houses when they wear out, like any other form of capital equipment'.[34] Significantly, in an urban modernist era, this notion of housing having a limited lifespan was broadly accepted across the political spectrum. Where Labour thinking differed from their political opponents, as Marsh went on to outline in a subsequent piece, was that housing should ultimately be a universal social service and a 'ceaseless concern' beyond 'special evils' such as slum housing.

The introduction of the 1954 Housing Repairs and Rents Act marked the beginnings of a renewed campaign of slum clearance. Going beyond previous legislation, the Act attempted to provide a universal standard of 'fitness' for slum housing.[35] Specifically, the 1954 Act listed key criteria which a property would have to meet in order to be declared 'fit' for human habitation, including the ability to be repaired; stability; freedom from damp; natural lighting; ventilation; water supply; drainage and an inside WC; facilities for storage, preparation and cooking of food, as well as for the disposal of waste water.[36] Back-to-back housing was uniformly declared 'unfit for human habitation'. This attempt to create a normative definition of 'slum' would later come in for criticism. In his 1970 study of the attempted clearance of the distinctive one-storey 'Sunderland Cottages' in the Millfield area of the city, the sociologist Norman Dennis argued the '*degree* of dampness and the extent of disrepair and so forth – the standards of the items – are matters with which the Act does not deal'.[37] Dennis took an exceptionally active role in his subject matter, chairing the Millfield Residents Association as well as being elected as a Labour councillor for the ward as part of the successful campaign to halt the slum clearance effort. In his 1979 survey of public housing policy, the academic Stephen Merrett asserted that 'the standard of fitness ... necessarily reflected both the social values of the time and the resources likely to be allocated to it'.[38] An October 1956 *Labour's Northern Voice* piece by the Manchester Councillor Edmund Dell reflected this, drolly asserting that 'some houses are built as slums, some become slums and some have slumdom thrust upon them'.[39] Dell suggested that the 'weary battle' of local authorities to force landlords to improve their properties was liable to continue, indicating that this would be the direction of travel for most Labour-run councils.

While Labour-controlled councils were bound by the Housing Acts, the notion of leaving near-slum houses standing was anathema to party activists committed to sweeping clear the detritus of the Industrial Revolution. In a 1954 briefing, Labour warned that 'dilapidated houses' could be made fit at an undefined 'reasonable expense' by the landlord, which the authors argued would be exploited by 'reactionary local [authorities]' on behalf of private landlords.[40] Dismay at the prospect of private landlords making their properties just about habitable signified both the seriousness with which Labour took reshaping the urban environment in a modern fashion and a fundamental issue with this aim. On the one hand, there were far too many slum houses to condemn all outright, whilst on the other, it would be near-impossible to simultaneously build houses in large quantities and clear away the slums. 'It would take at least twenty-five years of all-out effort by the building industry', claimed Michael Young in 1955, to replace the seven million unfit houses in existence.[41] Young contended that repairing 'structurally sound' slum properties would be a greater social good than slum clearance.[42] He was strident on this point, having previously suggested in 1954 that 'we have a strange attitude to old houses'. Young asserted that richer people (such as, he wryly observed, architects and town planners) seemed to prefer older houses aesthetically, but when it came to poorer people 'the sooner they are replaced by towering flats the better.'[43] There was an obvious qualitative issue with Young's claims. Life for overcrowded working-class inhabitants in a Georgian or Victorian house would be rather different to that of middle-class residents. He was nonetheless prescient on one point. Striving to remove all slums, Labour had to believe that slum dwellers could be rehoused *en masse* and that it would be politically possible to sustain long years of clearance.

Defeat at the general election of 1955 ensured that Labour would continue to conduct slum clearance policy at the local level. Whilst removing subsidies for public housing constructed outside of slum clearance provisions, the 1956 Housing Act created vague new powers but did not advance to local authorities any allowances to reduce the high cost of compulsory purchase. 'Local authorities have plenty of powers already to deal with slum clearance', claimed Labour in a briefing to members on the Act, 'what they need is more money.'[44] In their major policy statement *Homes for the Future*, Labour identified several 'housing needs', including 'slum clearance' and 'housing improvement'.[45] How the latter need might be met in practice was shown in a September 1956 *Labour Woman* piece, in which the regional organiser Florence Caruth described her visit to an exhibition of four 'improved' terraced homes in Labour-controlled Bristol. Caruth reported approvingly that the indoor bathrooms, gas hot water systems and 'gay, bright colours' of the improved homes were such that 'it is a home that any young modern couple would jump at'.[46] Not all within Labour would agree that old houses could be satisfactorily improved. Ralph Samuel would later assert that the mood of the age was that 'anything old was suspect and ripe for development'.[47] Others believed that bright colours or not, repairs could only ever be temporary at best.

An even more significant piece of housing legislation in Labour eyes was the 1957 Rent Act. The effects of the 1957 Act with regard to rent control will be examined at length in the subsequent chapters, but its effects with regard to slum clearance were more insidious. Through liberalising the private rental market, rents were raised on near-slum houses and landlords were able in some instances to skimp on repairs. The Act condemned 'hundreds of thousands of tenants to impoverishment by rapacious landlords', claimed the Labour newspaper the *Barons Court Citizen* in June 1963.[48] Worse, the *Citizen* went on, the Act had increased the 'evils of overcrowding' by forcing low-income households out of accommodation of a suitable size.[49] Just two years later in 1965, the investigation of the Milner Holland Committee into housing in London would confirm numerous bleak instances of tenants being forced into low-quality accommodation as landlords took the opportunity to evict them. Labour activists were convinced that without municipalisation, existing slums would worsen as greedy landlords economised on repairs, and new slums would be created as other homes deteriorated. Some within Labour went further – 'slum' equated to 'old house'. The architectural historian Stefan Muthesius wrote that housing reformers were mistaken in distinguishing between early- and late-nineteenth-century housing, pointing to the strictly enforced byelaw standards that later houses were built under.[50] But as he conceded, 'it was chiefly an aesthetic dislike ... of their overwhelming repetitiveness' that saw byelaw houses declared unsuitable.[51] In this sense, it did not matter if a designated slum was truly a slum. Responding to the Rent Act in a 1957 *Labour's Northern Voice* article, the Salford Lawyer and Labour Councillor Jack Goldberg recommended that Labour councils bring forward as many clearance areas as possible to protect tenants, as rents could then not be raised according to the 1936 Housing Act.[52] The assumption was, of course, that the tenants would not object to being subject to slum clearance procedures.

A further issue was that of compensation to owner-occupiers of 'unfit' properties. It was easier for Labour actors to advocate low levels of compensation to landlords than to the individual homeowner. 'We all know that some people make bad bargains', wrote the Bolton Alderman James Vickers in a 1959 LPRD circular, 'they may not get all their money back – nor should they'.[53] Vickers plainly believed that the business of home ownership could be a risky one. Of course, this did not mean that Labour voters were not caught out by this assessment. Dennis found in Sunderland that large numbers of his working-class respondents were owner-occupiers and were unwilling to give up their 'structurally sound' yet 'unfit' cottages, which helped to prompt Dennis's activism on their behalf.[54] Hilda Jennings identified a similar situation in the mainly owner-occupied working-class district of Barton Hill within Bristol.[55] Writing in *Labour Woman* of January 1964, the MP for Sowerby Douglas Houghton described a constituent who had bought a house in line for clearance for £240 three years previously.[56] Taking a similar view to Vickers, Houghton suggested that 'the shadow of a coming Clearance Order must have been evident' when his constituent purchased the property, making the 'site value' compensation offer of £22 hardly shocking.[57] In the late 1950s, many within Labour had little sympathy for those standing in the way of the future.

'The slum problem is not being solved – it is growing', lamented the social policy academic John Greve in a February 1961 *Socialist Commentary* article.[58] 'Public squalor' occupied the minds of Labour observers after a further election defeat in 1959, and would continue to be a key point of debate throughout the 1960s. Greve noted that of the 5 million households in the private rented sector, 52 per cent of tenants lacked access to hot water from a tap and 56 per cent were without access to a fixed bath. 'Tenants [were] probably doing more than landlords to improve landlords', Greve remarked, and the existing slum clearance programme did not allow for 'continuing obsolescence or for rising standards'.[59] This perception of stagnating or even worsening urban conditions was shared by others on the left. 'The slums remain a breeding ground of disease and unhappiness', lamented a 1960 Communist pamphlet on housing, which squarely pointed the finger at private landlords for exploiting a desperate situation.[60] Though the Communists principally referred to London, housing deterioration was a serious issue across Britain. Writing in *Socialist Commentary* of March 1961, a correspondent in Edinburgh claimed that the city had the worst housing conditions in Western Europe.[61] The correspondent considered Arthur Street such an 'abomination of squalor', that he believed it should be kept intact, like 'German concentration camps', as a memorial to a society 'which permits such degradation in these days of supposed affluence'.[62] Though this was an extreme position, the correspondent went on to note that Edinburgh's

Conservative council maintained the Georgian old town, but 'slums [had] no place in the briefs'.[63] It would be fair to say Edinburgh's old town was a special case. Sue Goss has observed how aesthetic arguments for retaining housing had little effect on Southwark councillors, largely because they were from slums themselves.[64] If Arthur Street was an especially dreadful example, it was by no means unique.

One such example was the Beaconsfield Buildings in the Barnsbury area of Islington, or 'Britain's worst slum', as a 1962 report in the West Ham Labour newspaper had it. The buildings in question were a series of late-nineteenth-century tenements built, as irony would have it, as superior housing for artisan workers. Now referred to as 'the Crumbles', a recent 'stream of sewage water' covering the yard children used to play, as well as the fear of polio, had prompted residents to organise a protest march against the landlords of the tenements. Summarising conditions, one schoolboy interviewed said, 'I don't mind sleeping with my three brothers and two sisters in one room, but I dread using those lavatories.'[65] Although the Beaconsfield Buildings were ultimately demolished in 1970, the poor state of such dwellings in the early 1960s reinforced arguments for slum clearance: it is significant that West Ham Labour's report focused on the fact that the tenements were 'eighty-four years old'. Again, the fact that private landlords continued to profit from ageing slum housing was an important feature to Labour arguments. The Labour Party Research Department estimated in a 1962 study on rented housing that virtually all privately rented accommodation at that point in time had been built prior to 1919, when 'standards which are broadly still acceptable today' had been introduced.[66] Of this stock, the researchers estimated that around 3.3 million houses had been built before 1875 when by-law regulation came into force, and were regarded as irredeemably bad. Though an enormous number of houses would need to be demolished annually to remove those from before 1875 that were 'rotten from bad materials and bad standards', the research department argued that there was no point in improving such dwellings.[67] Rather than improving all 'old houses', they went on, the model of the Labour-controlled Leeds City Council should be adopted. The council had designated areas of Leeds with large numbers of old houses as improvement areas, grants for such work as required being offered to the owners, with the houses compulsorily purchased if the owners declined to bring their homes up to a standard that could be maintained for at least fifteen years.[68] According to academic studies conducted at the time, there was a 'begrudging acceptance' of Leeds's policy among residents.[69] Yet popular tolerance rested on the notion that the process of clearing the slums was a temporary hardship. As the research department conceded, even at a demolition rate of 150,000 a year – more than double the early-1960s rate of around 61,000 a year – it would take twenty-two years to remove all incorrigibly bad houses. For the inhabitants of districts suffering the blight of clearance policy, it was probable that the 'exciting vista of the town of tomorrow leaves [them] cold', conceded Douglas Houghton in *Labour Woman*.[70] Nevertheless, the ambitious plan advanced by the party research department to raze the worst, and make-do-and-mend with the rest, would form the basis of Labour's slum clearance policy in the later 1960s when published in 1963 as *Labour's Plan for Old Houses*.

Race and 'squalor'

'Squalor' had a racialised dimension to it. While the process of slum clearance was stigmatising in and of itself, through the designation of some streets as 'unfit for human habitation' and others as suitable, there was a racist variety to this stigma, with deep historical roots. In particular, the Irish in Britain had long been a target of racist rhetoric directed at 'little Irelands', believed to be 'synonymous with poverty, filth, and squalor'.[71] Most British port cities had well-established ethnic minority communities, which grew in size as the British Empire expanded in the nineteenth century and, in accordance with the imperial project, became the subject of racial scrutiny. When racial tensions flared, housing was often a key factor, whether in terms of limited supply or false assumptions that particular ethnic groups could function as the carriers of disease. These antagonisms were key to the 1919 race riots across British port cities – including Cardiff, Glasgow, Hull, Liverpool, London and Salford – in which white mobs attacked Black sailors of mainly African-Caribbean, Somali and Yemeni origin. Squalor as a racist category would be increasingly deployed with the onset of decolonization and greater levels of migration to Britain from former imperial possessions after 1945. While the Nationality Act of 1948 essentially granted New Commonwealth migrants British citizenship and the right to settle in the metropole, the act was an attempt to foster post-imperial unity across the former empire rather than a genuinely egalitarian approach to race.[72] As in earlier eras, housing was a key focus of anti-migrant rhetoric, with the poor housing conditions afforded to migrants being incorporated into arguments to discourage further arrivals.[73] Areas scheduled for future clearance, known as 'twilight' areas, became places of settlement for some migrants in the 1950s and 1960s, owing to the high numbers of vacant properties, unwillingness of landlords to rent out accommodation anywhere else and an effective colour bar to council housing through residency requirements to qualify for waiting lists. This posed a problem for Labour, whose activists varied enormously in their empathy with migrant groups, with some content to deploy 'squalor' in an explicitly racist fashion for electoral means. While there were activists committed to antiracism, the project of creating socialist cities in Britain was fundamentally nativist and exclusionary in character, with the white family privileged over other groups.

The decaying terraces of Kensington, Hammersmith and Paddington were one such example, becoming the focus for the Irish community in London, with the cheap lodging rooms of the area fuelling a 'slum' reputation. The housing conditions of Irish immigrants in Birmingham became the subject of a 1951 Young Christian Workers' report by Maurice Foley (later a Labour MP and minister with responsibility for immigrants), who detailed migrants sleeping 'in public lavatories … in parks, air raid shelters and on railway stations', and overcrowded boarding houses with an atmosphere of 'depression, almost despair'.[74] Foley's findings were publicised by the Taoiseach, Eamonn De Valera, who emphasised what he saw as the moral and health hazards of life in Britain in an effort to stop the flow of migrants from Ireland. Notably, the investigation found that where Birmingham City Council were willing to offer Irish immigrants council houses, the houses were invariably located in soon-to-be demolished slum houses in inner areas such as Aston and Hockley.[75]

Black immigrants from the Caribbean and from the Indian subcontinent experienced similar conditions throughout the post-war period. In mid-1960s Bristol, Black newcomers had rented dilapidated property in the inner areas of Montpelier and St Paul's, as the white population moved out to the suburbs and newly built council estates.[76] The majority of Black households lived in exceptionally poor conditions, lacking the exclusive use of all four amenities defined as 'basic': hot and cold water; a fixed bath; and a toilet.[77] In Notting Hill and St Pancras, the Black community were forced to rent from slum landlords such as Perec Rachman, who tended to bribe or threaten rent-controlled white tenants to move out in order to raise rents under the 1957 Rent Act. Rachman then charged higher-than-average rents to his Black tenants, often described by migrants as a 'colour tax'.[78] The only alternative for Black immigrants, denied easy access to council housing, was to pool funds to buy slum houses, becoming landlords themselves in an often-uncomfortable relationship when the houses came with rent-controlled white tenants.[79] The 1958 Notting Hill race riots, in which gangs of white 'Teddy Boys' attacked Black people in the area over the period of a week, were framed against housing shortages, stoked by fascist agitators from Oswald Mosley's Union Movement.[80] While the local Labour MP and constituency party promoted immigration restrictions in a gutless attempt to outflank the fascists, the London County Councillor for North Kensington Donald Chesworth promoted antiracist community activism, which drew in young radicals of the nascent 'New Left'.[81] Housing was his core focus, with Chesworth working to organise Rachman's tenants in an effort to prevent areas such as Notting Hill becoming 'mere transit camps', though, as Ben Jones and Camilla Schofield have recounted, the early attempts of the New Left activists to challenge Rachman were undermined by the motives of ambiguous community figures such as Michael de Freitas.[82]

Race and housing were combined in the national consciousness most vividly, and unpleasantly, in the 1964 general election contest for the parliamentary seat of Smethwick, an industrial town in Staffordshire (though only a few miles outside Birmingham). Despite Labour's general election victory, the Labour MP Patrick Gordon Walker was unseated on a 7.2 per cent swing by the Conservative candidate, headteacher Peter Griffiths.[83] A *Socialist Commentary* report on the shock result claimed that Gordon Walker had been jeered at the count with racist chants. Griffiths had certainly not disavowed far-right activist support for his campaign, with the National Socialist Movement promoting the slogan 'If you want a nigger for your neighbour vote Liberal or Labour' on his behalf.[84] As a member of the Smethwick Immigration Control Association, Griffiths had worked to make 'immigrants and slums' synonymous in the eyes of voters, falsely claiming that leper hospitals were being built in Smethwick as a consequence of migration, that immigrants had high levels of tuberculosis and that race riots would occur if Labour won.[85] Gordon Walker's role as an opponent to the Commonwealth Immigrants Act 1962 was used by Griffiths to suggest that he was uninterested in white voters, with the charge seemingly sticking to the extent that Gordon Walker lost a subsequent 1965 by-election in Leyton.[86] In this he had been aided by the local press, with the primary newspaper, *The Smethwick Telephone and Warley Courier*, owned and edited by a Conservative activist until 1962, before being sold to the West Midlands Press, itself owned by the Conservative Iliffe family.[87] Though only 4,000 immigrants lived in Smethwick in 1964, out of a population of 68,000, the council house waiting list of 4,000 raised tensions further, with the Tories campaigning on a platform that white British families should be given council houses first. There was no small irony to this, given that the likelihood was, as leader of Smethwick's council Labour group Ernest Lowry put it, that immigrants would be forced to buy or rent slum housing at '10–33 per cent above the odds', standing little chance of joining the waiting list.[88] Nonetheless, playing on these fears was a potent tactic and as Anthony Nicholas commented in an article for *Tribune*, it had the added effect of making Labour wary of committing to anti-racist campaigning. Nicholas reported that Labour activists in Smethwick claimed that racial issues were a 'non-party matter', and would only admit to Nicholas that there were Black party members locally 'between ourselves'.[89]

Smethwick would be regained by Labour in 1966, but Griffiths made full use of his time as MP to promote a segregationist scheme by the Tory-controlled Smethwick Council to buy up all the houses on Marshall Street, to be let to white families only in a supposed effort to prevent 'ghettoization'.[90] Notably, this campaign was centred on a group of white housewives, who in an interview with Midland News cited unspecified concerns that 'cleanliness' of the street was in some way threatened by immigrants, as well as expressing unevidenced fears of tuberculosis.[91] Although the scheme made little headway, with the Ministry of Housing refusing to sanction a council loan to finance the purchases in spite of a delegation of Smethwick housewives petitioning Crossman, it attracted international attention, with Malcolm X visiting Marshall Street in February 1965 at the invitation of the Indian Workers' Association.[92] More broadly, as Elizabeth Buettner has commented, Smethwick marked the arrival of racialised rhetoric 'on the national political stage in hitherto unprecedented ways, never fully to disappear again'.[93] It is significant that housing and specifically claims made about squalor were a means of anchoring racist discourse to a supposed material reality.

The employment in Smethwick of faltering slum clearance and the fading promise of urban modernism to drive racist rhetoric was soon replicated on the national stage. While Labour passed a Race Relations Act in 1965, the legislation did not outlaw discrimination in housing. Sustained campaigning by the Campaign against Racial Discrimination (CARD), containing within their ranks a number of Labour activists, alongside lobbying by other groups, persuaded the Home Secretary Roy Jenkins to introduce a further Race Relations Act in 1968, legislating against race discrimination in housing, employment and public services.[94] It was at this point, ahead of the second reading of the bill in April 1968, that the Conservative MP and member of the shadow cabinet Enoch Powell delivered the infamous 'Rivers of Blood' speech to a group of Conservative activists in a Birmingham hotel, having prepared the local press in advance.[95] Having made a name for himself as an opponent of race relations legislation, Powell referred in his speech to a letter from an elderly female boarding house owner living on a Wolverhampton street, claiming that as the sole white inhabitant of the street she had been terrorised by her

Black neighbours. It remains unclear whether the woman to whom he referred existed, with recent speculation that the person in question may in fact have had a rather more complicated, and largely positive, relationship with her immigrant neighbours.[96] Regardless of the veracity of his account, Powell utilised the image of threats, taunts and excreta thrust through the letterbox of an elderly woman to add empirical weight to his prophecy of racial conflict.

As a consequence of the speech, Powell was sacked from his shadow cabinet role. While the official Labour Party reaction excoriated Powell, his removal prompted demonstrations across the country, notably by London dock workers and market porters, and in the latter case influenced by fascist organisers. In Wolverhampton itself, there were several workplace walkouts and petitions in support of Powell, though in workplaces where there was a strong presence of shop stewards this generally did not occur.[97] Labour responses to trade union Powellism focused closely on housing factors as the main driver of this support. Racial tensions were 'much smaller [problems] than the general problems of poverty, of replacing our slums, and providing social services for the old and disabled', argued Peter Townsend in his May 1968 *Tribune* article 'We Cannot Have White Socialism', calling upon his recent argument that the welfare state had changed the shape of poverty in Britain.[98] The academic James Jupp critiqued the operation of effective colour bars on council housing in cities of high migration such as Birmingham or Bradford, suggesting that the 'immigrant problem' was in fact 'poor host community attitudes ... slums and poor provision'.[99] Perhaps the most pointed response came from Frank Allaun. 'It might be salutary', suggested Allaun in a December 1968 *Tribune* piece, 'to remind anyone infected with Powellism of his part in the 1957 Rent Act, the Landlord's Charter' (Powell had been a key architect of the bill as a junior minister).[100] One year later, the paper which Allaun edited, *Labour's Voice*, covered the release of the Notting Hill Summer Project Report, based on a 1967 survey of continued poor housing conditions in Notting Hill by Chesworth and the Labour-aligned community activists in the area.[101] The 'reservoir of cheap privately rented accommodation' and serious overcrowding described in the report was seen by *Labour's Voice* as reinforcing the need for municipalisation of all private rented housing.[102] In this respect, the stance of Labour activists was in keeping with an 'ameliorative, welfarist approach to antiracism' on the left which largely discounted the structures of everyday racism, and which would be increasingly challenged by Black activists in the 1970s and 1980s.[103] The rigid focus of the left on common material inequalities had serious limitations, and called into question the inclusivity of their modern urban mission.

The move to improvement: 1964–70

'There used to be twenty-one of us living in this house, with one lavatory for all of us to use', remarked Rose Jackson, originally from St Vincent in the Caribbean and a private tenant of a Maida Vale flat without a bath.[104] Jackson made her comments to Frank Allaun in the early 1970s, as he investigated continued slum conditions across Britain for a book. Though Jackson's complaints included mice and 'sewage water from the toilet [coming] down into the cooker', she nevertheless stated that she would be content to stay if the council fixed up the house and gave her a bath, in part due to the high rents charged by the alternative, the Mulberry Trust housing association.[105] In certain respects, the situation experienced by Jackson is indicative of the shift in slum policy that took place during the Labour governments of 1964–70. While Harold Wilson had utilised the 'White Heat' motif of scientific progress in 1963 to present Labour as self-consciously modern, enduring housing poverty frustrated the aim of the party to build entirely new cities. Though Labour in government increased the rate of slum clearance, the party simultaneously expanded the rehabilitation of erstwhile slums as a long-term solution. Notably, Labour did so without a coherent policy of municipalisation, or taking these properties into public ownership, as had been the 1950s aim. Political debates within Labour around the 1960s phase of 'improvement', as it tended to be described, were distinct from debates in the late 1940s and 1950s. Arguments for improvement in this period started from the basis that the levelling of Victorian cities in their entirety was simply impossible, or at least hardly feasible at the rates of slum clearance and house-building in the mid-1960s. Nor was slum clearance judged desirable when rising standards meant in practice that 'Welwyn Garden City [had] the same proportion of unfit houses as Stoke Newington', or that 'Tonbridge had more slums than the Rhondda'.[106] While there was a certain snobbery to this account – and the curious proportions given had much to do with the under-reporting of slum housing by local authorities – it did lay bare the reality of continuous slum clearance. If clearance was to operate cyclically, all houses would eventually be slums, regardless of the wealth of their inhabitants. 'In the so-called affluent society and the so-called welfare state', Allaun wrote, 'we can send satellites to the moon – but cannot put a bath in a house'.[107] For left-wingers such as Allaun, the answer was to improve conditions at the present moment – specifically in terms of baths, hot water and inside toilets – but without either turning it into a substitute for new council house building or ending slum clearance entirely. In this, they were set against their own government.

The entry of Labour into government in October 1964 did seem to promise this combination. In the general election, the party had promised a target of 400,000 houses built annually – a response to a Conservative pledge – the acceleration of the slum clearance programme and mass improvement of old houses, with local authorities stepping in the event that landlords failed to modernise their properties.[108] The house building target was revised in November 1965 to 500,000 per year by 1970, as the housing section of the *dirigiste* 'National Plan', though the 400,000 figure would only be exceeded in 1967 with 415,460 completions across the UK. In 1968, house completions hit an all-time peak of 425,830 completions, but cuts to government expenditure forced the abandonment of the half-million target.[109] High levels of house building under the Wilson governments paralleled exceptionally high levels of slum clearance between 1966 and 1972, peaking at 71,586 properties demolished in 1968.[110] Scholarly consideration of this late phase of large-scale slum clearance has tended to focus on the relationship between the process and the building of high-rise housing, owing in part to the argument advanced by Patrick Dunleavy that the convenience of high-rise building, as well as collusion between building firms and local authorities, drove the spread of the architectural form.[111] Whilst land pressures and the speed of industrialised building certainly linked this period of high-rise building to slum clearance, there were important architectural, sociological and political dimensions to the spread of this type, which will be explored in greater depth in the following chapter. Perhaps most crucially, as has been reiterated throughout this book, it should be stated that urban modernism was not reducible to twenty-storey blocks of flats. Slum clearance was a key element of the urban modernist phenomenon and we should seek to understand how those within Labour understood the process at the time of it occurring, rather than attempting to interpret clearance through our contemporary lens, in which the demolition of old houses tends to be viewed as an aberration.

It was in this respect that rehabilitation became a permanent arrangement. 'Leeds is as proud of its policy of improving the old central areas as Manchester is proud of its policy of total clearance', diarised Richard Crossman after a visit to the latter city in January 1965, noting that he was 'wholly on the side of Leeds.'[112] He described how it was 'really a pleasure' to see the joy given to people by 'proper dry roofing and modern kitchens'.[113] As noted previously, the carrot-and-stick approach of Leeds City Council to induce landlords and homeowners to improve their properties in central areas had been elevated to a prominent place within Labour ranks. Substantial variation in the estimation of numbers of slum housing by local authorities in the 1954 council returns had also created added impetus to improve dwellings rather than to demolish, at least while alternative housing was not immediately available. Some councils, such as Liverpool, had counted all unfit houses in their reporting, while the London County Council gave a far lower and rather unlikely estimate, with this ambiguity carrying over to the 1965 council returns.[114] Part of the problem was that as it was technically impossible to clear all houses identified as unfit within a short time frame, councils avoided creating the notion that they possessed a backlog by gradually adding cohorts of unfit housing into each clearance programme.[115] In the March 1965 pamphlet *Facts on Housing*, circulated ahead of the council elections that year, Labour claimed that the Conservatives had deliberately 'double-counted' their total of 450,000 houses cleared between 1956 and 1964 by recording houses subject to a clearance order again when they were demolished. Labour pointed to figures compiled by the Town and Country Planning Association that suggested 364,000 houses had actually been cleared, arguing that the true number of slums still standing was likely to be far higher than the Conservatives had claimed while in office.[116] The difficulty of obtaining clear housing data at a central level led to the increased recruitment of research staff by the Ministry of Housing under Crossman, and a number of studies into housing conditions in urban areas were initiated, as well as a national House Condition Survey.[117] The report of the Denington Committee in 1966, charged with investigating present standards of housing fitness, recommended mass improvement wherever structurally sound houses were awaiting clearance.[118] Reporting in 1968, the House Condition Survey recorded 1,836,000 unfit houses across England and Wales, which seemed to justify the earlier propaganda claims by Labour.[119] However, as the social scientist David Donnison commented in his bestselling 1967 Pelican book *The Government of Housing*, one might take the view that as housing standards rose: '... conditions that should be regarded as intolerable depend less on the structure and equipment of individual dwellings, more on the way in which housing is used and on the character of the environment in which it stands'.[120] Donnison was questioning whether the existing definition of a slum – generally a pre-1919 house – was sufficient to deal with bad housing conditions, which could well be present in otherwise 'fit' housing. This was in itself a powerful argument for improvement along the lines that Crossman had observed in Leeds.

Donnison's suggestion that 'housing obsolescence' did not account for the complexity of poverty had become an increasingly common observation in the late 1960s. Donnison had sat on the Milner Holland committee, set up under the Conservative government in 1963 to report on housing in Greater

London, an area of study which had been given additional impetus by the Rachman scandal.[121] The 1965 report of the committee drew particular attention to the severe problems of the private rented sector in the wake of the 1957 Rent Act. The operation of the Rent Act as well as Labour's opposition to it will be discussed in greater detail in a later chapter, but a practical effect of the legislation was that while landlords could raise rents on rent-controlled tenancies through carrying out improvements, the majority of tenants could not afford these increases. Those tenants in decontrolled properties, at greater risk of eviction, were often too frightened to ask for repairs, even in the case of a Fulham house with a wash basin 'blocked for over a year' and a bath so filthy that water was 'taken into own rooms by tenants'.[122] As discussed in the previous section, immigrant tenants were confined to the worst slum properties. Structurally, the committee noted that while they had been showing examples of accommodation with 'walls so damp that mould appears and wallpaper will not stay in place', as well as 'defective lavatories' and 'positively dangerous appliances and fittings', these dwellings would not necessarily be designated as 'unfit' and thus strictly speaking were not officially slums, whether owing to their location within a structurally sound building or the possibility of repair.[123] Worse, 'it was clear that the [improvement] grant system was working very slowly' and 'has so far done little to improve the dwellings and areas in greatest need', with private landlords either unwilling or unable to fund their portion of the costs of improvement.[124] Notably, the committee recommended 'areas of special control' for neighbourhoods containing exceptionally poor housing conditions, which might bring together an authority with the power to 'demolish and rebuild as necessary', compel or carry out improvements, as well as to make improvement grants on a more generous basis.[125] To Labour activists, some of this sounded rather like an argument for putting municipalisation back at the heart of party policy. 'The municipalisation of rented housing has been postponed too long, because it was too technical, too controversial, too difficult', wrote Anthony Nicholas in a March edition of *Tribune*, shortly after the publication of the report of the committee, 'but it is not nearly as difficult as the situation in which many Londoners now live'.[126] Peggy Duff, founder of the Campaign for Nuclear Disarmament and Chair of the St Pancras Borough Housing and Development Committee, agreed that municipalisation was the right policy, but for it to succeed councils required 'cheap money' and the right to pay little compensation to the owners of 'semi-slums'.[127] The view of party activists that some sort of stick was needed in the circumstances seemed to be reinforced by the findings of Brian Abel-Smith and Peter Townsend in their landmark 1965 publication *The*

Poor and the Poorest, which identified seven and a half million people 'with low levels of living' below the national assistance scale based on data from 1960, large numbers of whom were children.[128] The emotional public response to Ken Loach's television play *Cathy Come Home* that year, which depicted the appalling state of housing in clearance areas through the tragedy of a young couple forced into homelessness – and led to the formation of the charity Shelter – further underlined the need to act quickly on slum housing. While Crossman's 1965 Rent Act did not return municipalisation to the party agenda, instituting instead a form of rent regulation, the limitations of focus on slum clearance alone without ameliorating conditions within slum properties were apparent, and as such, some form of housing improvement seemed desirable. Whether the Leeds model pursued by Crossman was necessarily the right approach remained open to question. 'It may be that rejection of [municipalisation] has been too complete', commented an unnamed researcher in a Research Department review of Labour housing policy conducted in 1967, 'and that the lesson to be learned from the operation of the 1965 Act is that municipalisation is the answer at least in certain cases'.[129]

A 1966 piece by Frank Allaun in *Labour's Northern Voice* conveyed the basic sentiment of Labour activists at the time for a comprehensive approach to the slums. Below a photograph of Ellor Street – Walter Greenwood's birthplace – being bulldozed in Salford, with several high-rise blocks of flats being put up behind it, a caption read: 'Down with the old, up with the new. What we want to see.'[130] This was modernity at work. Yet, with the appalling conditions described by Milner Holland remaining present for households throughout Britain, while the target of 500,000 homes built annually remained elusive, housing improvement began to be seen by the Labour government as a realistic alternative to future demolition. It is true, as several housing historians have argued, that there was an element of cost-saving in this assessment, particularly in the ever-more parsimonious economic circumstances of the mid-1960s.[131] But it is questionable whether improvement genuinely was cheaper in the long run, even if it was believed to be so at the time. The 1967 review of Labour housing policy ensured that the Leeds model became government policy in the 1968 White Paper *Old Houses into New Homes*. The document introduced 'general improvement areas' – often identical to existing slum clearance areas – offering landlords and property owners grants to improve older properties, with a further Housing Act in 1969 giving these proposals legislative backing.[132] From 1968, this effort had been reinforced by area-based social policy initiatives in several major cities, known as Community Development Projects.[133] Within

Labour ranks, this was seen as a compromise, not a retreat. A Housing Policy Study Group had been set up by the party NEC in 1968, charged to 'evolve a housing policy for the 1970s', and including within its membership Frank Allaun and James MacColl.[134] The 1969 report of the Study Group stated that improvement grants would 'alleviate' the problem but that 'this must not be seen as an alternative to new house building'.[135] Tellingly, the Study Group believed 'it should be possible to complete the clearing of the worst slums within ten years and the Government should aim for this target'.[136] In this view, improvement was a palliative, not a solution.

The move to improvement as primary policy coincided with a 'heritage' turn through an aesthetic reappraisal of Victorian architecture, as well as beginnings of gentrification in depopulated inner-city areas. Labour activists played a part in both cultural phenomena, and it is important to recover the strangeness of it at the time. Glendinning and Muthesius are prescient in their observation that 'before the 1960s, to praise Victorian terraces or tenements and attack Modern dwellings, however complex one's arguments, could only have seemed sophistic, if not incomprehensible'.[137] Although gentrification has more generally been understood as a process of reconstructing the inner city, led by the bourgeois and bohemian, the march of relatively smaller groups of the middle classes in the 1960s was accompanied by a strident appreciation for the 'period' home.[138] Michael Young had commented on the middle-class liking for Georgian and Victorian homes as early as 1956, contrasting it with the apparent unsuitability of terraced homes for the working classes.[139] The left-wing sociologist Ruth Glass coined the term 'gentrification' in 1964 to describe the displacement of working-class inhabitants by the middle classes in certain areas of inner-city London, including Islington, Canonbury and Notting Hill.[140] This was caused in part by the gradual decline of the private rented sector, as landlords began to sell large multi-occupied properties to middle-class buyers, forcing out lower-income tenants to cheaper rented areas or to council housing in outer-city areas. However, action against comprehensive redevelopment by the new arrivals was not widespread in Britain until the late 1960s, although in cities such as Cambridge and in the Barnsbury area of London, certain streets or neighbourhoods were preserved on the grounds of 'heritage' value at the discretion of the council.[141]

The redevelopment of the Victorian Packington Estate in Islington became the source of opposition from residents led by a Labour councillor, Harry Brack (an inhabitant of the gentrified Gibson Square in the borough), with Crossman recounting that he was initially minded to support calls for rehabilitation as it 'could become a second-class Canonbury', before being reminded by Evelyn

Sharp (the Permanent Secretary) that to do so would require the eviction of all existing working-class tenants.[142] Brack was expelled from the Labour Party for contesting the development on the basis that subsidies offered for improvement were far lower than those available for new building, and managed to force a hearing on whether the statutory inquiry had been mishandled in 1966, although the redevelopment was ultimately approved.[143] Considering the spread of gentrification in Islington and Canonbury in the mid-1960s, Joe Moran suggested that the 'cultural politics' of home refurbishment and urban conservation promulgated by this pioneering wave have been established in contemporary culture. Moran articulates the curious meeting of old and new in the habit of middle classes for 'knocking through' the interior walls of terraced houses and the removal of carpets to reveal the original boards as a 'signifier of modernity and freedom'.[144] The refitting of a terrace or villa into a bourgeois home was in this light not quite a refutation of modernity. Even so, as houses were 'simultaneously modernised and antiqued' in Raphael Samuel's memorable remark, the introduction of Conservation Areas through the Civic Amenities Act of 1967 was a clear impediment to the idea that modern dwellings should by necessity replace 'obsolete' older housing.[145]

While the left did not for the most part attack modernist housing, left-wing Labour activists were increasingly drawn into preservationist 'community action' campaigns by the close of the 1960s and into the 1970s, seeking to support the inhabitants of decaying housing to have their homes repaired and removed from the risk of demolition. The Notting Hill Summer Project provided something of a model for this work, influenced by New Left ideas of participatory democracy, in a rejection of the paternalistic view of Labour council leaders that slum clearance was the best outcome for the population of slum areas. It should be stated that the main period of preservationist campaigning goes beyond the scope of this book. Organised community opposition to slum clearance in most major British cities was relatively limited until the close of the 1960s.[146] 'They are pulling down the little cottages in the East End, but the "sub-standard" tenement blocks will stay for twenty years or more', observed James Kincaid, Raphael Samuel and Elizabeth Slater in a critical 1962 piece for *New Left Review*.[147] While 'Down with the old, up with the new' was a common left attitude, this sense that slum clearance was fundamentally failing to address housing needs – and through designating properties as slums, actually making conditions worse – led some within Labour to refute clearance, though not without reservations. The Community Development Projects, providing employment for a number of radical social workers, would become a focal point for left-wing activists engaged in opposition to slum clearance.[148] In their study of the St Ann's area of Nottingham, published in 1970, Ken Coates and Richard Silburn expressed their view that neither selective improvement nor wholesale demolition was likely to resolve the issues presented by long-standing slum areas. 'The only possible solution', they wrote, 'would be to treat housing as a welfare service rather than a marketable commodity, and to approach the housing problem with the urgency that a national crisis merits'.[149]

'I think we have had too much of the bulldozer, and have destroyed too many old houses and whole communities with them', stated Tony Crosland in a 1971 lecture.[150] After Labour's defeat in the general election, Crosland became Shadow Environment Secretary with responsibility for housing, and his speech was published as a Fabian pamphlet in 1971. Crosland appended extracts of his speech to a working group on housing in December of that year, and while he did not rule out slum clearance outright, it is striking that he was willing to critique it. In his appended remarks, Crosland stated that while 'we need an intensified effort [in house building] for at least a decade ahead' to resolve existing housing issues, he queried the idea of 'annual obsolescence', in which older houses gradually qualified as 'unfit'.[151] If slum clearance was increasingly viewed as a limited mechanism to address the problem of old houses by the 1970s, this did not mean that new houses were no longer a priority. Nevertheless, slum clearance was a phenomenon closely tied to the era of urban modernism: quite simply, it promised to remove the old in favour of a better new. Yelling remarks that slum clearance 'was never just a common-sense approach to dealing with inherited housing problems, but a profoundly political act', a key battleground of state intervention into the operation of the housing system.[152] Neither should it be forgotten that slum clearance aimed to serve a social purpose. The reaction to slum clearance in the 1970s, on aesthetic and communitarian grounds amongst others, has tended to obscure the political rationale behind it. Without dismissing the reasonable concerns over insensitive bureaucracies that negative accounts of clearance had, present-day commentators have begun to cautiously rehabilitate the process itself, with Owen Hatherley arguing that clearance meant being rehoused 'in something which was, more often than not, superior in terms of space, security of tenure and hygiene'.[153] For Labour activists, the demise of slum clearance as urban policy did not end the battle for decent homes. Rather, it was the faith that levelling the Victorian city could clear the way for modern, socialist cities that was ultimately checked.

2

Down with the old, up with the new

Labour and urban planning

'It will be said that mistakes may be made [in planning], but we must no longer be afraid of making mistakes', argued the Labour MP for Mitcham, Tom Braddock, in a House of Commons a debate on the 1947 Town and Country Planning Act.[1] He went on to remark that 'great town planners' such as Patrick Abercrombie had been denied the opportunity to practise their craft in the past, asserting that 'after all, in questions of design and of town and country planning, it is very often a matter of opinion'.[2] Braddock's comments encapsulate the attitude amongst Labour activists to urban transformation after 1945. In the opinion of many Labour adherents, British urban areas – and especially their housing – were unplanned symbols of an unwanted past. Any complaints about the modern moment were part of the process. Unusually amongst MPs, Braddock had actually been an architect before parliament: a direct meeting of contemporary urbanism with an imagined socialist future. Far beyond the doorstep of the home – whether council house, privately let or owner-occupied – Labour activists had a sense of a planned future cityscape. This was not solely idiosyncratic dogma, though there was, of course, some of that. Richard Hoggart's famous reference to Hunslet as 'a study in shades of dirty-grey, without greenness or the blueness of sky' captured the essence of many post-war British towns or cities that had developed throughout the Industrial Revolution.[3] In the eyes of Labour actors, a socialist city was one in which the iniquities of the Industrial Revolution could be swept clear and, in this bulldozing respect, their aims met that of the modern moment. Reshaping the city in a progressive manner would align with the architects and planners of the modern movement, removing the spatial obstacles to the success of cities and citizenry.

The power of political ideas as an explanatory factor has tended to be minimised in urban history, due to what Frank Mort has described as a 'particular reading' of urban planning as 'rationally judged political and professional initiatives'.[4]

None of the major histories of urban modernism address precisely why one of the two major political parties in Britain showed particular enthusiasm for, and came to be associated with what John Gold describes as 'the principle of progress through technology'.[5] Miles Glendinning and Stefan Muthesius focus more closely on political leaders of major cities as the driving force of modern housing production, and while acknowledging that virtually all of their subjects of study were Labour figures, they are less interested in the political hinterland of their subjects than their forceful personalities.[6] In this regard, discussions of post-war urban modernism in Britain can be so thoroughly stripped of political meaning that as Otto Saumarez Smith recently lamented, there has been a tendency to suggest 'that a set of architectural ideas were foisted upon the country'.[7] This book instead asserts that the political culture of Labour in the post-war era – focused as it was on a neoteric socialist future – meant that the basic ideas of urban modernism for light, order and space were, for a time, synchronous with the aims of the political left. Modernist ideas had strong purchase across all political parties in the post-war era, but the posthumous association of what is often termed 'welfare state modernism' with the political left is not without foundation. Pragmatic concerns had their place, but it is difficult to have a complete understanding of the post-war urban changes within Britain without accounting for political conceptions of the modern moment. As elsewhere in this book, I take a broader understanding of the modern moment as a set of normalising cultural ideas at a particular historical instance, underpinning urban transformation and the near-ceaseless post-war housing drive, rather than limiting my focus solely to modern architecture.

'To create cities worthy of twentieth century Britain we must see planning as a whole', proclaimed the 1961 party pamphlet *Towns for Our Times*. It continued: 'Our cities are cursed with traffic-choked central areas, misplaced offices and factories, decaying terraces of Victorian terraces and the sprawling flood of buildings bursting into the green belts.'[8] Advocating 'rigorous' control of the siting of industry, the replacement of 'outmoded' city centres and 'obsolete' slum areas, more New Towns, and the coordination of traffic policy and the public ownership of land, this was a reading of modernism for socialist purposes. This chapter examines how Labour activists understood and related to two key elements of urban planning: the planning and construction of the city; and the politics of land control. In each case, we can glimpse a socialist rationale for the urban transformations that would take place, and this chapter situates urban modernist planning as it was related to socialist ideals held by Labour adherents. 'Some good things can happen by accident', observed the 1958 policy statement

Leisure for Living, 'but not a decent building or a well-planned town'.[9] In the unsurprising view of those within Labour, it was the 'purposeful use by local authorities ... of the [planning] powers delegated to them' by the 1945 Labour government that had been responsible for the 'architectural achievements' of the 1940s and 1950s.[10] Confidence in the potentialities of modernist planning would ultimately prove historically contingent, broken by what Marshall Berman described as a growing 'split between the modern spirit and the modernized environment'.[11]

Towns for our times: Labour and the logic of urban planning

In a famous passage from his tour of the 1930s 'new England', the socialist writer J. B. Priestley identified 'three Englands':

> Old England, the country of the cathedrals and minsters and manor houses and inns, of Parson and Squire ... the nineteenth-century England, the industrial England of coal, iron, steel, cotton, wool, railways ... a cynically devastated countryside, sooty dismal little towns, and still sootier grim fortress-like cities ... the England of arterial and by-pass roads, of filling stations and factories that look like exhibition buildings, of giant cinemas and dance-halls and cafes, bungalows with tiny garages ... and everything given away for cigarette coupons.[12]

His rich description of what had changed, and what had not, was illustrative of the post-war landscape of Britain. Reshaping the sooty 'fortress-like cities' described by Priestley had been an aim of those within Labour since the party's foundation. Socialism was an international force and Labour had plenty of precedents to draw upon, both from the Soviet Union and from the democratic left. 'Red Vienna' of 1920s Austria had seen the Social Democrat Party attempt to make the city into a 'model of municipal socialism that would prefigure the coming socialist society'.[13] This was the context within which Labour activists understood planning: as an instrument for transforming cities to achieve socialist aims. Labour-led councils had acted on this basis in the 1930s, most significantly in the case of the London County Council, which built both vast suburban estates to reduce overcrowding and new urban estates with a range of amenities. The fact that planning schemes championed by Labour adherents sometimes had a contradictory outcome is, in some respects, beside the point.

There remains a powerful popular narrative that planning was unwelcome, with such sentiments characterised by Beach and Tiratsoo as 'ordinary people's wishes were ignored, as common sense was jettisoned in favour of dogma'.[14] It could be the case, as Scott comments, that the 'standardized citizens' envisioned by planners in modernist schemes were deemed 'uniform in their needs and even interchangeable', with the lived reality of such schemes frustrating these assumptions.[15] Yet this was not always so, and a rich vein of social history has begun to reclaim the rather more varied experiences associated with council housing in the urban modernist era.[16] Without a clear understanding of political reasoning for modernist urban planning and the context within which such schemes were taken up, we have only a partial view of the modern moment. It is necessary to bring to the fore the ideological foundations that informed how those within Labour saw urban planning.

Planning began to be established as a professional discipline in Britain in the early twentieth century, separate from architecture. By the 1940s, planning formed a major part of the policy landscape, aided by a 'vast framework of structural planning powers'.[17] A long lineage of utopian thought in urban planning influenced Labour thinking. The worst urban effects of the Industrial Revolution had inspired numerous attempts by enlightened eighteenth- and nineteenth-century businessmen to improve living conditions for the workers under their care, notable examples including Robert Owen (later a socialist) in New Lanark from 1800; George Cadbury in Bournville from 1879; and William Lever in Port Sunlight from 1888. More radical experiments, often with an agrarian, communitarian ethos though generally short-lived and relatively small-scale, were also a feature of nineteenth-century Britain, perhaps most successfully in the strawberry-growing Chartist settlement of Dodford in Worcestershire, founded 1849. Although these utopian communities were effectively anti-urban, the notion of a possible low-density, healthier urban existence did develop, such as the bucolic settlements depicted in the socialist and Arts and Crafts artist William Morris's 1890 novel *News from Nowhere*.

The Garden City Movement drew together these diverse utopian currents. Founded in 1899 by Ebenezer Howard and based on the ideals of his 1898 book *To-Morrow: A Peaceful Path To Real Reform*, the Garden City Association promoted Howard's dream of low-density, land-holding utopian communities surrounded by 'green belts' of undeveloped land. Only two were created, at Letchworth in 1903 and Welwyn Garden City in 1920, but a larger number of 'garden suburbs' were created and the basic conceptual features found their way into municipal schemes.[18] The American activist and community planner

Jane Jacobs would later criticise Howard's vision as 'almost feudal', claiming that Howard sought a 'static society' by resisting metropolitan fluidity.[19] Conversely, Glendinning and Muthesius argue that realising the 'Garden City' ideal 'would have required nothing short of political revolution' to allow for the relocation of enormous numbers of people.[20] Though many within Labour were suspicious of the bourgeois character of the Garden City Movement, Herbert Morrison – later leader of the London County Council (LCC) and Deputy Prime Minister in the Attlee government – was briefly a resident of Letchworth during the First World War, and suggested building twenty-three similar towns around London in 1920.[21] Regardless of Labour misgivings, Garden City principles of low density and pastoral placidity guided the development of inter-war LCC 'cottage estates', albeit with tram and London Underground connections so that cottage estate residents remained part of the city.[22]

The prominence of the Garden City ideal was in fact due to its adaptability. Raymond Unwin – a disciple of Howard – had served on the 1918 Tudor Walters Committee, which formalised standards for council housing in Britain. Unwin was an advocate of stripped-down satellite settlements for major cities, rather than full-fledged garden cities, and in his capacity as a senior government advisor his proposals were influential on peripheral housing schemes between the wars.[23] Patrick Geddes and Lewis Mumford were also to have considerable influence over the direction of post-war planning. Geddes – an early-twentieth-century planner principally known for his work across the British Empire, most notably in his modernist 'White City' core for Tel Aviv – believed it was the planner's job to discern the 'present tendency [of an urban environment]' from the 'phantasmagoria of change'.[24] Conversely, the American literary critic and commentator Mumford wanted 'communities' to transcend 'the sinister limitations of the metropolitan environment'.[25] This conception of physical 'community' as a means of building social solidarity in the modern age had a strong influence over Labour – which will be discussed in detail in a subsequent chapter – and Mumford's 1940 magnum opus on urbanism, *The Culture of Cities*, was distributed to Coventry's Labour council.[26] Tom Braddock, whose brusque dismissal of cautious approaches to planning opened this chapter, wrote in 1953 that great cities such as Glasgow and Manchester should be 'split up into their original small communities and great avenues of open space, horticultural and market gardens, parks etc., driven through the areas'.[27] In this he echoed the nineteenth-century socialist Robert Blatchford, who wrote in 1893 of a fictionalised Manchester filled with flowering public gardens.[28] Transcending the 'sinister limitations' of cities remained a key element of Labour thought. 'In place of the old disorder and ugliness we must build fine new communities', asserted a 1951 commemorative pamphlet issued by the party for the Festival of Britain. They went on: 'Town planning means that the health and the happiness of the people comes first.'[29] For all the distaste of party members for the deficiencies of urban capitalism, Labour was a profoundly urban force. The gaze of the party was – and still is – fixed upon the city, not the countryside.

The Second World War was the catalyst for urban planning on a scale far greater than had ever been attempted in Britain previously.[30] A total of 450,000 dwellings had been destroyed or were uninhabitable as a consequence of aerial attacks, with a further 4 million damaged.[31] The experience of total war exposed the inadequate conditions in which millions lived, which became still more desperate through the wartime suspension of house building.[32] Major wartime commissions on national planning issues – the Barlow, Scott and Uthwatt committees on the distribution of industry, use of rural land and on land compensation respectively – all recommended a centralised system of planning in the face of 1930s overdevelopment and economic decline in parts of Britain.[33] Labour were keen to seize the opportunity for change provided by war, which, as Stephen Brooke observes, seemed to activists to demand 'the tools of socialism for the purpose of victory'.[34] The party enthusiastically took up reconstruction planning. Bombing 'gives rise to unprecedented possibilities for re-planning', remarked a 1941 NEC paper on reconstruction, while a further 1942 memorandum asserted that 'whilst the demand for houses has been seriously increased, the possibility of [building] in a thoroughgoing way has also been increased'.[35] The opposite of 'thoroughgoing' development was Priestley's 'England of arterial and by-pass roads', which horrified Labour adherents, architects and town planners alike. Inter-war 'ribbon' developments had followed bus services along the new arterial and by-pass roads, with unplanned 'sprawl' vastly extending the urban environment into the countryside.[36] The effect of sprawl around London was especially significant, with the 1938 claim of the London Communist leader Ted Bramley that London was 'a monument to the anarchy of building' not especially hyperbolic.[37] Planning, for Labour, was a means of creating order from chaos.

Reconstruction planning found a wide audience – Patrick Abercrombie and John Forshaw's 1943 *County of London Plan* for the LCC sold nearly 10,000 copies.[38] Their vision saw London radically re-planned at low densities, to avoid the 'jumble of houses and industry' as well as the 'lofty close-packed tenements' that characterised the existing city.[39] Abercrombie and Forshaw also advocated the dispersal of a large part of the population to satellite towns outside of London.

This was a point of divergence with Labour municipal authorities, who were generally less willing to countenance the wholesale dispersal of the population beyond city boundaries without control of these new areas. In a 1943 housing pamphlet, Birmingham Borough Labour Party stated that 'Birmingham as a city is large enough', suggesting 'at least one satellite town' would be desirable, but emphasised that it would have to be closely linked to Birmingham by a 'fast electric railway service'.[40] The 1944 policy statement *Housing and Planning after the War* asserted that Labour were willing to countenance 'a considerable measure of decentralisation', but did not specify whether this was to be achieved via satellite towns or extensions to existing settlements.[41] Conversely, the Communists insisted in a 1944 publication that the low densities demanded by dispersal were impossible, as it would result in cities spreading 'two to three times as far out into the countryside'.[42] Roger Smith has claimed that the Abercrombie-authored 1947 Glasgow plan demanded such a high level of population dispersal that the Labour city council increased densities to ensure more residents stayed within the city.[43] This tension was essentially one of divergent ideologies. Planners like Abercrombie, influenced by the anti-urban Garden City Movement, aimed to radically reduce the populations as well as the pre-eminence of what they believed to be unhealthy and grotesquely oversized cities. While Labour activists also saw mid-twentieth-century cities as oversized and unhealthy, the party had an urbanist bent, preferring to reconstruct existing cities over mass dispersal. This tension would remain at the heart of how those within Labour saw urban planning: should the focus be on creating entirely new settlements or on building cities more amenable to socialism?

'The practical application of socialist principles': The New Towns

'The New Towns are ... the most complete of all attacks upon Squalor', claimed Beveridge in a 1959 lecture address to the Town and Country Planning Association.[44] Rather as with Beveridge's social policy prospectus, Labour were content to adopt similar views to him on dispersal, seeing the New Towns as an instrument to reduce the slums. Emphasising his interest in the concept, Beveridge went on to chair the New Town Development Corporations of Newton Aycliffe and Peterlee. Thirteen New Towns were designated under the 1946 New Towns Act, with further waves from 1961 creating twenty-one settlements in total.[45] The New Towns have been one of the most closely studied aspects of post-war planning, referred to variously as pandering to 'the suburban aspiration in English culture', as 'expressions of an architectural and environmental modernity, articulated through a language of nostalgia', and most recently, as mid-century vantage point to view a 'broadly social democratic political culture'.[46] Part of the appeal to scholars is the fact that the New Town concept was exported globally as a new planning paradigm, with varying degrees of success.[47] This being said, the New Towns only affected a relatively minor proportion of the British urban population.[48] Cities such as Labour-controlled Manchester attempted initially to build their own 'out-country' suburban estates by expanding their boundaries to include projects such as the colossal housing estate of Wythenshawe, rather than dispersing their population via New Towns.[49]

Whether in Basildon or Warrington, it was possible to see the New Towns as 'the practical application of socialist principles', as the Labour MP for Wellingborough George Lindgren proclaimed in a 1958 edition of *Socialist Commentary*.[50] The aim of this section is not to review the voluminous scholarship on New Towns, but rather to explain the New Town phenomenon within Labour political thought. Controlled development on these lines was more than a rejection of the Victorian city, but also a 'reaction against the soulless council estates and middle-class suburbs run up between the wars', as the left-wing journalist Norman Mackenzie put it.[51] In this regard, Clapson's contention that New Towns were the same as suburban estates seems misplaced.[52] The later phase of New Town design certainly became more suburban and indeterminate, as Ortalano has demonstrated in the case of Milton Keynes, but even in those examples, a unifying theory of self-contained settlement still drove the plans.[53] 'It is not just another housing estate', suggested the Labour activist Joan Harrison on a 1951 visit to Crawley, pointing to the fact that 'the idea is to build a town complete with industry so that its residents may work near their homes'.[54] While the industrial base of New Towns would not be a lasting feature of many, the enthusiastic attempt to create autonomous settlements rather than suburban extensions was sincere. More controversial within Labour ranks was that New Towns were not managed by the local authorities but rather by autonomous Development Corporations, with boards appointed by the Minister for Town and Country Planning and with direct financing from the Exchequer.[55] Some Labour members believed, largely correctly, that the New Towns would not be the radical alternative that they envisaged if left to Development Corporations.

Writing in *Socialist Commentary* in September 1954, the sociologist Michael Young argued that New Towns would fail, as the workers of the towns and their children 'will realise no new town can offer as wide a choice of employment as a city' and would eventually commute elsewhere.⁵⁶ He criticised the focus on 'overspill' development, claiming that 'for every bright new house put up at Harlow, Crawley or Basildon, a score are falling down in Birmingham, Bristol and Bradford'.⁵⁷ Versions of Young's argument would become familiar in Labour ranks as the post-war years went on. Rather than 'abandoning' the old, Victorian city, Labour should concentrate its efforts in reshaping it – Young's own quixotic reasoning for this is explored further in Chapter 4. The physician and former Labour MP for Barnet, Stephen Taylor, now a board member of Harlow New Town Development Corporation, replied to Young in the same issue of *Socialist Commentary*, under the heading 'Abandon our Cities? – Certainly Not'. Taylor claimed that the alternative to New Towns was not 'sardining' through higher densities, but 'it is more [peripheral] council estates of the kind he so rightly condemns, or an extension of the suburban sprawl, where a low level of human happiness seems to march in hand with a low Labour vote'.⁵⁸ Despite their differences over the New Towns there was much agreement between the two commentators. Both Taylor and Young felt that the inter-war 'out country housing estates' were a 'disaster', and both were opposed to private suburbs.⁵⁹ Taylor had written on 'suburban neurosis' for *The Lancet* in 1938, claiming that 'we have allowed the slum which stunted the body to be replaced by a slum which stunts the mind'.⁶⁰ Throughout the 1950s in particular, there was deep unease in Labour ranks about the supposed political consequences of suburban living, many party members suspecting that semi-detached family life would turn workers into Tories.⁶¹ Their fears were heightened further by 'Subtopia', a neologism coined in 1955 by the architectural journalist Ian Nairn to describe how the 'spreading thing' of the modern city was 'rendering meaningless the old distinction between urban and rural life'.⁶² Setting aside the obvious fact that plenty of party members themselves were suburban residents, Young's critique did give voice to the fears of some activists.

This being said, the New Town concept explicitly aimed to prevent the 'suburban neurosis' believed to exist by Taylor and others, by ensuring that residents lived within easy access of work and other amenities. Through the post-war nationalisation of transport services, Labour had considerable scope to achieve this.⁶³ The first wave of New Towns largely reflected the 1943 recommendation of the National Council of Social Service that 'most people should be able to live within about fifteen minutes' door-to-door travel from their work by bus, tram or cycle'.⁶⁴ In a September 1954 *Socialist Commentary* article on Harlow New Town, the author claimed that no one was 'more than twelve minutes by bicycle from his place of work', with 'fully used' and 'deservedly popular' cycle tracks enabling quick movement around the town.[65] A further piece on Harlow in the following issue by George Thomson, MP for Dundee East, also commented on the cycle tracks, with factories 'only a few minutes from the workers' doors', contrasting this with 'exhausting, overcrowded tube journeys' made by the same workers when they had lived in London.[66]

Urban transport policy had an important function in Labour thinking. In his 1913 pamphlet *Eight-Pound Cottages*, the Glaswegian Labour councillor John Wheatley planned to use the profits of the Glasgow Tramway Department to build his eight-pound cottages.[67] Wheatley justified the use of tramway funds by the fact that it was poorer citizens who were tram-users, asserting that the rich 'must be prevented from putting a finger into this poor man's purse'.[68] However, this novel form of redistribution did not form part of his scheme for increasing municipal house-building when Wheatley became Minister of Housing more than ten years later. In an era of urban expansion, the working classes were becoming commuters, particularly within London.[69] The 1918 Tudor Walters Report emphasised that local authorities should phase house-building plans in with tramway development.[70] Similarly, the Labour-controlled LCC aimed to ensure 'a rapid and cheap means of locomotion' in the planning of their 'out-country' housing estates, but this often did not occur.[71] The tram was gradually superseded by the bus throughout the inter-war period, due to the belief that buses would ease traffic congestion.[72] Herbert Morrison had attempted to rationalise bus services through limiting competition as Minister of Transport in the 1929–31 Labour government, and additionally initiated a bill to create a public London Passenger Transport Board (LPTB).[73] The inter-war preference of the LCC and other Labour-controlled councils for suburban housing estates made good transport imperative.[74]

In spite of the attention paid to transport, high fares and long commuting times alongside higher rents for council homes concerned some observers, with several inter-war sociological studies arguing that this combination was a key factor in causing tenants to leave peripheral estates.[75] Indeed, Jevons and Madge had concluded in their 1930s study of 'out-country' estates in Bristol that there was a pressing 'need for less segregation of estates from the life of the city as a whole'.[76] Labour's opponents on the left held similar views. In a 1938 Communist pamphlet, Ted Bramley decried the 'misery of queuing up, fighting for bus or tram in the pouring rain' before returning to one's home.[77] He continued this theme in a 1945 publication, claiming that 'to build houses in such a way as to isolate people unduly from the community is a crime'.[78] Nonetheless, as Orwell observed in a similar manner to Priestley, the 'germs of the future England' were to be found in those suburbs pioneered by 'cheap motor cars'.[79] This was especially true of the south and midlands, though car journeys only represented in total 9.1 per cent of journeys to work by 1939, with the train and bicycle only narrowly outstripped by walking.[80] This being said, it is evident that the provision of urban transport within New Towns was not always consistent. In an August 1956 piece on Peterlee for *Labour Woman* it was noted that 'there is a need for a better transport service – more buses in all directions'.[81] Car ownership did not begin its dramatic rise until the mid-1950s, tripling from 4.4 million in 1950 to 13 million in 1965.[82] For Labour, the urban experience, whether old town or new, remained principally one of Hoggart's romanticised childhood: one in which 'motor-cars seldom penetrated', trams remained the 'gondolas of the people' and the charabanc held its place as king of the road.[83]

By the 1960s, the purpose of the New Town was being reassessed in the context of dispersal at large: was the New Town a limited means of redistributing population and industry? Or was it the basis for a new way of living? In a 1960 pamphlet on overspill, the planning academic Barry Cullingworth reflected that 'the actual mechanics of developing non-dormitory towns has presented unexpected difficulties'.[84] He accused local authorities of 'wrecking the policy of urban dispersal' by building peripheral housing and increasing their industrial bases, as well as suggesting that many New Towns had not been able to employ their populations within them.[85] Conversely, some within Labour regarded this as evidence that New Towns should be supervised by their 'parent' local authority. Transfer of each New Town to an 'appropriate local authority' was reasserted by the NEC in 1959, with a transition period of additional funding to provide employment for the younger-than-average populations and to provide further amenities within the New Towns.[86] Covering the plans of Crawley Development Corporation to sell the leases they held on factories in 1956 – an unusual feature for a New Town – the journalist Mervyn Jones remarked that the ability of the town to develop to meet the needs and desires of working people 'was grounded in the fact of municipal ownership, which makes municipal planning possible'.[87] Yet as the Development Corporation was gradually wound up, the Chair of the Development Corporation, Sir Thomas Bennett, suggested that the Labour-controlled urban district council was not the 'proper body' to own the council houses or factory leases.[88] This stood in contrast to the usual process, by which New Town assets would pass to the elected local council. Attitudes such as this heightened the significance of democratically controlled industrial planning to Labour members, particularly in the context of a renewed 'drift south' of population and industry to London and the South of England in the 1960s, though it should be noted the Midlands remained an industrial beneficiary until the 1970s. *Towns for Our Times* compared this process to the 'drift west' of American population and industry to California, warning that 'the forces of expansion in this country will create a built-up area stretching from Dover to Liverpool'.[89] Tranter argues that the attempt to 'counter-urbanise' was able to reduce excessive population increase in London, but failed in attempts to shift the balance of industry elsewhere.[90]

A 'failure to plan' was the cause of industrial concentration in the Midlands and the South, according to *Signposts for the Sixties*, which advocated 'employment spread more sensibly throughout the country' via more New Towns.[91] It was clear, from a Labour perspective, that the New Towns were only useful to socialist aims if they were closely controlled. The draft of *Towns for Our Times* recommended using New Towns planned as 'counter-magnets to the great conurbation areas', suggesting far larger populations of 250,000 (they were limited at 100,000 in the published version).[92] The late-1950s plan for an LCC New Town at Hook in Hampshire by the Communist architect-planner Graeme Shankland was one likely inspiration. Hook was 'designed to celebrate urbanity', with high densities, the town centre set on a deck structure with roads banished below and housing within walking distance.[93] Hook was, however, never built, the project being abandoned by the Conservative government in 1960 in the face of local opposition.[94] This seeming reluctance to push ahead with New Town schemes galvanised Labour into promising more, and larger, New Towns that would be 'centres of expanding industry' as well as providing 'education, culture and recreation'.[95]

While New Towns would be a key feature of the Labour governments between 1964 and 1970, tackling urban decay remained a major concern. Some activists believed that the New Towns had wrongly taken precedence over reshaping cities. It was as if '… the conurbations in which most of our population live' had taken second place to the New Town project, argued the academic Paul Thompson in a 1963 Fabian pamphlet.[96] The accompanying reconsideration of urban transformation against dispersal in Labour ranks was perhaps most evident in an extended *Socialist Commentary* report on planning in September 1961 entitled the 'Face of Britain', which drew upon a host of high-profile contributors including Peter Hall and Peter Willmott.[97] It was an unabashed defence of planning by left-leaning architects and planners, including Shankland, and Alison and Peter Smithson. Responding to the 'reaction to planning' from local activists inspired by Jane Jacobs and heritage bodies such as the Victorian Society, *Socialist Commentary*'s editorial stated that whilst 'our deep-rooted passion for liberty makes us fiercely distrustful of interference', this could result in an 'absurd sentimentality'.[98] Jane Jacobs had led protests against urban motorway construction in late-1950s New York City, most notably defeating the city planner Robert Moses' scheme for a 'Lower Manhattan Expressway' that would have cut through the Lower East Side. However, Jacobs was more meditative than might have been imagined on the subject of the car, writing that though traffic was a 'powerful and insistent' force changing the city, 'we blame automobiles for too much'.[99] Jacobs argued that the problem was less the fact that cars existed, but rather that the 'orthodox planning' of the period demonstrated 'sheer disrespect for other city needs, uses and functions'.[100]

'The Face of Britain' was part of a general reaction to urban congestion in the early 1960s, which stimulated a wave of enthusiasm for modernist urban renewal across the political spectrum. In January 1961, an LPRD report on planning claimed that cities were being 'throttled by traffic jams', the automobile being a more popular choice for commuters than public transport.[101] *Towns for Our Times* contended that traffic was not 'an inevitable evil to be endured along with wet summers and the common cold', warning against giving the car a 'completely free run' as had happened in the United States with the introduction of the urban motorway.[102] 'Face of Britain' recommended the development of cities into a series of pedestrian communities, connected by public transport, contrasting this modernist vision with 'row on row of red-brick terrace housing, crammed in without a hint of green space anywhere' that characterised the inner areas of Birmingham and other major cities.[103] Private developers 'cannot redevelop congested or obsolete working-class districts', the report went on, stating that the need to rehouse the populations of said districts meant that this had to be a public undertaking, creating 'new towns within cities'.[104] Summarising this prevailing orthodoxy, the 1963 report of a government committee on congestion headed by the town planner Colin Buchanan entitled *Traffic in Towns* argued for a new 'traffic architecture', which would require nothing less than the total reconstruction of cities.[105] While the Buchanan Report, as it became known, was never implemented due to the high costs of remodelling cities to meet increasing motorisation, the primacy of the car was nevertheless entrenched in policy terms.[106] At the local level in Labour-controlled Bradford, Gunn has shown that those within Labour were attracted to the brash modernism of the City Engineer Stanley Wardley, whose urban motorway system, pedestrian subways and car parks built from the late 1950s onwards were 'the most visible embodiment of the post-war city as a networked infrastructure'.[107] Coventry, too, was held up as an exemplar, with one such 1959 *Socialist Commentary* piece remarking approvingly on the 'inner circulating traffic route' formed around the pedestrian shopping area of the city centre and its preservation of pedestrian access 'in the face of modern traffic'.[108] The influence of the car had effects on both inner-city and dispersal planning, with roads given prominence over the pedestrian street in the former case, and in the latter, Los Angeles having a long ascendancy as a planning archetype.

'Britain's planning needs are Labour's great opportunity', stated the *Socialist Commentary* editorial for the edition in which the 'Face of Britain' report was published, adding 'planning is basic to its beliefs'.[109] What we might designate an 'urbanist turn' of the early 1960s towards reconstruction seemed to affirm Labour's commitment to urban transformation: demolition of an 'obsolete' urban past while simultaneously reducing overcrowding through a rejuvenated New Towns programme. Anticipating a more munificent era when Labour next entered government, the 'Face of Britain' authors commented that Labour's previous term of office had been 'hamstrung' by recurrent financial and economic crises, meaning that housing was pursued only as an 'end in itself' rather than as part of a holistic approach to planning incorporating all elements of the physical environment.[110] There was no small irony to this: financial stringency would again curtail urban modernist radicalism from the mid-1960s onwards. Nevertheless, the outlook for urban transformation on radical terms was highly promising in the earlier part of the decade. Proclaiming the success of the New Towns programme as 'self-evident', the 'Face of Britain' authors pointed to the redevelopment of central and inner urban areas as a priority for the next Labour government, contrasting their approach to the 'multiplication of brick and asphalt deserts' characteristic, they claimed, of Conservative policy.[111]

The heights of modernity: High-density housing and urban transformation

The most aesthetically striking element in the modernist reimagining of British cities was high-density, mass housing in urban redevelopment schemes, captured in the popular imagination by high-rise 'tower blocks' of flats. This high-density revolution was one of public housing and unlike in the New Towns, development was controlled by local authorities. Three factors prompted the move to high-density development. Firstly, high-density mass housing formed part of the urban modernist moment, which saw a sincere belief that improved living conditions and the benefits of urban life could be distributed to the greatest number through greater densities. Secondly, a trend towards technological optimism within political circles that enough homes could be delivered through new building techniques – and in the case of Labour, council workforces – that all could escape inadequate housing. Thirdly, there was a pragmatic recognition by policymakers that dispersal had limits: not all would choose to move out of the city if offered the chance to do so, and most would continue to live within cities rather than in New Towns or expanded towns. For a period in the late 1950s and 1960s, high-density housing promised open space in the centre of cities, signifying to progressive planners 'the freeing of the lower classes from the darkness of the slums'.[112] But how was this received by those within Labour: what were the processes that took Labour from cottage estate to Trellick Tower?

High-density development was not initially a part of Labour's urban thought. Some Labour-controlled councils had built flats in the inter-war years, especially the LCC across a range of slum clearance estates, with notable examples including the art deco Ossulston Estate in Somers Town and the White City Estate in Shepherd's Bush.[113] The most ambitious scheme to be built was the Quarry Hill Estate by Leeds City Council, a megastructure influenced by the Karl-Marx Hof estate in 'Red Vienna'. In spite of these efforts, large-scale flat schemes would not become the norm until the late 1950s.[114] Though they would fervently embrace flat-building in the late 1950s, Birmingham Labour Party expressed their preference for houses over high-density construction in a 1943 policy pamphlet, pointing out that Conservative plans for forty-two dwellings per acre in the central area of Duddeston and Nechells were more than three times the density of suburban areas. They noted that 'as a general principle the Labour Party are against the policy of housing the working people by means of flats' – presumably overlooking the examples of their LCC and Leeds comrades – and went on to outline their aim that average densities in central areas should not exceed '25 [dwellings] to the acre'.[115] This seemed optimistic: Patrick Abercrombie's 1944 London plan would go on to propose forty houses per acre in central areas, with two-thirds of that population in flats, although most inter-war building in Birmingham was of the large cottage estate model such as those at Kingstanding and Weoley Castle.[116] In contrast to the Birmingham Labour viewpoint, the Communist Party claimed in 1944 that existing cities would 'spread two or three times into the countryside' if suburban-style housing densities were attempted in central areas.[117] The Communists believed, not without reason, that 'reactionary influences' had made modern flats sound worse than they were and their argument on densities proved prescient when viewed in a contemporary light.[118] In a 1943 survey of housing preferences, Mass-Observation suggested that 'flats are not the sort of dwellings that people want to live in all their lives', though they noted that an overwhelming proportion of the flat residents surveyed across medium-rise blocks in Fulham and Kentish Town were satisfied with their current homes in spite of indicating a future preference for a garden.[119] Responding to the Birmingham Labour policy statement, delegates of the Birmingham Trades Council claimed that they '[represented] a younger age group than the Borough Labour Party' and while acknowledging popular desire for gardens, felt flats might well become more popular when they were not 'gloomy tenements in undesirable surroundings'.[120] Though it was evident that the cottage estate model of homes with gardens remained dominant, it did not necessarily follow that the inter-war experience of flats had been unsuccessful.

By the mid-1950s, Labour had become increasingly concerned with the lack of house-building in central urban areas, as well as the advanced decay of the older housing stock. Urban dispersal had created 'two nations', claimed Michael Young in 1955, one living in 'modern houses in the suburbs', the other in 'old houses at the centre'.[121] The 1956 housing policy statement *Homes for the Future* indicated that if slum areas were to be redeveloped, multi-storey flats would be the only way in which similar densities could be provided with improved living conditions, to enable those who wished to stay in slum areas to do so.[122] Flat-building offered the tantalising possibility of quickly solving housing shortages. Bristol City Council – who had built a large number of flats in the late 1950s – reportedly felt that their housing problem was 'solved' in a 1960 NEC Home Policy sub-committee paper.[123] *Towns for Our Times* alluded to the possibility of flats as a means of replacing 'slums and obsolete twilight areas' with the ambiguous term 'modern development'.[124] The renewed focus on central urban areas was both a product of stalled slum clearance and a response to urban sprawl. 'If we allow suburban sprawl to continue unchecked', the author of an LPRD paper on the 'quality of living' reflected in 1964, 'we shall end up with a subtopian wasteland where the benefits of both the town and the country have been destroyed'.[125] '[Experimenting] with high density building' was the recommendation in this case.[126] In most cases, this meant high blocks, although the mid-1960s low-rise, high-density developments designed by Neave Brown for Camden Borough Council would prove that this assumption was unfounded.[127] With the striking developments of Communist Europe serving as an inspiration, high-density development was, to many Labour activists, symbolic of cities reconfigured to serve their populations.

A 'culture of technological appreciation' was a crucial element in how high-density urban development was understood by those within Labour.[128] There was a long-standing socialist fascination with the use of technology to accelerate change. 'Today ... science is the pace-maker in politics', claimed the journalist Ritchie Calder in a 1948 discussion pamphlet *Science and Socialism*, issued by Labour.[129] Science and socialism were 'mutually dependent and inseparable' in his argument that the Labour government needed scientific ingenuity to realise utopia, pointing to the role of applied research units such as the Building Research Station.[130] In 1950, two trade unionists visiting the USSR – Patrick Devanny of the Amalgamated Society of Woodworkers in North-West London and James T. Stark of the Amalgamated Union of Building Trades Workers in Edinburgh – reported of Moscow that 'it is a pleasant sight to see modern blocks of flats going up at the back of old wooden houses'.[131] Their visit was the consequence of an invitation for British workers to see the Soviet Union by the Moscow Trades Council, organised through the propagandist British-Soviet Friendship Society (BSFS), with twenty trade unionists attending the Moscow May Day celebrations and then touring the country for a further two weeks. While membership of the BSFS was proscribed within the Labour Party, the 1950 workers' delegations were nominated by shop floor vote. It must be presumed that not all delegates were BSFS members, given their numbers included at least one serving Labour councillor and others holding CLP positions. A further BSFS workers' delegation in 1952 included the Labour activist George Elvin, General Secretary of the Association of Cinematographers and Allied Technicians, as well as two further Labour councillors.[132] A wide range of Labour figures and architects had toured the Soviet Union in the 1930s under the guidance of the Society for Cultural Relations, which included Lewis Silkin, then Chair of the LCC Housing Committee and then Minister of Town and Country Planning in the 1945–50 Labour government.[133] Devanny and Stark remarked that most of the blocks being built were around six or seven storeys high and 'not too different in appearance' to similar blocks built in Britain, with the exception that lifts were provided.[134] Such largesse would not continue: the later wave of 'Khrushchyovka' blocks built between the late 1950s and early 1960s were deliberately built at five storeys to justify not including lifts. The 1952 delegation were similarly impressed by apparent Soviet dynamism, Crosbie M. Hall from the Association of Building Technicians in Stirling recounting that 'all the resources of science are used by the [Soviet] building industry'.[135] Hall paid particular attention to the use of pre-cast units in flat building on a trip to Dnipropetrovsk, remarking that a five-storey block of sixty-two flats could be 'built by 200 workmen in 100 days'.[136] Whether or not these flats were still paradigms of scientific socialism after a few years is beside the point – what mattered was that those on the left believed that technological innovation could deliver the New Jerusalem in built form.

The new world would, as Hall's comment indicates, be one built by the hands of free workers. Whether the building industry should be under public control or not was a consistent post-war theme of discussion within Labour. Throughout the inter-war years, the building trade unions had pushed for sectoral bargaining and experimented with guild socialism, having syndicalist sympathies and believing that the longer-term housing programme implied by the 1924 Wheatley Act offered the opportunity to de-casualise an industry in which the demand for labour fluctuated wildly.[137] Their stance began to change in the 1940s as a Fabian view of state-led socialism became dominant in Labour thinking. In a 1945 pamphlet, Harry Barham claimed that the basic problem of the building industry was inefficiency, with labour casualised and distributed between small, competing companies, though the effects of war had meant that these companies had begun to amalgamate into larger firms.[138] Barham recommended the creation of a 'National Building Corporation', claiming that with job security through a 'socialised industry', workers would be motivated to be more productive more and 'more bricks laid will mean more houses more quickly'.[139] If Barham's assumption that builders would be galvanised by a nationalised industry was open to question, there was a clear logic to centralising the labour pool. Yet the 1945–51 Labour governments made no move to create any such body, with a National Building Agency created by the Conservative government in 1963.[140] Prior to this, 'direct labour' was advocated by Labour, which meant increasing the public works units of local authorities.[141]

It would not be until the 1950s that a move would begin within Labour to make a nationalisation of the building industry a policy priority, with votes in favour of doing so failing to pass at the annual conferences of 1950 and 1953.[142] Bevan spoke against the latter vote, arguing that 'if you want to do it, do it, but it does mean the immediate socialisation of the vast number of industries of Great Britain'.[143] The secretary of the principal building union body, the National Federation of Building Trades Operatives (NFBTO), Richard Coppock, had been opposed to a national body throughout the inter-war period and remained so into the early 1950s, despite endorsing Barham's pamphlet.[144] This was in part due to union concerns that the use of industrialised building techniques would result in de-skilling and thus lower wages.[145] In the event, the greater volume of work in the 1960s resulted in a higher rate for the job, though this was provided through the 'lump': labour-only subcontracting in which nominally self-employed workers were hired for the construction job in question, cutting building unions out the process.[146] Coppock – and the unions he represented – became increasingly in favour of nationalisation, writing in a December 1956 edition of *Labour's Voice* that 'building as a social service' was only possible under public control.[147] In a 1961 NFBTO pamphlet, Coppock argued that the enormity of the slum clearance project invited the question: 'Why not have a publicly controlled building force doing the actual work?'[148]

In spite of the conversion of the building unions to nationalisation, this force would, in most cases, remain a municipal one. Whilst the idea of a 'National Building Corporation' failed to become policy, Labour-controlled councils began to make heavy use of direct labour. Labour strongholds such as Bermondsey, Salford and West Ham had especially powerful direct labour organisations, which could, as Glendinning and Muthesius observe, 'act as a powerful brake on involvement of national firms, or innovative policies such as prefabrication and high flats'.[149] Direct labour could result in 'institutionalised chaos': the architect of the high-rise Red Road Estate in Glasgow, Sam Bunton Jr, contrasted the careful approach of workers in Sweden who wore sandals after each floor layer was put in with those in Glasgow who 'trod their pieces into the floor and wrecked the place'.[150] By contrast, the direct labour organisation of Edmonton Borough Council in North London were early adopters of battery-cast prefabrication and carried out all building work in the area.[151] Similarly, Sheffield Council utilised their direct labour department to build the iconic, modernist Park Hill development: 'proving beyond any doubt', to Bob Gregory in *Tribune*, 'the value in any municipality of a Public Works Department'.[152]

Marking the successful completion of several eleven-storey flat blocks a full six months ahead of schedule by Salford City Council's direct labour force in July 1959, Frank Allaun asserted that this success showed what could be achieved if 'Labour men and trade unionists [have] guts'.[153] Salford were an especially committed socialist council, but the belief that private builders were responsible for high building costs and poor working conditions was widespread throughout the party.[154] Building workers in Stevenage New Town – in common with other areas in which there was not a dominant direct labour organisation – spent much of the post-war period engaged in a bitter battle with firms using 'lump' labour, eventually gaining the agreement of Stevenage Development Corporation that such firms would not be given contracts.[155] By 1966, Labour had amended the law so that local authorities did not have to offer contracts for open competition, enabling direct labour units to commit to continuous industrialised building.[156]

This was a significant step, albeit short-lived, as Labour would rescind this change to return to open competition in 1969. The Liverpool Walton MP Eric Heffer – a former joiner sponsored by the Amalgamated Society of Woodworkers – called for a National Building Corporation to absorb direct labour organisations in response to this 'partial retreat'.[157] It is evident that direct labour had a mixed record in high-density building, though it is difficult to critique the ambition to ensure sickness pay, holiday pay and continuity of employment were part of building contracts. Shapely, Tanner and Walling observe that in Salford, it did not really matter how efficient direct labour was to the Labour council, but rather, 'direct labour showed that the people – and collectivism – were capable of competing with capitalism'.[158]

The rapid building methods utilised in high-density construction offered the potential for enormous numbers of homes to be built annually. When flats were a significant part of the total, it became relatively easier to achieve the high targets set for building homes. The use of prefabricated 'systems' for building council homes was a key part in this. Michael Harloe comments that the status of council housing as a 'plannable instrument' meant that it became 'the test-bed for most of the innovations in building techniques, new materials and so on which were developed in the post-war years'.[159] High targets were enthusiastically taken up by the Conservative government, with Keith Joseph as Minister of Housing raising the target from 300,000 homes built per annum in 1962 to 400,000 in October 1963.[160] Labour responded in kind, with the party stating in the 1964 general election manifesto that 400,000 homes were a 'reasonable target', through the use of industrialised building.[161] As discussed in the previous chapter, the extent of the slum problem added further impetus to high targets, as the rate of clearance could not realistically rise without an equally large stock of new homes for those displaced to move to. This being said, the rapidity with which these homes were to be built was often at the expense of quality, with a wide array of off-the-shelf industrialised 'systems' in circulation. Equally, as Glendinning and Muthesius remark, 'in the prefabricated schemes of the mid-sixties, architectural theories of mass-production were unrealised in the face of municipal demands for limitless minor variations'.[162]

After a year in office, Richard Crossman felt confident – with the support of Wilson – that he could increase the target to 500,000 homes per annum. By January 1966, with a general election to be called that year, Crossman was assuring the readers of *Labour Woman* that '500,000 houses a year is only the first step. The 1970's will see even higher targets'.[163] Ironically, house completions fell drastically in February 1966 and, ahead of the April general election, Crossman reflected in his diary that '… we haven't delivered the goods; the builders are not building the houses'.[164] As noted in the previous chapter, the building programme peaked in 1967, with 415,460 completions in one year. By June, with a large Labour majority secured but an ominous economic picture developing, Crossman was having to fight off efforts in the Cabinet Housing Committee to scale down the housing programme.[165] With Crossman's replacement by the less forceful Anthony Greenwood as Minister of Housing in a subsequent reshuffle, the 500,000 target would be quietly dropped in 1968, bringing an effective end to an ever-increasing national housing programme, though energetic campaigns continued in Labour-controlled London boroughs.[166] Finnimore notes that 'the seriousness of the 1967 economic crisis in Britain was matched by the speed with which the vision of a "revolution" in building evaporated'.[167] A 1969 *Tribune* editorial reflecting on the fall in output suggested that the problem was the Conservative takeover of many major councils in the late 1960s, with the solution to 'leapfrog local Tory obstructionism' through a national building agency that would deliver the housing programme.[168] Although the reduction in housing output had much to do with spending cuts, there was something in this. The massive Conservative municipal victories in the mid-1960s were won on the back of anti-flat campaigning, opposition to direct labour, and programmes of council house sales rather than construction.[169] In 1967 and 1968, the Conservatives took control of Bradford, Cardiff, Coventry, the Greater London Council, Leeds, Leicester, Liverpool, most London boroughs, Manchester, Newcastle, Nottingham, Sheffield and Southampton.[170] One might wonder why, with ambitious policy aims of high housing output, Labour chose to continue to work through local authorities to build homes rather than to coordinate house-building nationally.

Owing to the significance placed on this factor in surveys of the phenomenon, it is important to address the question of subsidies in high-rise housing. In 1956, the Conservative government doubled the subsidies on high-rise blocks over six storeys in height from that given per standard house, with the subsidy rising by fixed increment for each additional storey. This system would be retained until 1966.[171] In places such as the London borough of West Ham, high-rise blocks of flats had been built from the late 1940s, but with traditional brick-based methods. The role of this generous subsidy system in supporting the growth of high-rise building – or 'a climate of encouragement' as John Gold put it – seems evident, though it is difficult to separate this out from the trend for high-density developments in this era, and indeed Gold is adamant that the subsidy regime did not 'create' the high-rise boom.[172] Saumarez Smith emphasises that the slow pace of slum clearance and need to rehouse those whose homes had been demolished made faster building methods an enticing possibility to both of the main parties.[173] Finnimore argues that the removal of the progressive height subsidy in 1966 was the 'beginning of the end' for high-rise, whilst Glendinning and Muthesius have pointed out that local authorities could negate subsidy changes in the short term 'by pooling rents or subsidies on existing properties, or by drawing further on rate revenue'.[174] This being said, Glendinning and Muthesius believed that 'subsidy manipulations' by central government had some effect in the late 1960s, though still more significant was a general withdrawal of Treasury funding for local government.[175] It would be reasonable to assert that building costs were not the sole cause of enthusiasm for high-rise dwellings. A 1969 memorandum by the Housing Policy Study Group of the NEC stated that 'there is growing evidence that Tory authorities are reducing or cancelling council house building projects' despite continuing to receive central government funding for priority housing areas.[176] Significantly, the Study Group also suggested that high interest rates and building society issues had meant a slowdown of private sector construction projects.[177] Given that the post-devaluation economic crisis was hitting both public and private finances in the late 1960s, subsidy withdrawal seems more a symptom than a cause of a reduction in high-rise building. Indeed, the Study Group claimed that the overall house building problem was one of finance, Britain spending proportionately less of its gross national product on housing than other Western European nations.[178] Nicholas Bullock considers the basic failings of the industrialised manner of building, and a change in architectural practice to low-rise, high-density dwellings to have been of equivalent importance.[179] Most symbolically, the 1968 collapse of the twenty-two-storey Ronan Point block on the Clever Road estate in West Ham, with four fatalities, had a major effect on public perceptions of the safety of high-rise housing and strengthened the position within government of high-rise detractors.[180] High-rise building for public purposes was already on the way out by the time subsidies were withdrawn.

The fate of high-density building was closely linked to the phasing out of slum clearance in favour of rehabilitation of older houses. The previous chapter has discussed the discomfort that this shift induced within Labour, with some activists feeling that the project of urban transformation was far from complete. High-density construction did not end entirely: Labour's return to power in number of London boroughs in 1971 laid the foundations for a brief renaissance, particularly in those boroughs experimenting with low-rise, high-density construction such as Camden and Lambeth.[181] Nevertheless, we might see the 1969 publication of the Report of the Committee on Public Participation in Planning – more generally known as the Skeffington Report after the committee chair Arthur Skeffington, MP for Hayes and Harlington, and Parliamentary Private Secretary to Greenwood – as auguring the end of grand projects in housing. The Skeffington Committee had been appointed to look into ways by which local communities could contribute to local plans, largely in response to popular reaction against redevelopment schemes which, more often than not, involved large roads and high blocks. In 1968, the basic principle of public consultation on planning decisions at an early stage had been enshrined within the Town and Country Planning Act of that year.[182] It was part of a broader trend in 'participation', which included a series of twelve Community Development Projects across Britain seeking to stimulate community action. John Gyford notes that the defeats of the mid-1960s in local government meant that the succeeding generation of Labour councillors in the early 1970s were committed to a 'more open style of government'.[183] Yet the published report took a cautious line, stating simply that 'opportunity should be provided for discussions with all those involved'.[184] This was still too much for paternalistically minded Labour councillors and the Skeffington Report was 'greeted with derision' at the 1970 annual conference.[185] Not all activists responded negatively. A 1969 letter to *Tribune* from an A. Killick suggested that the new doctrine of 'participation' meant that the Development Corporation of Basildon New Town had finally been forced to consult the public, with 300 turning up to one meeting in a demonstration of 'the real democracy that is necessary to counteract bureaucracy'.[186] Reflecting positively on 'participation' in 1971, David Winnick (previously MP for Croydon South and later MP for Walsall North) suggested that 'there still remains among some [councillors] a feeling that council tenants should be damn grateful for being rehoused', despite it being a local authority duty to rehouse those in need.[187] In the event, the Report helped create 'a presumption in favour of preservation', consolidating the ongoing rehabilitation of old houses.[188] Significantly, the Report did not herald an end to expert planning more broadly, concluding that 'the public should react constructively to the facts and ideas put before them … the preparation of plans … must move on smoothly and with reasonable speed'.[189] It did, however, mark an end to top-down attempts to build socialist cities of the kind Labour had envisaged throughout much of the post-war period – high blocks and all – setting the scene for increasing interest on the left in smaller-scale, grassroots work.

Labouring the land: Labour and the politics of land control

'At the heart of nearly all town planning problems', the authors of the 1961 'Face of Britain' report remarked, 'lies the question of the land.'[190] Labour's relationship with the politics of land control is integral to understanding the party view of post-war urban policy. For urban transformation to take place, a high degree of state control over the supply of land would be required. It should be noted that rural policy and land policy as a whole were often intermingled, with urban land rarely mentioned separately.[191] Policy on land put forward also addressed a practical issue in urban development: should state-led projects be hindered by private ownership and high land prices? Equally, for Labour, the terms by land should be controlled were ambiguous. There remained throughout the post-war period a tension between public ownership – generally expressed as nationalisation or legislation – and forms of land taxation. Labour's discussion of the merits of land control also challenged the party's radical self-identity: if the party wished to take away the power of 'landlords', this theoretically had to apply to all landholders. The politics of land control are revealing both of the pressures building upon urban planning from the 1950s onwards and of the difficulties faced by Labour in utilising the modern moment for their socialist aims.

The 1937 policy statement *Labour's Immediate Programme* listed nationalisation as the second of 'four vital measures of reconstruction'.[192] The commitment seemingly held firm throughout the Second World War, to the extent that a major row broke out between Labour and their Conservative coalition partners over the level of compensation for land acquisition for local authorities in the 1944 Town and Country Planning Act, as well as the lack of provision for future nationalisation within the Act.[193] In the 1945 manifesto *Let Us Face the Future*, the party stated that 'Labour believes in land nationalisation and will work towards it, but us a first step the State and local authorities must have wider and speedier powers to acquire land wherever the public interest requires'.[194] In spite of the reaffirmation of land nationalisation, the 1945–51 Labour governments pursued only 'wider and speedier powers to acquire land', through the 1947 Town and Country Planning Act. The removal of land nationalisation as a 'vital measure' has led scholars to conclude that Labour did not take the subject seriously. Clare Griffiths has suggested that land nationalisation was gradually moved out of Labour's focus after non-implementation in 1945, with a brief re-appearance in 1960 in comments by Hugh Gaitskell.[195]

In fact, the subject was 'live' within the party in the early 1950s, and remained prominent until the late 1960s, with the introduction of the 'Land

Commission' to buy up development land. Peter Weiler has argued that the 'Land Commission' was an ideological rallying point, a 'continued hope for a new moral world'.[196] Glen O'Hara notes that successive Labour leaderships took care to avoid committing to land nationalisation, despite it being the clear preference of party activists.[197] He characterises the Land Commission as being an attempt to 'short-circuit' the constraints of the 1947 planning system.[198] I am concerned here less by the policy history of the Land Commission during Labour's term in government than what it might reveal about the mutability of Labour's political thought on land, and perhaps more importantly, land in the context of housing plans. It is arguable that land nationalisation was for Labour activists both a rallying point and a pragmatic recognition that planning for large-scale housing drives was difficult without land control. Crosland observed in *The Conservative Enemy* that 'land is not an ordinary commodity, to be bought and sold like toothpaste or detergent', as it affected far more people than the purchaser.[199] In this respect, Labour's attempt to bring land under public control was as much about a planning quandary as it was about a socialist aim.

The politics of the 'land question' had a long history and land agitation can be dated back to the Chartist movement of the 1840s.[200] At the beginning of the twentieth century, the 'land question' began to develop on an urban character, beyond previous debates about agricultural land, as overcrowding in British cities seemed to suggest to Liberal Party reformers that only land controls would solve the slum problem.[201] Attempts by the Liberals to impose land value taxation during the 1906–10 government failed and land reform as a single issue – focused on removing land from the control of great landowners – fractured into several connected subjects.[202] Labour took a similar view to the Liberals with regard to urban land, viewing control of it essential to building generously apportioned working-class housing to replace the slums.[203] John Wheatley wrote approvingly in 1913 that German cities had wide-ranging powers over the land, '[recognising] the controlling influence of the land on the life of the community'.[204] The 'land question' encompassed the challenges of urbanisation, as well as reversing the deterioration of rural life and confronting the power of the landed classes.[205]

In spite of the recognition of the party that urban land was integral to their future plans, land reform remained primarily an agricultural point of contention for Labour throughout most of the inter-war period. Greater state supervision of land was about improving the lot of the tenant farmer, as well as ensuring urban workers had a constant supply of butter for their bread.[206] This did not preclude moves towards full public ownership of land, with the 1932 party document *The Land and the National Planning of Agriculture* making the 'obviously socialist' declaration that agricultural planning required land control.[207] Labour's growing interest in 'town and country planning' marked a shift towards land nationalisation. The policy began to be presented as a 'functional solution', principally in agricultural terms though increasingly on the question of urban development, as the party became less suspicious of the Garden City Movement. Its inclusion in the 1937 *Immediate Programme* was based on a rural understanding of the need for land reform, with some recourse to town planning.[208] Notably, unlike other nationalisation commitments, there was not a detailed model of how land nationalisation might work in practice.[209]

The Second World War changed the terms of debate from pastoral to urban. During the war, the Uthwatt Committee assessed the possibility of post-war land speculation, recommending local authority compulsory purchase powers for land in post-war planning in their 1942 report, with compensation set at the value of the land on 31 March 1939.[210] Land controls were, as Griffiths puts it, 'a pragmatic answer … to the urban and suburban challenges of post-war rebuilding'.[211] The wartime shift within Labour to seeing land controls as pragmatic urban policy was indicative of party interest in comprehensive planning. In a 1942 report by the NEC Housing and Planning Sub-Committee, it was suggested that without land control, 'planning cannot even begin to be effective'.[212] The report went on to argue that immediate post-war land nationalisation set at 1939 land values was an 'extravagant method' of taking control of land.[213] Given that the row between the wartime coalition partners over the 1944 Town and Country Planning Act was partly based on Labour's refusal to compromise over the 1939 value as the basis for compensation, it seems surprising that internally the party were inclined to moderation.[214] It raises the question whether Labour had a more complex view of public ownership than most accounts of the period suggest. Indeed, the 1942 Housing and Planning Sub-Committee report listed alternatives to land nationalisation, with municipal ownership being seen as the preferred option to 'permanent ownership pooling'. The latter method involved the local authority in question compulsorily purchasing all land, re-planning the area in full and handing back new plots to the owners. Alongside the obvious potential for dissent from disgruntled landowners under this method, the report authors felt that local authorities were comparatively 'strong candidates for the job of owner', as long as they didn't 'make a principle of it'.[215] Tichelar argues that it was in fact Labour councils who were least keen on nationalisation, seeing it as a threat to their own independence and preferring limited (and cheaper) powers of compulsory acquisition.[216] Pragmatically, the loss of rate income by councils during the war meant that low compensation and local control were of greater interest than land nationalisation.[217]

The path taken by the 1945–51 Labour governments was thus focused on controls rather than nationalisation. Compensation to landowners affected by compulsory purchase was to be paid at existing use value under the terms of the 1947 Town and Country Planning Act – far less generous than the 1939 value proposed during the war – with any land value increase accrued from development to be paid to a Central Land Board.[218] In effect, the Act '[nationalised] the development value of land' to guard against inflated land prices.[219] Critiquing these proposals, the socialist writer Douglas Brown argued that the absence of land nationalisation had allowed great landowners to '[carry] on a guerrilla war against the post-war plans for reconstruction' by frustrating local authority plans.[220] John Davis remarks that the complexity of the Act was recognised even by those charged with overseeing it, with the first Chairman of the Central Land Board, Trustram Eve, pointing to the fact that the average landowner would struggle to understand why local authorities could buy the land for far less than its market value, but that the same land could be sold privately for whatever price purchasers might pay.[221] Discretion was the better part of valour when it came to land policy under the Attlee government. In a February 1948 report by the NEC Social Services Sub-Committee on planning, it was suggested that 'there are powerful arguments against nationalisation until the new system has been given a fair trial'.[222] The report went on to suggest that the issue should 'lie dormant until at least 1953', betraying the assumption that Labour would still be in government at that point.[223]

The issue was far from dormant in 1953. In August of that year, the Labour newspaper *Forward* featured a debate over the relative merits of land nationalisation versus land value taxation. *Challenge to Britain*, the party policy statement released in June 1953, had simply confirmed the existing 1947 Act as party policy, after the position of Bevan and his supporters for nationalisation of all rented agricultural land was defeated in the NEC.[224] Advocating land nationalisation was the former MP for Wellingborough George Dallas, while his opponent, Richard Stokes, the MP for Ipswich, was a long-standing supporter of a single land tax.[225] Nationalisation would cost, according to Stokes, 'not less than £20,000,000,000!' in compensation, with tax money being used to pay off landlords.[226] He argued that Labour should instead 'make the landlords pay for the privilege of ownership' through land value taxation.[227] Stokes' reasoning was in essence identical to the Liberal argument of the 1900s, although, as Tichelar suggests, the development charge was a far more limited form of taxation than that sought by land tax advocates.[228] In his response, Dallas noted that party policy was to nationalise agricultural land, and Stokes had been elected on a manifesto pledge to enact it. He critiqued Stokes' use of 'grotesque figures' to attack nationalisation, pointing out that Stokes 'was a member of the Government which nationalised the mines'.[229] Curiously, though the Conservative government had abolished the development charge in 1952 – a key element in the 1947 Town and Country Planning Act as regards urban land – the discussion was confined to agricultural land, but the logic for and against either land taxation of some kind or land nationalisation remained the same. One reader writing into *Forward*, W. E. Fox of Battersea, claimed that land nationalisers 'not only [want] us to buy out the land … but to provide [landlords] with capital', while Dallas asserted that land taxation 'entrenches private landlordism … pay your tax and the land is yours for ever'.[230] In 1954, the suicide of Edward Pilgrim, a toolmaker ruined by the compulsory purchase of development land he had bought, enraged Conservative activists and would ultimately lead to the end of compulsory purchase at existing use value in the 1959 Town and Country Planning Act.[231] It was this later abolition that would return the focus to urban land. The problems faced by large cities attempting to expand began to renew interest in the nationalisation of urban land, as it became apparent to those within Labour that without an effective monopoly of development land to build on, the housing drive would suffer.

Whilst the 1947 Act was 'a brave effort to control the land', wrote John Mackie in a 1960 edition of *Labour's Voice*, it was 'far too complicated … and far too easily dismantled'.[232] Arguing that Labour should avoid 'half-hearted schemes' such as this, Mackie advocated nationalisation, with urban land taken into public ownership first.[233] O'Hara notes that while land price rises may have had a more limited effect on house-building costs than observers at the time believed, the sharp rise in the price of land that increased by 50 per cent during the 1960s compounded existing concerns about ready access to development land for local authorities.[234] Planning policy had been partially liberalised by the Conservatives through the 1952 Town Development Act, which required urban councils to negotiate with other local authorities for development land, and through the 1959 Town and Country Planning Act, which obliged local authorities to pay market rates for compulsorily purchased properties.[235] Urban developers were the beneficiaries of rising land values and accompanying rents, building large numbers of office blocks on central development sites as a consequence of the rise in service industry employment, as well as the fact that the 1947 Act had not designated offices as subject to the same controls as other industrial sites.[236] Speculative investment in the projected future rental value of office blocks created a situation in which there was considerable profit in leaving buildings empty, with the deliberately untenanted office skyscraper Centre Point in the central London coming to symbolise this practice.[237]

The office boom threatened Labour plans for urban transformation of central areas, which had become the priority development area in the early 1960s as discussed earlier in this chapter. *Towns for Our Times* pointed to the success of the redevelopment of Coventry and Plymouth city centres as underscoring the importance of 'unified ownership' of building land, warning against allowing developers to dictate the process.[238] Frank Allaun claimed in 1962 that the 'fantastic racket' in land values had added substantially to already-high housing costs, meaning that the average council flat in Birmingham cost up to £500 'before a single brick is laid'.[239] Allaun asserted that the 'Socialist principle' that increased land value should return to the community meant public ownership of building land, noting the proposal for a Land Commission to do so in *Signposts for the Sixties*, the 1961 Labour policy statement.[240] The question was whether such a proposal would complicate the land situation rather than resolve it.

'It is now clear', stated *Signposts for the Sixties*, 'that public ownership of building land is the only way in which we can expand and renew our towns and villages without being held to ransom by the landowner or the speculator'.[241] Gaitskell himself wrote the land section, having made high land prices a major political issue in repeated attacks on the Tories in 1960.[242] *Signposts for the Sixties* proposed a Land Commission to acquire 'the freehold of all land on which building or rebuilding was to be authorised' at site value plus a further amount 'to encourage the willing sale of land' by landowners.[243] The building land acquired in this way would then be leased to private developers or local authorities as required, ensuring in the former case that development value passed to the public purse as per the 1947 Act.[244] While professional bodies such as Town and Country Planning Association and Royal Institute of Chartered Surveyors were supportive of the Land Commission concept, it had critics within Labour.[245] The authors of the 'Face of Britain' report in the revisionist organ *Socialist Commentary* – most of whom were architects, academics and town planners – critiqued the 'extraordinarily vague' Land Commission plan, recommending instead a more 'bold and far-reaching measure' to acquire the freehold of all land, noting that 'our proposals can … be described as nationalization'.[246] Somewhat surprisingly, the *Tribune* editorial reviewing *Signposts for the Sixties* was far more complimentary, describing the Land Commission as 'one of the most beneficial things the party has ever put forward', though they contrasted this with the absence of municipalisation from the document, wondering whether ambitious land policy would be dropped to secure 'a warm reception from the capitalist press'.[247]

Rather than outright nationalisation in the form more commonly demanded by the Labour left, the 'Face of Britain' proposal was for the owners of freehold land to remain *in situ* as leaseholders on eighty-year leases. An extensive programme of valuation would take place, with the compensation when the leases expired being limited to whatever the use of the land or building might have been at state takeover.[248] Though the report authors claimed that their plan limited ambiguities, as it covered 'all land at the same time', the fact that it contained a large number of leases potentially subject to change and a vast valuation programme meant that it was in practice hardly less complex than the Land Commission.[249] They received some support from Crosland, who stated in *The Conservative Enemy* that nationalising all land would be more effective than limiting plans to simply building land.[250] Assessing the *Socialist Commentary* proposal, the LPRD claimed that 'it does not seem to us that the fact that large areas fall into public ownership together necessarily achieves anything', though they rightly perceived there were more similarities than differences between the two schemes.[251] Giving some indication of the direction of thought, the researchers examining the proposal noted that the emphasis on encouraging 'willing sales' of land in the Land Commission idea was borne of the 'recognition that for any policy to have any hope of becoming a permanent solution it must be seen to be fair'.[252] The risk of land policy being unwound as the 1947 Act had been by the Conservatives was central in the minds of the Land Commission architects, not least Gaitskell.

To develop the Land Commission into a workable form, a Study Group on Land was formed, chaired by Arthur Skeffington.[253] In a memorandum prepared for a Study Group meeting in April 1962, Lord Silkin – Minister of Town and Country Planning in the 1945–51 Labour governments – argued that in order to avoid 'a confiscatory element' to the Land Commission, compensation to bought-out landowners would have to be at market value.[254] Silkin had famously been confronted with a 'Silkingrad' sign on a visit to Stevenage New Town put up by locals opposed to compulsory purchase, and it was evident that the hostility shown to the 1947 Act by the propertied classes had induced caution in his approach. But his objection was exactly the reason upon which those supporting public ownership justified themselves: land was seen to belong to the community, not to the individual. 'All urban land should belong to the community', stated a North Kensington Labour Party study on housing – which had been sent to the Research Department and, we might assume, circulated to the Study Group – 'but it should be leased to private developers so long as the proposed development does not conflict to that of the community'.[255] A paper prepared for the Study Group by the LPRD the previous month had taken on the criticism, prolific in the popular press, that market value was the only means of ensuring 'willing sales' of land, commenting that 'today's market values are far higher than is necessary to induce an owner to sell his land willingly for development'.[256] Silkin was ultimately overruled by his fellow Study Group members, with the final proposals for the Land Commission remaining on the original Gaitskellite lines of *Signposts*, recommending compensation at 30 per cent of market value.[257] Meaner compensation reflected the Labour view that landowners had no right to profit from land that could be used for social purposes. '[The] land racket burdens tenant, rate-payer and tax-payer and hampers the building of houses, schools, hospitals', claimed the Shadow Housing Minister Michael Stewart in *Labour's Northern Voice*, whereas the Land Commission would lead to 'more new towns, more council houses, lower interest rates, and more [municipalisation]'.[258]

When put into practice following the Labour electoral victory in 1964, the Land Commission faced opposition from the start. Considering the operation of the Commission, O'Hara focuses on the 'administrative and political problems inherent in the venture', not least nowhere near enough valuers to assess building land ahead of compulsory purchase.[259] He observes that the creation of a Ministry of Land to oversee the Land Commission prompted a counter-attack from the Ministry of Housing and Local Government, from both the Civil Service and Crossman.[260] Crossman believed that monopoly powers on land purchase for the Commission would do little more than 'gum up the works and destroy any chance of building the houses we would require', believing that it should simply collect taxes on land value increases and buy land where required.[261] Fred Willey, the Minister of Land, had added to the Study Group proposal a tax on all land transactions as a means of getting around the lack of valuers: an act of laudable pragmatism, but one which seemed to return to the 1947 Act in all but name.[262] Much to the consternation of Wilson, who remained keen on the Land Commission proposal, Crossman had no intention of following party policy. His opposition ensured the 'Ministry of Land' merged into the Ministry of Housing and Local Government following the 1966 election, rather than vice versa as had been the aim of *Signposts*.[263] When a much-reduced Land Commission was eventually created in February 1967, the task of buying up land on a scale at which it could be effective proved difficult. Only 1780 acres of land had been bought by 1970 and, rather ironically, given the constant anxiety of Labour in opposition over encouraging 'willing sales' of land, the popular press cited the Pilgrim case of the 1950s as an example of why land controls were unjust.[264] Conservative opposition to the policy encouraged landowners to withhold their property from sale on the assumption that a Tory government would simply abolish the Commission.[265] A Housing Policy Study Group, set up by the NEC in 1968 to develop policy for the 1970s, stated in their 1969 report that 'although the Land Commission is now beginning to justify its existence, there is still some suspicion that it is becoming a political liability'.[266] Rather unrealistically, the Study Group suggested that 'the future of the Land Commission may well be bright', but all but admitted that it had failed in their recommendation that a 'Strategic Land Use Planning Unit' be created as a complementary body to the Commission.[267] This body would deal with another form of opposition to the Commission: local authorities refusing to cooperate with it.[268] Given the scale of opposition, both bureaucratic and landowner, to a policy that purportedly was not land nationalisation, one wonders whether there was any point at all in stepping away from land nationalisation in the hope of a better reception.

Labour's land policy was aimed, as Greenwood asserted in 1967, at 'one of the most gross forms of exploitation – the power of a landowner who renders no service to take large sums from both private and public concerns'.[269] Yet by the dawn of the 1970s, the landowner continued to have the upper hand. Poignantly, the Land Commission was quickly broken up by Conservatives following their election victory in 1970, having been consigned to what Weiler terms an 'Orwellian memory hole' by Labour, with no mention of it during the election campaign.[270] Labour would make only one further serious attempt at land reform in government with the Community Land Act of 1976, which empowered local councils to buy development land at existing use value, and lease it to developers at a market price reflecting future development gains.[271] Considering this final endeavour, Weiler contends that the over-reliance by Labour on a land market in which councils could act as profiteering landlords was a 'fundamental contradiction' if the aim was to cut out speculation.[272] The 1976 Act was repealed by the Conservatives when they came to power in 1980, and land reform has not re-emerged as a significant issue in British politics since, though the proposal for an 'English Sovereign Land Trust' in the 2019 Labour manifesto had some uncanny similarities to the Land Commission.[273]

Regardless of the mechanism by which they were to be gained, Labour's housing plans meant some strategic powers over land were clearly necessary. Labour's evolving interest in controlling land was fundamentally indistinguishable from their wider aims for British cities in the post-war period, given the need for readily available housing sites at a price that did not seem to reward speculators.

The power of ideal environments

What can be taken from Labour's attempt to reshape the urban environment between 1945 and 1970? It is clear that party activists had a socialist vision of urban Britain which drew upon prevailing cultural ideas of modernism. The socialist future – orderly, strikingly modern and well-served by public transport whether New Town or inner area – was set against a reviled urban past, characterised by dark, dirty places of the sort described by Orwell and Priestley. When the significance as well as sincerity of Labour urban thought in the period are understood – all of which was believed to be in service of a well-housed populace – the enthusiasm of Labour activists for urban transformation can be correctly located as a commitment to the modern.

The vision of an urban environment that transcended the limitations of the 'Victorian' city had a clear effect on Labour's urban thought. Whilst the future that would replace 'Industrial England' in the eyes of Labour actors was generally inspired by urban modernism, that image was not uniform and those within the party retained a number of anachronistic preferences. The greatest flaw to this vision was the most prosaic: it rested on a 'complete trust in the power of "ideal" environments to bring about ... reform'.[274] The planning of the post-war cityscape of the future was more than the physical plans of post-war experts, or decisions in the council chamber. While this vision was unstable, and much of it did not come to pass, the political possibilities of British cities 'levelled' in terms of class as well as physical environment appealed to those within Labour as much as it did to other socialists globally in the post-war era. It is difficult to appreciate in the present day how forceful these ideals were and what they meant to those advocating them.

This faith in utopia owed much to the fundamental basis of party culture. Labour's urban policy rested on the assumption that their vision of progress could deliver what the people wanted, without necessarily inviting comment from the people. In matters of policy, Drucker comments that there is a conflict between 'the instantaneous advantage to be gained from expedient political decisions and the slow maturation needed for any policy to be effective'.[275] This was especially true in terms of the built environment in the post-war period. Short of the collectivisation of national resources, translating Labour's modern, socialist vision into reality could only be a long, drawn-out process.

3

'An elementary social need'

Reconstructing housing for the twentieth century

'Good housing is an elementary social need as much as water', wrote Jean Copeland in 1948, 'but it continued to depend on cash for very much longer'.[1] A key Labour objective after 1945 was to create a socially just housing system. Bevan's focus on 'quality' and 'need' in his role as Minister of Health from 1945 to 1951 (with responsibility for housing) has been cited as evidence of 'specifically socialist content' in Labour planning.[2] But where did socialist aims of high-quality homes for all interact with the modernist phenomenon? 'In the twenty years between the two wars it was largely assumed', Copeland went on, 'that the only necessary action was to permit the red-brick blotches to break out all over the countryside and let the first-comers buy them'.[3] In contrast to the sprawling home ownership of Conservative-led government, Labour argued that a socially just housing system would be planned and ultimately of a similar status to other welfare state institutions. 'Of all the social services – though it is often not regarded as a social service – the needs of housing are the most pressing', stated the party research department in a 1965 *newsletter* to Labour councillors.[4] This chapter explores how and why Labour aimed to create a 'social service' in housing – even if their efforts to do so were occasionally contradictory – as a means of understanding how the ideological aim to radically reshape housing related to the modernist moment. In doing so, the chapter suggests that Labour contributed to the expansion of a 'dual tenurial pattern' in which council housing and owner-occupation became the dominant tenures and private renting declined to become a marginal section of the market. For Labour, a socially just housing system was as futuristic as novel architecture.

Housing had – and continues to have – a special place in the Labour tradition. Although housing was undoubtedly an emotive issue for all political parties in the post-war era, Labour had associated itself with not only better but a fairer distribution of housing since its foundation. Whilst the key features of the welfare state retain a certain purchase on the popular mindset – in the respective forms of the National Health Service, state education and public pensions – the state role in housing is rarely registered as an integral part of contemporary welfare. Almost a third of British households lived in a council house or flat by 1971.[5] When we add to that number all who lived in a rent-controlled private house or flat, or all who may have directly or indirectly benefitted from a state-sponsored or state-supported mortgage (or mortgage relief) on their property, the hypothetical total for whom housing policy mattered is considerably more significant. As Danny Dorling has recently stated, 'policy on housing is different from policy on employment, crime, defence, health or education. Policy on housing touches everyone'.[6]

Dorling's assertion is backed by the sheer number of homes built between 1945 and 1970. Table 1 shows the permanent dwellings completed in these years, with the exceptionally high completions in the 1960s particularly eye-catching. The period 1945–70 saw a radical shift in the proportions of public housing and owner-occupation, with a synchronous fall in the numbers of persons renting from private landlords. Martin Daunton has suggested that this was a continuation of changes that had been occurring since 1918, asserting that 'a new tenurial pattern emerged between the wars, based on two main features: owner-occupation and public rental'.[7] Indeed, even in 1967, the highest ever year of completions by local authorities in which some 199,749 homes were built, private builders constructed 204,208 dwellings. Conversely, private renting fell from around 58 per cent of all housing in 1938 to 20 per cent in 1970, and would collapse still further to just 9 per cent in 1991.[8] Yet existing scholarship affords little weight to what housing policy meant for the political aims of Labour.[9] The muscular Conservative approach to housing policy after the election of Margaret Thatcher in 1979 – anti-municipal and committed to housing privatization – was largely left intact by a New Labour leadership committed to burying 'Old Labour' when they entered office in 1997. Notably, more council houses were sold between 1997 and 2000 than in the previous nine years of Conservative rule.[10] The relative stability of scholarly focus on a supposed political 'consensus' surrounding the welfare state pre-1979 has tended to downplay the ideological distinctiveness of Labour approaches to housing in an era of monumental urban transformation, limiting our understanding of how housing figured in party thought.

Figure 1 shows a 1955 recruitment leaflet by Birmingham Borough Labour Party. Their rhetoric stands as an effective summary of Labour attitudes towards housing throughout the period. Knocking 'louder and louder for higher rents', the

Table 1 Permanent dwellings completed in Great Britain, 1945–70

Year	Local authorities	Private	Total
1945	1,936	1,099	3,035
1946	25,245	30,566	55,811
1947	98,028	41,487	139,515
1948	193,548	34,390	227,938
1949	170,806	28,457	199,263
1950	167,917	30,240	198,157
1951	166,483	25,485	191,968
1952	199,177	36,670	235,847
1953	244,916	64,867	309,783
1954	239,318	92,423	331,741
1955	196,024	116,093	312,117
1956	167,710	126,431	294,141
1957	169,629	128,724	298,353
1958	143,283	130,220	273,503
1959	124,545	153,166	277,711
1960	128,216	171,405	299,621
1961	116,118	180,727	296,845
1962	128,577	178,211	306,788
1963	123,903	177,787	301,690
1964	154,754	221,264	376,018
1965	164,547	217,162	381,709
1966	176,871	208,647	385,518
1967	199,749	204,208	403,957
1968	187,964	226,067	414,031
1969	180,958	185,917	366,875
1970	176,926	174,342	351,268

Souce: B. R. Mitchell, *British Historical Statistics* (Cambridge: Cambridge University Press, 1988).

private landlord is the villain of the piece. Labour had a contentious relationship with the private landlord throughout the period, veering from calling for the outright abolition of private renting and, on the other hand, attempting to create a fairer renting system. At the heart of this was a sense by those within Labour that tenants stood to be exploited by the private landlord – and indeed, in the leaflet they are the supposed 'losers' from Conservative policy. Tony Crosland would write in 1962 that 'private landlordism is not an appropriate

Figure 1 Birmingham Borough Labour Party Recruitment Leaflet, c. 1955.

Source: Birmingham City Archives, 329.94249, Birmingham Borough Labour Party, Recruitment Leaflet c.1955.

form of house-ownership in an advanced society' and his view was relatively commonplace amongst Labour members.[11]

Another 'loser' in the leaflet was the owner-occupier, with their mortgage and rates being increased by the Tories. Owner-occupation remains, curiously, to be believed an anathema to those on the left of British politics. This assumption is in spite of work by Ben Jackson on the Revisionist interest in owner-occupation and Guy Ortalano's ambitious study of what he terms a 'property-owning social democracy' in Milton Keynes, which this chapter builds upon. Indicative of this trend, in his widely read 2011 *Chavs: The Demonization of the Working Class*, Owen Jones felt compelled to state that owner-occupation did not lead working-class families to become middle class.[12] Similarly, in the course of explaining

Labour decline, Ross McKibbin has recently insisted that 'governments have long favoured, in one way or another, private home ownership', though his assertion is heavily based on the manner in which the housing system has changed since the 1980 Housing Act, which introduced the Conservative 'Right to Buy' scheme of selling council housing in England and Wales.[13] Far from uniform condemnation of the 'property-owning democracy' of mass owner-occupation cherished by the Conservatives, Labour both engaged with the concept and offered their own socialist alternative to it. Governments of all political characteristics have certainly favoured access to housing, but the Conservatives are the only party to have explicitly specified the private home as the ideal form in the post-war era.

Conversely, Labour undoubtedly promoted council housing as something of a 'vanguard' tenure, acting as an indicator of the socialist future to come. In the leaflet, the removal of subsidies for council homes was stated to lead to unfair rents for many. Throughout the post-war period, Labour expressed considerable uncertainty on how public housing should be financed, and at what level rents should be set. Equally, alternatives to the state provision of public housing struggled to gain traction within Labour, in a manner that would seem to echo Simon Szreter's comment that the welfare state was formed of 'benevolent and paternalistic' class prejudices.[14] Drawing together the changes to the 'tenurial pattern' allows for a clearer understanding of what housing meant for Labour's socialist ambitions than has previously been possible. What part did Labour's socialist urge for change play in the reshaping of the housing system in the context of urban transformation?

Housing as a social service: Labour and council housing

More than any other tenure, council housing has been central to narratives of Labour housing policy after 1945. The council house and especially the flat remain an emblematic feature of the built landscape, inviting both contemporary acclaim and critique. Historians have been drawn to Labour's preference for state intervention in housing, pointing to this variously as a paternalistic 'civilising mission' of the middle classes, an expedient post-war solution to housing needs, and, less commonly in the present day, as a working-class triumph.[15] Few, however, have questioned how council housing served broader Labour objectives within the wider urban environment. As with other forms of tenure, Labour's relationship with council housing in the years 1945–70 was complex and shifting – indeed, as labyrinthine as wider ideals of modernity. This section examines two illustrative, if overlooked, areas of Labour thought. Firstly, this section describes party deliberations over the appropriate level of rent or subsidy for council housing, which fed directly into the wider Labour conception of housing as a social service. The focus here is on debates in the 1950s and 1960s, after the provision of council housing had been widened under the 1945–51 Labour governments, rather than the Bevan years specifically. As council housing as a tenure grew in size, so too did concerns over whether housing could conceivably become a social service on the same terms as education or health. Secondly, this section discusses 'social' alternatives to state provision of housing, the failure of which further emphasises the statist character of Labour's approach to urban transformation. If Labour's vision of the future meant, in the words of one 1955 party publication, '[removing] housing from the field of profiteering and [treating] it as a social service', then how did the party go about doing this?[16]

Speaking in a Commons debate on housing in July 1946, the Labour MP for Acton, Joseph Sparks, stated that Conservative government between the wars had meant 'a policy of refusal to exercise the housing powers which existed to build houses at decent rents'.[17] Labour's championing of council housing was a refutation of this 'policy of refusal', in the belief that the needs of most people would be best served by subsidised council homes to rent. It would be 'the first time in history', Tom Braddock, MP for Mitcham, asserted in the same debate, 'that the ordinary people who do the work ... have been reasonably and properly housed'.[18] Through the provision of council housing, Labour could physically build their own vision of the future and it was for many activists 'the gateway to health, education, higher domestic standards'.[19] Stephen Brooke notes that Labour's social policy proposals for 1945 'evinced a sense of vindication', and this was as true of housing as of social insurance.[20] The 1946 Housing (Financial Provisions) Act was instrumental in this process, trebling the Exchequer subsidy for local authority houses and extending the subsidy period for sixty years.[21] 'Quality' was a key aim for Bevan, even during the conditions of severe shortage of building materials: Hugh Dalton described him as a 'tremendous Tory' for insisting on two bathrooms for all three-bedroom council homes.[22] Of a total of 1,016,349 dwellings completed in the years 1945–51 some 806,857 were council houses.[23] While the pivotal role of Bevan in the post-war housing drive hardly needs restating, he nevertheless subordinated housing to the overarching mission of creating the National Health Service: in contrast to the nationalisation of health provision, local authorities remained dominant in housing.[24] The absence of a national body for housing in Labour plans relates closely to the muted approach to universalism. Although the 1949 Housing Act removed the provision that council housing was for the 'working classes', rents were not set so low a level as to be truly open to all, being rather more than controlled rents for private rented houses.[25]

Following the Conservative takeover of government in 1951, a rise in the Exchequer subsidy for each new council house in the 1952 Housing Act was matched by a concurrent increase in building licences to private builders. This being said, the new Minister of Housing, Harold Macmillan, was under no illusions about the need for public house-building to achieve the target of 300,000 homes per year.[26] From Labour's perspective, the impetus was that council homes should continue to be built as a priority, at relatively low rents: as long as Labour controlled the municipality in question, this could take place on a smaller scale in reflection of significantly reduced funding. Nonetheless, it is apparent that Labour engaged in a continuous process in defining their commitment to public housing. 'In housing, [the Conservatives] assert that people with money can have a house: those without must get back in the queue', asserted a 1952 edition of *People's Pictorial*, with the clear implication that those without money came first under Labour policy.[27]

Rent policy was a central feature of Labour's approach to council housing, although the party remained conflicted throughout the period 1945–70 as to exactly the level that rents should be set at, as well as precisely how any subsidy scheme should operate. Throughout the 1950s and 1960s, the debates within the party on the question of rents for council homes are highly revealing of the shifting manner in which housing was seen as a means to end urban deprivation. Debates centred on whether tenancies should be reserved for those unable to pay market rents, or whether council homes could be a means of overcoming the private sector, available to all at the point of service like the NHS or education system. The key moment came in the mid-1950s, with a major change in Conservative government policy with the 1956 Housing Subsidies Act, which removed the subsidy for public housing not built for slum clearance tenants as well as removing the obligation for local authorities to contribute to their housing activities through their local rate fund.[28] This effectively meant that more of the costs of public housing would be shifted onto tenants, in direct opposition to Labour's aims. Combined with the move to decontrol the private rented market with the 1954 Housing Act, this presented a considerable challenge to Labour attempts to provide for their idealised 'ordinary people who do the work'.

Of course, those within Labour were not unaware of the high costs of providing council housing. Writing in *Socialist Commentary*, Peggy Crane, a Kensington councillor and LPRD local government officer, stated in 1950 that high building costs threatened to jeopardise the effects of existing housing subsidies unless local authorities dipped further into their rate fund, with the risk of antagonising ratepayers.[29] Crane suggested that Labour councils might have to consider 'differential' rent or rebate schemes, so 'the community is not asked to subsidise those who can afford to pay an economic rent'. However, as she went on to note, the schemes 'raised certain administrative and psychological problems' for the Labour movement, as it reminded many of the hated inter-war means test.[30] It was true that the schemes had first been introduced in the 1935 Housing Act, which had also linked public housing to slum clearance, rather than to 'general needs'.[31] Nonetheless, Crane pointed to Leeds, which had operated a differential scheme since the 1930s, and to a rent rebate scheme in the London borough of Lambeth, as a means of maintaining a 'socialist rent policy': given, she implied, the difficulties of drawing too heavily on rate funds or paying out high Exchequer subsidies indefinitely.[32] Indeed, Crane had presumably been involved herself in gathering a large tranche of LPRD information on differential or rebate schemes, which appeared as an LPRD internal memorandum in February 1950, and may even have written the proviso that those councils that did operate schemes did so 'on quite different lines from each other'.[33] Simply put, the 'differential' scheme in Leeds worked on the basis of rent calculated from the full family net weekly earnings, with rent relief applied according to the circumstances of the person(s) in question – an old-age pensioner might pay half of a 'normal' net rent for a council home.[34] Conversely, Lambeth's rent rebate worked through the setting of a fully subsidised 'standard' rent, with a possible maximum and minimum rent fixed either side. Tenants were then informed of the maximum rent they might pay and invited to apply for a rent rebate based on information provided about income. Lambeth council found that of 160 tenants taking part, 113 paid above the standard rent, 3 paid the standard rent and 44 paid less than the standard rent.[35] Lambeth had noted in their report to the LPRD that they were 'mindful ... that housing is a form of a social service, and the fair selection of tenants a serious business'.[36] Whilst it was clear that Lambeth had considered how to keep housing a social service, without putting themselves into financial difficulties, the principle of differential charges was likely, as Crane had noted, to cause conflict.

Such conflict over differential rents was probable when there existed the possibility of even cheaper rents. A 1950 visit by a delegation of trade unionists to the USSR, organised by the British-Soviet Friendship Society (BSFS), reported that the maximum rent was just 10 per cent of the highest individual income, including all utility charges. 'Just imagine', exclaimed one delegate, 'paying 7.s a week out of a £7 wage for a flat and nothing to pay for rates, electric light, electricity for cooking or central heating!'[37] Though it should be noted that the enthusiastic correspondent in question was the Communist activist William Wainwright, all of the other trade unionists expressed similar sentiments, and as a previous chapter recounted, several were Labour councillors. Similar regard for low Soviet rents was expressed in the 1952 BSFS delegates' report.[38] There were enticing possibilities on the other side of the Iron Curtain, too. A 1954 *Labour Woman* article by Mary Sutherland, the party Chief Women's officer, spoke of 'incredibly low' rents evidenced on a visit to Vienna, where the average worker spent only 5 per cent of their income on rent in 1945.[39] Rents had been fixed to cover the cost of maintenance only, with house-building financed primarily from municipal taxes, and whilst Sutherland seemed sceptical of how well such a scheme would operate in Britain, she conceded that 'it must certainly be popular with the tenants'.[40] It is quite likely that some *Labour Woman* readers would have been similarly persuaded by such comparatively cheap rents. In point of fact, the April 1954 edition of *Labour Woman* had run an article by W. J. Gilroy, the Labour agent for Chislehurst – then a highly marginal constituency – which described how houses completed in 1952 were being rented at almost £1 more a week than houses built two years previously, despite being smaller.[41] This was in part due to the higher cost of building the newer houses, and the policy of the local Conservatives to charge the tenants more to cover costs.[42] The Conservative policy in Chislehurst actually pre-empted government policy nationally, which contrived to raise council house rents by a gradual reduction of subsidy, and had by the end of 1956, under the new Housing Minister Duncan Sandys, removed the subsidy for general needs housing altogether.[43] Some Labour actors might have seen this as a good opportunity to introduce a differential or rebate scheme, which was, of course, the Conservative intention. Indeed, James MacColl proposed in 1954 that the greatest 'social advantage' would be gained from using housing subsidies to ensure 'that young families get better housing than they can afford and to keep a roof over the heads of old people'.[44] Others, however, were likely to see low rents as a sacrosanct part of the 'social service'.

Trying to devise a 'national' Labour solution to rent policy in 1955, David Eversley commented that 'emotionally … the pressure is in favour of the general subsidy out of national taxation'.[45] Even with this in mind, Eversley argued that taxation was probably as high as it could go, and given that in his estimation not everyone wanted a council house, he favoured a universal system of rent rebates: his preferred scheme was for 'those with the smallest incomes and greatest responsibilities to rent the best houses'.[46] Similarly, the Labour councillor

Arthur Marsh argued in a February 1954 edition of *Socialist Commentary* that as houses were 'durable consumer goods', and more difficult to supply free of charge than healthcare or education, then some form of differential or rebate scheme was required.[47] Interestingly, Marsh believed that the crux of the issue was in the system of local rates, hinting that some form of local taxation based on income would be far more effective.[48] Though Eversley conceded that many Labour members might be 'horrified' by his proposal, he felt that most would agree that a universal rebate policy would do more to 'help further our social aims' than 'old slogans and nostrums'.[49] One party figure who would certainly have agreed with Eversley on the latter point was Crosland, who argued that Labour should champion 'universal *availability*' of public housing, rather than '*universal free* availability'. In Crosland's view, linked to a wider revisionist notion of social equality, it was more important that an income test simply determined the question of free access to a social service such as housing, rather than determining the right to utilise public housing.[50] Peter Baldwin has argued that welfare states are in essence 'broad [communities] of risk', and have been most durable when the middle classes as well as the poor are favoured by 'statutory generosity'.[51] Whilst the positions advocated by Eversley and Crosland still fell within the logic of 'communities of risk', charging higher rents for middle-class or even better off working-class council tenants threatened to undermine the shared 'statutory generosity'. There was some irony, then, in Crosland's praise for the marginalising effect on private services of the 'high qualitative standard' of Swedish social services.[52] This had only been possible by a 'deliberately pro-bourgeois' policy of relatively low rents for all, rather than the more focused attempt on those in need that Crosland and other reforming thinkers called for.[53] In this regard, the reasoning for universal rents was to a degree more lucid than might otherwise have been suspected.

Writing in a June 1955 edition of *Labour's Northern Voice*, Councillor Price Jones offered 'a personal illustration' of why he believed that 'economic rents' for council homes were fair. Jones was a miner, 'struggling to pay off a mortgage on a not very modern house', whereas his wealthier colliery manager lived 'in a council house in the same town'.[54] 'Can anyone see Socialism in that', asked Jones, suggesting that there was a clear difference between a public park or the NHS where all paid and all benefitted, and housing subsidies 'where all pay and only a few may benefit'.[55] Responding to Jones the following month, the Manchester councillor Edmund Dell argued that differential schemes created 'unnecessary bureaucracy' due to their complexity. Instead, he remarked that a 'good Socialist principle' was not that some should benefit less from the common tax pool, but that they should pay more tax or, as he put it, 'differential tax payments but equal benefits'.⁵⁶ Curiously, both arguments evoked a socialist vision – but whilst Jones' addressed an immediate attempt by the Treasury to reduce the cost of housing subsidies, Dell's suggested that compromising the principle of a universal housing system in practice would frustrate it philosophically. It is notable that Labour groups in local authorities seemed to agree with Dell, at least until the withdrawal of subsidy. When surveyed on the question of differential or rebate schemes by the Local Government Sub-Committee of the NEC in 1954 and 1955, most Labour groups opposed them in principle as an extension of the long-despised means test.⁵⁷

Similar debates raged across the pages of *Labour Woman* and *Tribune*. Arguing for differential rents in the August 1955 edition of *Labour Woman* in a near-identical reprise of her 1950 *Socialist Commentary* piece, Peggy Crane asserted that housing could only be a social service if Labour enabled 'good houses to come within the reach of all'.⁵⁸ Conversely, a letter from Councillor M. Sivill in the October 1955 issue stated: 'Identical houses, like identical bedsteads or T.V. sets, should fetch an identical price.'⁵⁹ *Tribune*'s acceptance of differential rents in January 1956 – following a directive from the NEC that councils should consider implementing such schemes as a consequence of subsidy withdrawal – provoked a storm of largely hostile letters from its readership. 'This may be the intellectual's idea of Socialism, but it isn't mine', asserted Ralph Leader of Loughton, whilst Jack Pennington of Stoke Newington pointed out that 'nobody expects medical attention to be rationed according to income'.⁶⁰ Most who wrote in recommended raising local rates to keep housing as a social service. The issue was an especially emotive one: *Tribune* had reported on the expulsion of twelve Camberwell councillors in February 1956 for voting against the decision of the Labour group to implement differential rents, the latter being contrary to the policy of the local constituency party.⁶¹ The editors of *Tribune* – the lead editor at this point being Michael Foot – were unmoved, arguing in their response that 'differential schemes will in many places be the fairest way to share the burden and the *only* way to give the poorly paid worker a house'.⁶² In a very different instance to Camberwell, a left-wing leadership took over Labour-controlled St Pancras in 1956 and proceeded to scrap the differential rent scheme. 'It was probably the last time a council in Britain actually *lowered* rents', recalled Peggy Duff, then Housing Committee Chair.⁶³ It is clear from the debate that the limitation on funding available to councils put Labour in a difficult position. If housing was to be an agent of change, it had to apply to all equally: but if economic circumstances were beyond the control of Labour municipalities, then some measure of adaptation was required.

The conversion from universal to differential or rebate schemes was easier said than done. In January 1961, H. W. Lodder, Secretary of Watford Borough Council Labour Group, contacted the LPRD asking whether there was a party 'yardstick' for an 'economic' rent, as 'there is a difference of opinion between my members as to what constitutes a reasonable rent'.[64] In her response, Peggy Crane admitted that there was no official policy as to what a 'reasonable rent' was, but where councils had introduced differential schemes, the 'economic rent' was 'between one-sixth and one-seventh of gross income (including wife's earnings if she is working) or one-fifth of income if rents and rates are taken together'.[65] To add a further layer of complication, Crane added that some councils based their rent on 'two and a half times the gross [rateable] value of the property'.[66] Another party member writing to the research department was simply told, 'This is essentially a matter for Labour groups to decide for themselves in the light of local circumstances'.[67] Although leaving the matter up to local councils accounted for regional variability, it could also cause serious problems. Shapely has noted that the introduction of 'economic' rents by Labour councils was more often than not met with furious protests, as tenants 'were not interested in the council's increasing financial burden'.[68] In this regard, Frank Allaun was rather prescient in a 1956 edition of *Tribune*, where as one of the aforementioned letter-writers, he advised, 'If Labour controlled local authorities increase their rents it will be on Labour councillors that the tenants vent their wrath'.[69] Duff recalled how the efforts of Labour councillors in St Pancras to avoid raising rents led to them being surcharged, and then the temporary loss of the borough to the Conservatives in 1959, council tenants being 'unmoved by all our efforts on their behalf'.[70] While Labour would go on to benefit from the Tory decision to immediately introduce differential rents – which prompted large-scale rent strikes by council tenants – upon her return to the Housing Committee in 1962, Duff found that abolishing the scheme was easier said than done.[71] She recalled that the District Auditor would inform the council 'how large a deficit on the Housing Revenue Account he was prepared to accept', with the threat of surcharge should a flat rent be set.[72] The housing academic David Donnison acknowledged in 1967 that differential or rent rebate schemes based on household income failed to counteract the fact that relatively poor or otherwise precarious units had 'difficulty even paying a reduced rent'.[73] However, he did not advocate low rents, believing rather that a system of local housing allowances to 'top-up' the income of low-income households would be more effective. Such a system remains in place today, albeit in circumstances of relatively higher council rents.[74]

'The Labour Party has never really decided to what extent it regards housing as a social service to be available to all according to need not income', stated a Research Department review of housing policy in 1967, going on to note that policy as a result had not been consistent.[75] Following their entry into government in 1964, Labour had certainly put council housing at the centre of their plans rhetorically, but remained imprecise about whether the tenure would transition towards becoming a social service after a period in which the Conservatives had sought to residualise it. A 1963 editorial in *Labour's Northern Voice* had sought to explain the contradictions in Labour rent policy, suggesting there were 'two differing conceptions' by which local authorities approached public housing. The first view was of public housing as an investment, with the aim of councils to 'maximise the rent income', while the second was of housing as a social service, in which rents were instead a means of writing off the capital cost of building.[76] Favouring the latter approach, *Labour's Northern Voice* argued for flat council house rents with rebates for the poorest tenants, noting that 'all council houses offer the same utilities to tenants, and it is on this basis that rents should be assessed, and not on ability to pay'.[77] Throughout the 1960s, the Conservatives sought to use the 'myth of the oversubsidized council tenant' as a political attack line, playing upon a popular belief that 'middle-class ratepayers were subsidizing feckless workers' to justify council house sales in municipalities such as Brighton.[78] Stories of lavish council estate living often involved a 'tenant with [a] Bentley in front of his house', as a 1970 pamphlet issued to Labour members acknowledged.[79] In his 1967 survey of housing policy, Donnison noted that council tenant households tended to have more dependants and thus lower incomes per head than other tenures, meaning that their actual economic position was not as secure as the income of the highest (male) earner would seem to indicate. 'Stories of Jaguar-owning council tenants might be true in freak cases', Donnison commented, 'but for the vast majority of these tenants the car could only be a very ancient model'.[80]

The National Housing Programme in the 1965 White Paper on Housing aimed at 500,000 dwellings built per year, with the majority council homes, though in return for increased subsidy the government expected local authorities to charge an 'economic rent' (without giving an indication of what that might be). Crossman himself took the view that council tenants were a 'cosseted and privileged class', in unguarded remarks during a 1966 *People* interview, going on to state that councils should 'charge the rich man £1,000 a year rent' to convince them to leave the tenure.[81] While he was embarrassed that his views were widely reported, Crossman was quite content to lean into popular prejudice. He recorded in his diary that 'I am in favour of putting up the rent of tenants who can afford to pay and using the pool of money we collect for a decent system of rent rebates'. This being said, he acknowledged that 'it is not a popular view in the Labour Party'.[82] Although Crossman was seemingly not rebuked publicly by his party colleagues, in an issue of *Tribune* published a few days later, Allaun suggested that 'the only real complaint against council housing is that we need millions more of them'.[83] Yet it was not until the end of Labour's period in government that the question of council rents – and by extension the exact purpose of council housing – began to be seriously addressed.

A Housing Policy Study Group was set up by the NEC in 1968 to consider policy for the 1970s, with its membership including Allaun and MacColl, the latter being at this stage Parliamentary Secretary to the Minister of Housing and Local Government. In a 1969 memorandum, MacColl suggested that 'in our discussions there has been some confusion about what we are trying to do'.[84] He stated that the public sector should be the dominant supplier of rented accommodation and expressed his scepticism of the view that prosperous tenants 'have a duty to become owner-occupiers'.[85] Recommending relatively low average rents against a regional standard alongside generous rebates, MacColl reasoned that 'selective help of the low income tenant means letting the rent for others rise more'.[86] In a separate memorandum the same month, William Hilton, MP for Bethnal Green and Parliamentary Private Secretary to Bob Mellish, Minister of State for Public Buildings and Works, critiqued the notion of a 'economic rent'. Hilton argued that 'an economic rent ... is wrong in principle when seen against [tax] advantages given to owner-occupiers', suggesting that all council tenants should be equally subsidised, on the basis that a council house when paid off was a 'valuable asset' for the community.[87] Of the two memorandum writers, it was MacColl's view that seemingly won out. Council housing 'must provide really cheap rents for those whose means are limited', read the final report of the Housing Policy Study Group in June 1969, and avoid '[sucking] dry other social services' through high deficits.[88] This seemed to imply 'economic rents' for most, with the report going on to recommend a rationalisation of 'chaotic' rents via the pooling of risk across larger, regional bodies.[89] Laudable as the aim might have been to keep rents cheap for the poorest, it was a recipe for residualisation: if an 'economic' council rent became too high for those who did not qualify for supplementary assistance, the risk pool would invariably narrow as the less-needy left the tenure. This rather undermined the point of 'housing as a social service', or at least as Labour activists had understood it. For housing to function as a durable vehicle of welfare with the largest possible risk pool, it required what Baldwin describes as 'statutory generosity', or legitimating social solidarity through 'giving the affluent a share of what had been reserved for the poor'.[90] The residual policy choices advocated by the end of the 1960s were far from the modern promise of 'differential tax payments but equal benefits' that Edmund Dell had suggested as a core socialist aim in 1954.

'Is there something peculiarly wrong about you', asked Enoch Powell of a group of Scottish council tenants in January 1970, 'so that you cannot provide yourself with housing?' He went on to suggest that there was indeed something 'peculiarly wrong' about council tenants: that their rents had been 'too low for too long'.[91] The surprise Conservative election victory in June 1970 signalled a much harsher attitude on council rents, Powell's comments betraying an orthodox Tory view on the place of council housing that went far beyond Labour discussions about 'economic rents'. In June 1971, the government published a white paper proposing to introduce a 'fair rent' system, removing the freedom of local councillors to set council rents and allowing rents to reach market rates.[92] This was followed by the Housing Finance Act of 1972, which in implementing government proposals was 'designed to hasten the residualization of the local authority sector' through the re-introduction of means tests for rent assistance and a rapid rise in rents to encourage tenants to become owner-occupiers.[93] In some instances this did occur. A Liverpudlian steel erector named Joe Beckett told Frank Allaun he intended to buy his council house 'though it's against my own principles', believing that his £4.40 a week rent would likely double under the fair rent scheme.[94] Some Labour councils fought back against the 1972 Act, most notably at Clay Cross, where councillors refused to increase council rents and were ultimately surcharged.[95] Although Labour's return to government in 1974 marked a brief respite, the scene was set for a more aggressive Conservative assault on council housing, which would introduce further sharp rent rises as part of the Housing Act 1980.

'The essence of socialism appertains not just to the quantity of goods we make', asserted a research department memorandum in 1964 'but of the quality of life we lead'. It might be considered that if Labour were concerned with providing a quality of life that best reflected their ideal of a socialist future, then inexpensive, decent houses run by a 'public landlord' were a major part of this. However, the difficulty of making this vision fit within a model of economic viability threatened the intellectual basis of council housing as a 'social service'.

The various differential and rent rebate schemes could ensure that the neediest were provided for, but they had the disadvantage of reducing the attractiveness of the council waiting list to those with better incomes.

Private property or public ownership: Labour and the private landlord

In September 1958, *The Times* reported on a reception at Brown's Hotel in London, held to launch a new pamphlet by the great-grandson of Charles Dickens: *Whose Home?*, by Harry Dickens.[96] Yet this Dickens did not attack the slum landlords of 'tumbling tenements' or 'black, dilapidated streets' as his predecessor had done, but instead would claim that the landlords of the 1950s were now the victims.[97] In the setting of Brown's Hotel, *The Times*' political correspondent reflected that Dickens's attack on 'the Labour plan for the municipalisation of rented houses' was not as independent as it might have appeared. 'It ... seemed civil', remarked the correspondent, 'to move around the cocktail room to congratulate several old friends from [Conservative Party] central office on having maintained their high standards of workmanship'.[98] Though the correspondent noted that the Tory staffers 'modestly ... disclaimed the booklet', the appearance of the former Conservative minister Lord Woolton to 'wish [the pamphlet] well on his own account' seemed to confirm his suspicions.[99] But there is more to this than a Conservative false flag operation in a London cocktail room. Dickens' pamphlet was above all a response to the Labour Party policy of municipalization: the local authority takeover of private rented property. Municipalization represented a point in modern British history at which the private rented market appeared to be failing, with both major political parties consequently contemplating radical policies. Examining the thinking behind arguments for the effective abolition of private landlordism allows us to understand how Labour understood the tenure in the context of the Modern moment.

Whilst it is true that the Labour Party had never been the most strident supporter of the landlord, the vehemence with which the party attacked private landlords in the 1950s and the early 1960s far exceeded anything that had gone before. The assault on 'landlordism' was closely connected to what the party perceived as the Conservative government's failure in housing. Indeed, the Tory emphasis on increasing owner-occupation and linking public housing to slum clearance was thought to be excluding significant numbers of those trapped within low-quality inner-city privately rented stock.[100] The core Labour policy of municipalization – the local authority takeover of rented property – grew into an attempt to abolish private landlordism for the vast majority of renters. This was the continuation of a rapid decline in private renting across Britain for much of the post-war period, with the privately rented dwellings comprising barely 11 per cent of all housing in Britain by 1981.[101] Conversely, in 1938, private rented homes still formed 58 per cent of housing tenure in England and Wales.[102] Perhaps surprisingly, Labour radicalism towards landlords and private renting in the period has been largely overlooked by scholars. Although Peter Weiler has examined municipalisation in the context of Labour thought on land control, whilst Alan Simmonds and John Davis have both discussed the political impact of the 1957 Rent Act, no study (beyond an article by the author of this book) has examined the place of the private landlord in wider Labour plans for urban transformation.[103] Problems with private rental identified prior to 1945, and seemingly rampant by the 1950s, gave Labour strong grounds to argue that the housing system was failing and that the state needed to step in even more decisively. In spite of attempts to rectify the situation, many of the core problems – not least the question of how best to ensure tenants could afford to rent a home in a reasonable condition of repair – have returned in the present day. Many within Labour believed that it was not a coincidence that many of Britain's slums were rented homes, and saw the removal of these dwellings as a necessary step to sweeping away the rotten remnants of the nineteenth century. Indeed, Tony Crosland would claim in 1962 that 'much of built-up Britain is little better than a Victorian slum, a drab and oppressive legacy of the first Industrial Revolution'.[104] This move against rented slum housing was part of the destructive tendencies of the Modern moment aimed at the Victorian legacy of urban Britain, described in more detail in Chapter 1. Labour policy was conflicted, however, about whether the state should simply demand greater improvement of private rented property, or 'municipalise' rented property through local authorities. Party perceptions of whether a modern, socialist approach would be to manage or abolish 'landlordism' would have major consequences for British cities in the mid-twentieth century.

Writing in 1913, the Scottish Labourite John Wheatley attacked the private landlord as responsible for the slum living conditions of the Glaswegian poor. He claimed that slum life was so dreadful that it had finally eliminated the notion 'that an individual or family can have security for its own health and happiness in a community where thousands are being physically and morally ruined'.[105] Wheatley set a precedent for Labour thought, advocating the municipal oversight of landlords because of the effect of unfair rents on the wider housing system. In

1913, Glasgow actually had large numbers of empty houses at rents the working-class populace could not afford.[106] The absurdity of crowding the city's poor into low-quality property that they could barely afford whilst houses lay empty, was in the view of those within the Labour movement, evidence of the inability of the market to provide adequate housing at a fair price. Correspondingly, Wheatley played a major part in the 1915 Glasgow Rent Strike (which caused the first phase of rent control) and later, as Minister of Health in the first Labour government of 1924, introduced legislation to vastly increase the provision of public housing as a direct riposte to the private sector.[107] Labour actors believed the private landlord meant exploitation at best, and prevailing slum conditions at worst, and by the close of the Second World War the party directly associated landlordism with the ills of British cities. In a 1945 Birmingham City Council discussion, Councillor Jim Simmons argued against compensating slum landlords, should property be taken over and repaired, suggesting that the council health inspectors did not compensate for 'diseased meat'. He continued: 'Why should we compensate for diseased houses? We have paid compensation already – in the higher infant mortality rates of our central wards.'[108] If the slum landlord was little better than the butcher with flies buzzing in his shop, then Labour intolerance to the landlord could only grow.

However, Labour's tenure in government between 1945 and 1951 saw very little slum clearance. Instead, Aneurin Bevan led a close focus on public house building. As Martin Francis has commented, Bevan failed '… to adopt a coherent policy towards those aspects of housing that lay outside the local authority building programme [existing owner-occupation and private rented]'.[109] Peter Malpass remarks that the 1945 manifesto commitments on housing did not resemble a 'socialist housing policy', supposing that it 'might have been expected to refer to a universal right to decent affordable housing and to include proposals to municipalize the failing, declining private rental sector'.[110] Similarly, in his study of Southwark Labour and housing policy throughout the post-war period, Harold Carter found that whilst 'there was widespread agreement about the need for slum clearance', it was very slow to start.[111] There was an ongoing debate throughout the 1940s over local authority improvement of decaying properties, initiated through attempts by Westminster City Council to carry out improvements in Pimlico during the Second World War. However, initial Labour opposition to paying grants to private owners to improve their properties stalled the process. Jim Yelling has noted that Bevan would have preferred local authorities to take over substandard housing, but he recognised that this would be difficult due to the need to simultaneously increase public house-building. This meant a combination of local authority improvement within redevelopment areas and private improvement formed part of the 1949 Housing Act.[112] Repairs were even seen as a diversion by some local parties, who had been campaigning against slum housing before Labour's election victory. In the same 1945 Birmingham Council discussion in which Jim Simmons had referred to slum houses as akin to 'diseased meat', his wife, Beatrice, also a Labour councillor, claimed that to do anything to extend the life of slum houses 'would be a retrograde step'. Other councillors concurred, seeing building new houses as the priority.[113] Labour's overriding concern for increasing public housing would leave the private rented stock largely in a state of stagnation during their six years in government.

The strength of Labour disdain for 'landlordism' became most apparent in the context of opposition following the party's defeat in the 1951 general election. Whilst the Conservative government did not immediately seek an end to the existing system of rent control in the private rented sector, the two major landlord organisations – the Association of Land and Property Owners (ALPO) and the National Federation of Property Owners (NFPO) – campaigned against rent controls and held influence in Tory circles.[114] By the early 1950s, much of the private rented stock for those of lower incomes was in a state of decay, and a large part was subject to rent control. Two distinct phases of rent control had occurred, both prompted by war: first, houses controlled during the First World War, which in many cases were still let at almost the same rent as in 1915 (provided the tenant was the same person); and second, tenancies were held at levels set in 1939 under the Rent Mortgage Restrictions Act, which had increased the number of controlled dwellings to 10 million.[115] Rising repair bills – estimated to have increased by 316 per cent between 1939 and 1953 – had meant that by the 1950s landlords could not hope to recoup their losses through rent.[116] Additionally, the fact that rents could only be raised if the sitting tenant was ousted resulted in some more unscrupulous landlords resorting to harassment or deliberate neglect. Conservative opinion was largely sympathetic to the seeming plight of the landlord – Tories tended to believe that rent control was a negative force on the housing market, allowing tenants to benefit from 'cheap housing'.[117] At the same time, the Conservatives had reduced subsidies for public housing on taking office in 1951 and did not undertake to clear the slums.[118] Whilst the Tories saw the dilapidation of the rented housing stock as an indication that landlords were struggling, those within Labour began to conclude that the private landlord was guilty of a callous disregard for healthy living conditions – willing to take the tenants' rent, but not to patch a leaking roof. Worse still, the image of decaying, Victorian slums posed a clear challenge to Labour visions of an orderly urban future.

In 1952, the Labour-supporting economist Denys Lawrence Munby remarked in a pamphlet that '... the continued private ownership of houses to rent is likely to become more and more incompatible with modern techniques of planning in towns'.[119] Munby had considered how the system of rent control might be reformed, whether returning to free market principles, patching the existing system or local authority acquisition of low-rented housing. He saw the latter option as the most rational, arguing that whilst it was 'not recommended as a panacea', it would remove the slum landlord who was 'by ignorance as much as deliberate exploitation, merely a rentier who battens on the bad conditions of the poor'.[120] Munby followed his pamphlet in a 1953 letter to the Labour newspaper *Forward*, suggesting that the principal concern of the party should be that landlords were denied unreasonably large profits.[121] This belief in the 'character' of the slum landlord as an antiquated, grasping figure was further reinforced by Tory proposals to allow controlled rents to rise should the landlord carry out repairs, which eventually manifested as the 1954 Housing Rent and Repairs Act.[122]

The act additionally contained subsidies for slum clearance. A December 1953 article in *Labour's Northern Voice* discussing the White Paper for the 1954 Act argued that there was a danger of '... rent increases following repairs staying on for ever and never another tap done to the house'.[123] The author went on to assert that Labour should aim to take over the properties, but only with a view to re-housing the tenants as soon as possible and protecting them from 'Tory benevolence'.[124] In late 1953, Labour's policy statement *Challenge to Britain* had stated that local authorities should 'gradually' take over rent-controlled properties, as it was 'idle' to expect landlords to improve their houses.[125] The Labour-run Birmingham City Council had actually already done so earlier in 1953 – moving to take over and begin to improve some 30,000 slum houses.[126] Indeed, in a *Labour's Northern Voice* article, a councillor from one of the slum areas asserted that 'something had to be done' while the slum tenants awaited future rehousing, owing to the 'appalling conditions' of the houses.[127] If the party had been ambivalent about the place of landlords previously, they were now far less so – whilst the people awaited the modern, urban future, it should not be under rentier capitalism.

The move to full 'municipalisation' came at the 1954 annual conference, where Bevan backed a CLP motion on the subject, claiming that '... private ownership of rental property ... results in a progressive deterioration of an invaluable part of the social equipment'.[128] Labour saw the 1954 Housing Act as deliberately exploitative. In a Commons debate that year, the Labour MP James MacColl claimed that the 'vague' standards of repair of the act enabled a landlord to simply whitewash the walls of the property in question and hike up the rent, asserting that 'the Bill is a cynical attempt to break down the Rent Acts and to put the tenant at the mercy of the landlord'.[129] An unusually overlooked figure in housing discourse, MacColl was a prolific Labour contributor to housing and local government debates, having previously been Mayor of Paddington and later serving as Parliamentary Secretary to the Minister of Housing and Local Government between 1964 and 1969. In a 1954 pamphlet, MacColl stated his support for local authority takeover on the basis that houses were 'part of the nation's capital', remarking that '... landlords and tenants come and go but the home goes on for several generations'.[130] However, he was cautiously critical of a state monopoly in housing, noting that 'it is going to be hard to get away from the all-seeing eye'.[131] This wariness about the consequences of effectively collapsing the housing system from three tenures to two – public housing and owner-occupied – would be a continued element of Labour deliberation. Nevertheless, the prospect of bringing the vast majority of housing under public control – around 6 million houses were rent controlled of a total 15 million households, with almost 3 million of the remainder council houses – offered a significant means of advancing Labour's plans for modern cities.[132]

In a 1955 report to the Social Services sub-committee of the NEC, the sociologists Peter Willmott and Michael Young claimed that without municipalisation, the 7 million controlled houses that they had identified would be slums in ten or twenty years.[133] Willmott and Young suggested that the re-introduction of large-scale slum clearance through the 1954 Housing Act had heightened this process, with most landlords seeing little point of improving their properties with compulsory purchase looming – as they put it, 'the more slums are cleared, the more slums there are'.[134] The 'social case' for the abolition of the landlord was examined still further in a 1955 pamphlet by the economist David Eversley. In Eversley's view, municipalisation would allow for the comprehensive urban transformation that Labour sought, as well as ending a broken system of renting.[135] On this point Eversley was prescient – rent control was self-evidently not a particularly good system for anyone, though Labour would hardly countenance decontrol without ensuring tenant protection. It was in some senses then a logical step to remove the threat to tenants from landlords by removing landlords from the equation entirely. Willmott and Young asserted that falling values heralded the 'unscrupulous, bucket-shop landlord', supported by 'bucket-room lawyers', characterised by undertaking the minimum amount of repairs possible, as well as supposedly taking large bribes to allow new tenants to take over vacancies.[136] However, Eversley noted that Labour would have to proceed cautiously – there would have to be a slight rise in rents under municipalisation given how low the levels of some rent-controlled properties were, despite Labour's campaigning against these provisions in the 1954 Housing Act.[137]

Labour's proposals for municipalisation and an end to the 'bucket-shop landlord' were not sufficient to convince the electorate at the 1955 general election, with the party suffering a further defeat. Covering the election campaign, an April 1955 Daily Mail piece contrasted the 'property-owning democracy' of the Tories with the supposed 'nationalization of homes' proposed by Labour. The author of the piece argued that 'the only homes to have rent increases without restriction are council houses', unwittingly reflecting Eversley's assertion that rent rises would indeed occur.[138] This defence of rent control against Labour's municipalization plans would be somewhat ironic in hindsight, given the major decontrol of rents that would occur under the Tories in 1957. In spite of the election defeat, Labour began to craft a more sophisticated case for an end to private renting.

A party publication in 1956 attacked Conservative claims that amenity improvements could be carried out by private landlords, suggesting that '[Landlords] are not philanthropists, most of them – but business men. They are not going to bother to improve or maintain their properties unless they can see some return on their investment'.[139] Clearly, Labour were appealing to pragmatism, rather than just moral impulses. Following the 1955 defeat, the NEC had created an ad hoc Housing Study Group, headed by Anthony Greenwood (later Minister of Housing from 1966).[140] The deep distaste that the party felt for landlords was apparent in the discussion of the draft policy statement that the Housing Study Group prepared, in which the question was raised: 'Is it to be an offence to own a house let to other people?'[141] Labour clarified their position with the 1956 policy statement *Homes for the Future*, which utilised the discussions of the Housing Study Group. Although municipalisation would be strictly temporary, the party accepted that it would take some time to build replacement homes and that the homes taken over would need improvement. Rather troublingly, a future Labour government would take no steps to coordinate municipalisation, asserting that local authorities would have 'the task of planning and operating the largest public ownership project yet undertaken in this country'.[142] Given the different sizes, budgets and, perhaps most significantly, the political make-up of local authorities in the country, the likelihood of a unified policy taking shape seemed rather slim.

Nevertheless, *Tribune* welcomed the commitment to public ownership, arguing that it recognised that 'wealth in bricks' was the source of power for the landed class, funding 'the Eton master's mortar board, the debutante's bromo-seltzer, and the Archbishop's mitre'.[143] There remained an obvious issue – given the volume of repairs that local authorities would have to undertake, the 'unfit' character of much of the private rented stock would likely remain so for some time. Tony Crosland noted this in his 1956 magnum opus *The Future of Socialism*, remarking that if substandard property was taken under state control *en masse*, 'we should find a pattern of social inequality in housing which bore no obvious relation to the size or distribution of housing subsidies, but depended solely on physical differences in housing standards'.[144] In effect, Labour were falling into the trap that James MacColl would later warn of, namely, that 'the hanging of a landlord for his sins of the past will not mend a leaking roof'.[145] Whilst the public ownership of most rented housing made sense in terms of planning for modern cities, the severe dilapidation of the rented stock meant that nineteenth-century decay would be a feature of the urban environment for an indefinite length of time. The context of continuing slum clearance and, as previously noted, a greater number of properties falling under the slum designation created still more difficulties.

The response of the Conservative government to the poor condition of the private rented stock was to seek to remove rent control entirely. Their thinking was motivated by an ideological ambition to recreate a free market in housing, which they believed would solve the repairs issue. Another impetus for the removal of rent control came from the Treasury, who believed that some of the increased profits for landlords would fall to them as income tax.[146] The eventual manifestation of these deliberations was the 1957 Rent Act, which removed control from all unfurnished accommodation rated above £40 in 'block decontrol'; below £40, rent increases were limited to twice the annual gross value of the property in question, though if the tenancy changed the property could be entirely decontrolled.[147] John Davis has referred to the act as a 'maladroit liberalization of the rental market', the provisions of which allowed for a process of 'creeping decontrol' of rent-controlled properties and raising of rents.[148] He remarked that the effects of the 1957 Act on the lower end of the rental market were the most 'socially pernicious', given the incentive for the landlord to move the sitting tenant to make a profit – according to a 1960 survey into the act, where this had occurred tenants faced a 145 per cent increase.[149] Indeed, a visit by the *Tribune* correspondent Mervyn Jones in early 1957 to the 'irregular rows of brick houses' comprising Lavender Street in Reading found sharp rent increases for tenants, with the Barker family's rent rising from 9 shillings to 15 a week, and an elderly Mr Absolom's 'tiny house' going up in rent by over 50 per cent.[150] Jones suggested that the local landlords were neither little old ladies nor big corporations, but simply people 'in business as landlords'.[151] Surveys in the early 1960s by Barry Cullingworth and John Greve determined that private landlordism was indeed a 'cottage industry': based around an individual owning a few houses rather than corporate entities.[152] The average landlord was elderly, had a moderate income, two or more houses, and had inherited their property portfolio.[153] Jones was not quite right: the 'little old ladies' were exactly those in 'business as landlords'. Examples such as Lavender Street seemed to confirm Labour's worst fears – landlords profiting from slum property, with no discernible stick to accompany the carrot of increasing rents.

Labour's determination to municipalise rental housing increased, but the party remained unclear about the form it might take. Hornsey CLP passed a resolution to commit a Labour government to take over all rent-controlled housing within twelve months of taking office, with the author of the resolution Lyn Mostyn arguing that '… if need is not to be exploited by greed, housing must be taken out of the realm of profit. But the job must be done completely'.[154] Mostyn's assertion was a case study of the moral style of argument Labour deployed: to profit from another's need for shelter was simply wrong, in this view. However, when brought to annual conference in September 1957, the resolution was soundly defeated on the basis that it was unrealistic to expect *all* local authorities to take over housing at the same rate.[155] Nonetheless, a March 1957 edition of *Labour Organiser*, the magazine of party election agents, carried an article arguing that the Rent Act had been a good opportunity for 'pointed propaganda' when campaigning in Reading.[156] Perhaps tellingly, the Reading Labour Party had omitted to emphasise the Labour commitment to municipalisation in their leaflets. In spite of this, H. E. Newbold, secretary of Salford and Manchester Trades Council, wrote in late 1957 of the 'thousands' of letters from tenants expressing 'shocked indignation' at the Rent Act, who had written to the Labour Party and Trades Council offices requesting the trade unions' Labour Research Department one-penny pamphlet on the Rent Act.[157] The pamphlet detailed how the act would affect tenants, and explained how to get a certificate of disrepair to prevent rent increases.[158] Newbold went on to state that the next Labour government would not only repeal the act, but make 'all rented property into an effective social service'.¹⁵⁹ In this vision of an equitable future, there was no place for the private landlord.

Property owners were not slow to recognise the threat that Labour's robust policies posed to them. The ALPO and NFPO formed the Rented Homes Campaign to resist municipalisation, with the assistant editor of the *Economist*, Norman Macrae, as a leading spokesman.¹⁶⁰ Helpfully for Labour, many of the leaders were members of the Rented Homes Campaign and were exactly the sort of big landlords that Labour railed against. For example, the campaign's council included Lord Brocket, a Conservative peer and the chairman of five companies, as well as the construction magnate Sir Richard Costain and the Conservative MP for West Harrow, Albert Braithwaite.¹⁶¹ The *Daily Mail* found in November 1958 that a retired Under-Secretary at the Ministry of Housing, Harold Symon, was the secretary of the Rented Homes Campaign (and ALPO).¹⁶² Symon came to prominence during a minor scandal involving the use of Ministry of Housing stationery in 1958, when a Ministry press officer had happened to 'lend' his mailing list to Harold Symon, who then used it to send his Rented Homes Campaign material. Part of the list included a pre-addressed stick with the legend 'On Her Majesty's Service' printed on it. The scandal ended with the press officer reprimanded, and Symon 'ticked off' by the prime minister.¹⁶³ Even with the benefit of insider knowledge, ALPO's propaganda was not especially sophisticated. One leaflet circulated in 1959 claimed that 'if the local council became your landlord, your rent could be raised whenever the council thought fit', ignoring the fact that the 1957 Rent Act had presented a similar threat to tenants.¹⁶⁴

In a similar vein, the Conservative fifth columnist introduced at the opening of this section, Harry Dickens argued incongruously in his 1958 pamphlet that the 1957 Rent Act was 'working smoothly' and that a 'council dictatorship' of 'The Official Knows Best' would occur under municipalisation.¹⁶⁵ Whilst Dickens had a point in terms of the bureaucratic tendencies of some Labour councils, his focus was narrowly partisan. Indeed, a 'staunch Tory' talking to *The Guardian*'s correspondent at Dickens's launch event claimed the pamphlet formed the basis for a new 'ginger group', based on vigorous opposition to Labour housing plans.¹⁶⁶ Moreover, this was very much an opposition led by large property holders. The *Daily Mail* pointed to the admission of former Conservative publicity chief Toby O'Brien – Dickens's publisher – that 'the venture was backed by some property owners'.¹⁶⁷ Given that the other members of Dickens's anti-municipalization 'ginger group' included Reginald Sizen – secretary of the NFPO – this was no popular revolt.¹⁶⁸ Yet there was a clear danger in bringing all rented property under state control, and some Labourites were alive to it. James MacColl warned in 1957 against a rigid approach by the public landlord, suggesting over-use of 'the chilling refrain, "By Order, The Town Clerk"' would not convince tenants that their new public landlords were better than the old, private one.[169] Rather less credibly for tenants, Dickens asserted that the landlord would 'lose his stake in British land', the meaning of which he claimed could not be understood by 'left-wing socialisers'.[170] This being said, even if private tenants were not inclined to sympathy for landlords in terms of their profits or property, they were not necessarily going to be persuaded that municipalisation would improve matters. In spite of some perceptive figures, Labour activists did not always appear to realise the enormity of municipalisation, whether in terms of the increase of state control or the difficulties of taking over thousands of dilapidated properties.

In a 1958 policy pamphlet, *100 Questions Asked and Answered on Labour's Housing Policy*, Labour asserted that 'the case [for municipalisation] in a nutshell is the failure of the private landlords ....the private landlord who owns property in order to make money must be replaced by a public landlord treating housing as a social service'.[171] Weiler has suggested that the fact that such a pamphlet was issued 'indicates the difficulty [Labour] was having in selling its policies', though he draws his criticism for the policy from *The Economist* and *The Times*, hardly the most impartial critics of socialist ideas.[172] Given the magnitude of change to the housing system municipalisation demanded, it might be considered that excessive prudence by the Labour leadership was unsurprising and, indeed, municipalisation enacted would have caused serious controversy for years to come.[173] Labour were careful to allow room for manoeuvre, however scant. In a 1958 letter to *The Times*, the party General Secretary, Morgan Phillips, assured readers that municipalisation was a temporary measure to repair and improve properties.[174]

Attempts like Phillips's to soften the policy were not entirely accepted across Labour – a 1958 article in *Labour's Northern Voice* by a Stoke-on-Trent councillor complained of 'wobbling' by 'some prominent members of the party'.[175] Indeed, MacColl identified that the very vagueness of when municipalisation might actually occur was a severe weakness of the policy. As he put it, 'the dates might of course be the Greek Kalends but presumably something in the near future is intended'.[176] In part, as the LPRD local government officer admitted in comments to MacColl's draft pamphlet on the issue, it was because in Leeds and elsewhere 'councils are refusing point blank to acquire and patch on the grounds that they do not wish to become slum landlords ... it would be physically impossible ... to replace these properties within 20 years'.[177] This notwithstanding, if slums were 'the product ... of private landlordism' as Labour asserted, then their very existence was an argument for municipalisation.[178] Chapter 1 has discussed in greater depth the move towards improvement and Labour deliberations on this point. If slums could not be replaced within twenty years, and 'rewarding' landlords through further profit was an unappealing option, then mass improvement was logically the solution most likely to overhaul the slums in the short term.

Labour's defeat at the polls in 1959 made mass municipalisation an impossibility, though councils did continue to acquire large numbers of properties in slum clearance schemes. Was municipalisation in part to blame for the 1959 defeat? Examining why the 1957 Rent Act did not significantly damage the Conservative vote in a later study published in 1969, M. J. Barnett argued that whilst the Tories feared that tenant anger would have an impact on the 1959 general election, housing was not the decisive electoral issue.[179] Surveying Gallup poll data, Barnett suggested that housing fell behind pensions and the cost of living in terms of voter importance.[180] Indeed, Labour led on pensions policy in their series of party political broadcasts, 'Britain Belongs To You', during the 1959 election campaign.[181] It is tempting, therefore, to agree with Barnett's conclusion that Labour's municipalization commitment was, in the eyes of the electorate, nothing more than 'traditional statements'.[182] Even so, Labour's deliberate unwillingness to clarify the cost of the scheme may not have helped matters. The left-wing MP for Reading Ian Mikardo had argued to the Local Government Sub-Committee of the NEC in 1958 that major savings could be made if the owners of municipalised properties were given an annual payment or council stocks rather than a lump sum, making as he put it 'nonsense of the talk our having to find millions of pounds in compensation'.[183] Mikardo's suggestion was indeed taken up, and Labour's *100 Questions* pamphlet recommended an annual interest payment to landlords rather than cash payment. However, the document also drew a line between the 'good landlord' and the 'bad landlord', noting that the latter 'who has neglected repairs in order to get a higher net income will get a lower income after municipalisation than he gets now'.[184] As Labour's rhetoric had classified the majority of landlords of rent-controlled properties as belonging to the latter category, it would perhaps have been more realistic to advise that the costs for the scheme would be relatively limited. Mikardo had also noted that a rent rise would be inevitable to cover improvement works to low-standard housing.[185] Given previous rhetoric, it is difficult to see how Labour might have reconciled itself to raising rents on controlled tenancies, and this was precisely the claim made by their adversaries in the Rented Homes Campaign.[186] Labour were vehemently opposed to private landlords, but unwilling to contemplate the enormity of municipalisation.

In a November 1960 edition of *Labour's Northern Voice*, the Salford councillor Eddie Hough claimed that the 'creeping decontrol' of private tenancies was forcing up weekly rents by as much as a pound.[187] Worse, repairs were being neglected and Hough went on to note with some horror, '... workers are comparing excessive rents, as against less excessive payments for purchasing houses ...'[188] Hough argued that this was part of the wider Conservative ploy to create a 'property-owning democracy'. Whilst the place of owner-occupation in Labour thought will be discussed in the following section, it is clear that Labour viewed with dismay the prospect of the Tories creating new voters from deficient housing policies. Salford City Labour Party called for greater unity between private and council tenants in 1961, arguing that both were 'subsidising the enhanced profits of the landlord and the moneylender'.[189] Council tenants were experiencing rent rises due to the increase in interest rates nationally, as well as central government pressure for councils to set 'fair rents'. In drawing together the council tenant and the private tenant, Salford Labour psychologically made all tenancies the responsibility of the state. Nonetheless, the idea that all rented property would be part of the welfare state seemed to be losing favour within Labour.

In a 1962 NEC paper, outright takeover of private rented homes was dismissed and encouraging private landlords to make improvements to their properties became a clear policy aim.[190] Decisively, this was followed by the dropping of municipalisation as Labour policy at the 1962 party conference.[191] This was in part a recognition of appalling slum conditions across Britain, with a sluggish pace of slum clearance under the Conservatives and some 600,000 slums still standing in 1961.[192] The NEC paper retained the possibility of temporary municipalisation, asking 'why should incompetent private landlords be left to benefit from higher rents'.[193] Where slum clearance was occurring, previously private tenants of cheap if inadequate housing were unimpressed by the prospect of paying higher council rents. As David Eversley had observed in 1955, the rents of controlled houses were artificially low, as were those of slum areas, and there would invariably be rent rises in the move to local authority control.

Writing to the LPRD in 1961, the Secretary of Swansea East Labour Association, J. G. Davies, noted that tenants from Swansea's slum clearance areas were subsidised on being relocated to council homes.[194] However, Davies expressed concern that the ex-slum tenants had supposedly been informed that if they moved back to new homes and flats built on the slum clearance site, they would lose the subsidy.[195] Replying to Davies, the LPRD's Local Government Officer, M. J. Ward, referred him to Swansea Borough Council's Labour Group, but did explain that tenants from former slum areas were subsidised as '... they have been used to unusually low rents and the adjustment is sometimes difficult'.[196] Although he was aware that subsidy was a 'controversial matter', Ward stated that the high interest rates required for loans to finance construction meant that subsidy could not be maintained, though he acknowledged that sometimes councils did temporarily subsidise the rents of new homes in clearance areas.[197] In this light, the financial cost of building council houses and carrying out slum clearance was difficult enough for local authorities without adding low rents and compulsory takeover of private rental properties. The problem, as Labour perceived it, of greedy landlords and crumbling rented properties remained. How, then, to solve it?

The publication of the 1963 pamphlet *Labour's Plan for Old Houses* marked a change of pace. Labour asserted that 4–5 million rented houses were in need of improvement – with only 25,000 being improved by landlords annually, it was suggested that 'private landlords will take over a century to provide all their houses with baths if the job is left to them'.[198] Indeed, official figures for the period 1960–4 indicated that only a fifth of rent-controlled properties and a quarter of uncontrolled rented homes had a sink, bath, hot water to a bath or sink, satisfactory conditions for storing food and an inside toilet.[199] In spite of this, *Labour's Plan for Old Houses* adopted a hesitant tone on whether councils should take over houses in the event of improvements not being made, arguing that 'it would not be practicable ... to insist that *every* old house must satisfy *all* the requirements of the new standard. There will be cases, for example, when a tenant objects to turning a bedroom which cannot be spared into a bathroom'.[200] This seemed an impractical solution – Labour councils would be unlikely to accept any diminution of standards, and those who did would be left with a stock of private rental housing in need of improvement.

During the summer of 1963, the existing scandal of the 'Profumo Affair' grew to encompass the slum landlord Perec Rachman, who had dealings with some of the figures in the case. Though Rachman had in fact died in November 1962, his activities in using intimidation to force a change in tenancy – and thereby decontrol – were demonised by the press, and 'Rachmanism' was used to encompass all unsavoury landlord practices.[201] The Conservative government felt compelled to set up an inquiry into housing in Greater London in August 1963, chaired by Sir Milner Holland and with reference to the private rented sector. When the inquiry reported in 1965, it included brief case studies of landlord abuses, ranging from 'petty irritation' to 'intimidation or actual violence'.[202] 'Anti-social behaviour by disreputable owners of property should be condemned in the gravest terms', stated the September 1963 editorial of *Labour Woman*, but registration of landlords was recommended rather than local authority takeover.[203] 'Rachmanism' made it clear that 1957 decontrol had gone too far, but the sheer scale of the problem in rented housing made municipalisation unviable. A few voices were to be found in favour of a harder line. Renee Short, the Prospective Parliamentary Candidate for Wolverhampton North-East (and MP from 1964), argued in *Tribune* that enforced improvement was a 'poor substitute' for municipalisation, stating that it was as much a part of 'a really comprehensive housing policy as the public ownership of land'.[204] In a similar vein, the local Labour paper the *Baron's Court Citizen* claimed in June 1963 that the 1957 Rent Act had condemned 'hundreds of thousands of tenants to impoverishment by rapacious landlords'.[205] Though Labour were gifted an enormous piece of political capital by the Rachman scandal, they appeared less sure of their attitude towards private landlords. Were they now an acceptable part of the modern housing system – or yet a symbol of Victorian capitalism which had to be tolerated in the interim?

In February 1963, Mrs R Chambers, a private landlord owning a 'compact block' of forty-nine 'superior artisan dwellings', wrote to Harold Wilson complaining about the high cost of improvement works that had been demanded by her local Labour council without prior payment.[206] Surprisingly, given who she was addressing, Chambers claimed that she had a link to two Conservative MPs 'ready, if necessary, to ask a question in the House on my behalf', but asked 'how many private landlords have these advantages?'[207] Chambers did not appear to be an especially typical landlord, though she professed to have a sort of *noblesse oblige*, claiming she had forsaken a high profit from selling her property to 'protect my decent loyal tenants'.[208] Although this case appeared to confirm Labour suspicions of rent-seeking recalcitrance, the LPRD local government officer responded by criticising the council in question for not dealing with the matter sooner, and making it clear that councils ought to pay the landlord by instalment for improvements done.[209] This sympathetic attitude demonstrates the change in Labour sentiment, from one of outright opposition to the landlord as a symbol of anachronism, to grudging encouragement.

On entering government in 1964, Labour found themselves in a strange position. Far from demanding that the Mrs Chambers of Britain should have their property expropriated without delay, the party moved towards a means of re-imposing rent control and improving the lot of tenants within the existing system. Some indication of this strain of Labour thinking was present in a 1965 *Socialist Commentary* article by Ivor Richard, MP for Baron's Court, in which he argued that despite the Labour usage of the slogan 'Repeal the Rent Act' (that he himself had used), few parliamentary candidates '... really assumed that it meant a straightforward simple repeal of the 1957 Rent Act'.[210] Whether or not this was so, Richard went on to suggest that any new system should be based on 'the freedom of landlord and tenant to fix their own terms', adding only that tenants in low-rated accommodation should have security of tenure.[211] This was quite a departure from past Labour rhetoric. Rather than viewing the tenant as the victim of exploitation, and the morass of rent controls best overcome by fully incorporating private renting into the public system, Richard placed the private rented sector as primarily outside the business of government.

Indeed, whilst Labour had pledged to crack down on 'Rachmanite' practices prior to taking office in 1964, they instead used their entry to government to impose a 'compromise between control and freedom', in the form of the 1965 Rent Act.[212] Significantly, the Act also created security of tenure for those in unfurnished accommodation who did not have controlled rents. As Martin Daunton has pointed out, security of tenure had been solely associated with rent control, 'so that a tenant had both or neither'.[213] Devised by Crossman and his advisors, the act created an independent cadre of 'rent officers', empowered to assess property standards and to set 'fair rents' appropriate to the value of the property as a whole as a means of adjudicating between landlord and tenant. Crossman did not define precisely what he believed to be a 'fair rent' or how it should be determined, noting simply that he intended that it should be 'fair to landlords as well as tenants'.[214] Moreover, it enabled a system of what Malpass has described as 'moderated market rents', by allowing increases to 'fair rents' to be phased in subject to review by local Rent Assessment Committees.[215] In this respect, the 1965 Rent Act made rent regulation feasible, through lifting ultra-low rents, and through creating security of tenure, certainly made life better for tenants. Yet it was manifestly not a challenge to the private rented sector in the manner that previous proposals had been.

Cracks in the new system appeared relatively quickly. Frank Allaun had been a leading critic of the fair rent concept from the outset, claiming in a 1965 debate on the Rent Bill: 'Whatever method or formula we reach [to set a fair rent], the aim must be absolutely clear – to keep rents down.'[216] He and other critics from the Labour left were especially sceptical about the role of Rent Assessment Committees, fearing precedent-setting sharp rent rises, which was indeed what occurred as the 1960s wore on. The belief that 'rents should be taken out of party politics' was the basis of the Rent Act, noted a 1967 LPRD review of housing policy, 'but this principle is of questionable validity'.[217] Revealing considerable weaknesses in the fair rent formula, the review noted that the rent-fixing process was accessed only by 'well-informed' tenants, with decisions in London tending to 'emphasise the difference in income between east and west ... no matter what the surrounding amenities are like'.[218] Criticisms of the Rent Act were not taken terribly seriously by Crossman himself, who claimed that 'the tenants have let us down' in their failure to apply for rent reductions (which may or may not have been granted).[219] Yet the critiques ranged far and wide. One 1968 *Socialist Commentary* article asserted that the Rent Act had created a 'hotch-potch of *ad hoc* rules', most glaringly failing to ensure that rented property was maintained and improved. The author of the piece went on to recommend 'public control', through a system of compulsory registration for private landlords with rent-fixing as standard – in effect, a state-managed private market.[220] Such a scheme could have required selective municipalisation where landlords were found to be unfit for a housing register, though the author was at pains to assert that municipalisation was no longer the right option.

In a 1968 memorandum to other NEC members, Allaun cautioned that the move to encourage landlords to make improvements could be counter-productive: tenancies could be decontrolled if a house gained a bath, hot water and inside toilet, even if installed by the tenant.[221] He noted that 'fair rents' fixed for unimproved properties in London, Birmingham and Southampton had tripled controlled rents, meaning tenants would 'bitterly resist' bathroom installation if it meant high rents.[222] Responding to Allaun in a separate memorandum, Anthony Greenwood suggested that 'the keynote of the whole exercise is persuasion'.[223] Rent increases, argued Greenwood, were the only means of encouraging landlords to improve the housing stock.[224] Ironically enough, this was one of the justifications for decontrol under the 1957 Rent Act. Greenwood echoed Crossman in his commentary on the fair rent system in a 1969 *Labour Woman* piece, remarking that though the 'machinery' of fair rents existed, but 'not enough tenants have taken advantage of it'.[225] However, the mood within the party was rather more in sympathy with tenants. In their published report of August 1969, the Housing Policy Study Group accepted that only around 10 per cent of households subject to rent regulation had applied for a fair rent, but felt that the rent tribunal process should be simplified to make it less intimidating for tenants.[226] Indicating the direction of travel for Labour policy in the 1970s, the Study Group also recommended that furnished accommodation be regulated, 'rent aid' for private tenants and registration of all private rents.[227] While Labour would go on to lose office in 1970, the private rented sector had declined to just 20 per cent of all dwellings by 1971.[228]

'To socialists … the ownership of one man's home by another has always been repugnant', stated the housing group of the Society of Labour Lawyers in a 1973 pamphlet advocating municipalisation.[229] Municipalisation remained a key commitment for the Labour left into the 1970s as that wing of the party began to exercise greater power. Though there was truth to the claim by the Labour Lawyers that state action would be 'less acute and socially harmful … than allowing private landlordism to die in its own way', Labour ultimately took the simpler route of extending security of tenure when the party returned to office in 1974.[230] If the failure to municipalise when in government was in part reflective of the difficulty of implementation, it was also indicative of a lack of clarity by Labour activists surrounding the place of private landlordism in their vision of the future. Labour had contributed to running down private renting as a form of tenure, but were both unwilling and unable to remove it entirely. Given that the failure of rent decontrol confirmed many of Labour's critiques of landlordism, it is surprising that the party committed to the complex, quasi-voluntary 'fair rents' system, not least as Crossman seemed to be the only real champion of it. The temporal restrictions of Labour's attempt to transform the urban environment offer one explanation: the vision of socialist modernity that those within Labour sought would not happen immediately. In this light, private rented housing would have to remain standing for some time. By 1970, a significant proportion of the remaining private rented sector was not much better than it had been in 1957. The shrinking of the modern future was part of the reason why, but Labour's unwillingness to bring an end to the 'wealth in bricks' of private landlordism was still more damaging.

Castles for all: Labour and owner-occupation

'There is secret applause', wrote David Eversley sardonically in a 1956 *Socialist Commentary*, 'every time a man takes himself off the [housing] register and buys his own solution to the problem'.[231] He went on to claim that 'the problems of the owner-occupier are receiving as much attention as those of the homeless', arguing this undermined the concept of 'housing as a social service'.[232] Though the 'property-owning democracy' is a familiar slogan to historians of post-war Britain, it is near-unanimously associated with Conservative thinking, and as a consequence, so too is owner-occupation.[233] The nature of Labour's relationship with owner-occupiers and indeed the wider politics of the 'property-owning democracy' in the period 1945–70 is a subject largely neglected by historical scholarship. Ben Jackson has demonstrated that the revisionist wing of Labour in particular were far more interested in owner-occupation than might have been imagined.[234] Far from lambasting the 'property-owning democracy' as a Tory fiction, revisionists tried to move Labour towards ending a 'false dichotomy' of Conservative exaltation of private property and Labour attempts to socialise it.[235] More recently, Guy Ortalano has through his study of Milton Keynes made a broader case for the existence of the 'property-owning social democracy: a managed housing system including both the public and private sectors, in which a controlling authority prevented residualization in the public sector while facilitating entry into the private'.[236] How, then, did owner-occupation fit into a modern, socialist housing system? And why has Labour interest in property ownership been overlooked?

Private home ownership had exploded in size as a tenure in the inter-war period. This was in marked contrast to the situation prior to 1914: as Malpass has recounted, owner-occupation may have been as low as 10 per cent of overall housing before the First World War, but the majority of the four million homes constructed between the wars were sold to private owners.[237] Around 32 per cent of the British housing stock was owner-occupied by 1938.[238] By 1939, George Orwell was able to write of the 'long, long rows of little semi-detached houses ... as much alike as council houses and generally uglier', that symbolised the pre-eminence of home ownership in 1930s Britain.[239] Although Noel Skelton, the Conservative MP for Perth, had coined the term 'property-owning democracy' in 1923, it was not until after the Second World War that the Conservatives began to seriously explore the concept of owner-occupation as a hegemonic tenure.[240] Following their victory in the 1951 general election, Conservative housing policy focused on building homes for sale, though the promised 300,000 houses per annum included council homes.[241] 'Ideological corners [had] to be cut' to meet the target, as John Davis puts it, meaning that private enterprise only accounted for 30 per cent of all completions before 1954.[242] The Tory dream of a 'property-owning democracy' was far from a reality in the early 1950s, even if owner-occupation was gradually increasing.

In marked contrast to Conservative sentiment, Labour policy after 1945 had emphasised the provision of rented housing, identifying an over-focus on private ownership in the inter-war period. In this they were supported by the findings of the 1944 Pole committee, which had investigated private enterprise house-building during the war and concluded that more rented housing was needed.[243]

Whilst Bevan has been charged by historians such as John Campbell as being opposed to home ownership, evidenced by the fact that he ensured far more council houses were built than houses for sale, Martin Francis argues that Bevan was concerned simply by 'provision on the basis of need'.[244] In this regard, he was not fundamentally opposed to home ownership, simply where it overshadowed rented housing. The problem with the inter-war period, as Labour's *Guide to Post-War Housing Policy* put it, was that 'most new houses ... were not being occupied on the basis of need, but money'.[245] This was not simply a Labour view. 'Only the man who could put down £50 or £100 in ready cash', remarked the anarchist writer George Woodcock, 'and looked like he was holding down a safe and respectable job was a suitable candidate for one of these jerry-built villas'.[246] Labour activists had a certain disdain for the ability of private enterprise to serve the needs of the working classes. Birmingham Labour Party had suggested in 1943 that 'the average working man cannot afford to buy his own house and rear and educate a family at the same time'.[247] However, Jon Lawrence has convincingly argued that this was something of an illusion: working-class home owners made up a substantial part of the inter-war boom.[248] Nevertheless, for Labour activists, the future of housing was municipal: 'They, and they alone, are able to assess the relative housing needs of different families.'[249]

The 1950s saw a gradual change in attitude. Labour had proposed giving leaseholders of private houses the option of buying the freehold of their home in their 1951 election manifesto, which was reasserted in the 1953 policy statement *Challenge to Britain*.[250] While anxious that Labour did not indulge in 'me-too-ism' with the Tories over owner-occupation, James MacColl observed in 1954 that for party activists, 'there is no fundamental objection to a man owning his own house any more than to owning his own trousers'.[251] Most audaciously, the Labour MP for Oldham West, Leslie Hale, suggested in a 1953 edition of *Labour's Northern Voice* that tenants of rent-controlled properties should be allowed to buy their home as a freehold as an alternative to municipalisation.[252] Hale proposed that the tenants in question could acquire their homes with 'no question of mortgages or deposits', remarking that 'the average person does not feel secure so long as he remains a tenant'.[253] Had Labour actually pursued this idea it could well have been popular, but Hale's sentiments were certainly not conventional Labour wisdom. This said, a similar idea was proposed by the LPRD local government officer in comments on the draft of MacColl's 1957 pamphlet *Plan for Rented Houses*. In order to reduce the number of municipalised dwellings, the officer argued that 'there is a strong argument for encouraging tenants to purchase [slum properties]'.[254] Surprisingly, the left-wing Labour campaign Victory for Socialism (VFS) argued in 1958 that municipalised tenants should receive 100 per cent mortgages.[255] This was all the more extraordinary, given that Harry Dickens had claimed that municipalisation would end property ownership and prevent tenants from escaping 'the regimentation of the Red Heaven'.[256] Although Labour activists would not privilege owner-occupation, there was no contradiction between individual property ownership and Labour's modern, socialist vision.

Where Labour were far more cautious was on the question of individual financing of property ownership. MacColl warned in 1954 that if mortgage repayments outstripped the cost of repairs, owner-occupied property became a 'wasting asset': he believed that a relatively high wage of £12 a week was required to avoid this.[257] 'Wasting assets' were also the concern of Munby, who argued in 1957 that the 'small man' should hold liquid assets such as stocks and shares, as 'if one's savings are tied up in a house, they cannot easily be mobilised in a crisis'.[258] Slums could therefore develop in entirely owner-occupied areas, as became the case in parts of inter-war Bristol.[259] In his study of 1960s Sunderland, the sociologist Norman Dennis focused on an area of owner-occupied single-storey cottages. In spite of his claim that the cottages were not 'structural slums', it is clear from his findings that many cottage inhabitants lived in poor conditions.[260] Building societies – responsible for much of the inter-war housing boom – were generally seen as the villains of the piece, running the 'cleverest racket of modern times' in the view of Orwell.[261] In 1955, David Eversley alluded to this in his description of the 'grand-parental system of finance', with parents tied in mortgage repayments for private homes in the hope that they might be able to help their children with deposits.[262] Munby also referred to the 'racket', arguing that building societies were concerned simply with making a profit, despite the fact that 'the propaganda of politicians has apparently convinced these admirable money-lenders that they perform a social service'.[263] In spite of the abject inefficiency of the owner-occupied sector, it clearly provided a rival housing service, if not exactly a social one.

Labour's solution was to cut out the 'admirable money-lenders' where possible. One hundred per cent mortgages were proposed in *Homes for the Future*, and the party stated that '[our policies] will provide the incentive for a vast extension of owner-occupation'.[264] However, Labour made it clear that government-assisted loans would be subject to strict conditions. The mortgager was required to install modern amenities in the house in question, contribute to a repairs fund and to give the local authority the first opportunity of buying the house at a price fixed by the district valuer.[265] This was owner-occupation articulated in the terms of the Labour movement: controls preventing the individual from benefitting at the expense of the collective community. In a similar vein, MacColl had suggested that Labour should only offer leaseholds so the state remained in control of the land supply. He felt that this was an acceptable price for an efficient housing system, remarking, 'There is ultimately no room left for the Englishman's sovereignty over his castle.'[266] Victory for Socialism proposed that housing sales become a local authority practice: local authority surveyors would be used instead of private individuals, and the group recommended the abolition of stamp duty to encourage house buying.[267] Similarly, in a 1956 *Tribune* piece, Albert Evans, MP for Islington South-West, approvingly commented upon the West German use of tax deductions to encourage owner-occupation.[268] Ironically, VFS was viewed as a hard-left vehicle, and the NEC acted to limit its ability to organise, but its housing policies were not so distant from Labour thought in the period.[269] The declared position of VFS – 'we seek in short only two tenures of residential land-holding: the freehold of the owner-occupier, and the Council tenancy' – was essentially the same sentiment as expressed in *Homes for the Future*.[270]

Other left-wingers remained suspicious of home ownership. Ian Mikardo sardonically defined the 'property-owning democracy' as a system 'under which a few people own property and the rest democratically decide that the same few shall go on owning it'.[271] Writing to *Tribune* in 1956 on the subject of 'housing as a social service', Mr M. Wales of South Shields argued that owner-occupiers were not playing their part in the financing of the housing system due to low rates and that many 'bought their homes before the war when property was cheap'.[272] It is probable that some Labour activists in the 1950s regarded property ownership as little more than a distraction to the task of building public housing. This was particularly so when owner-occupiers were often the source of disquiet about paying rates: the key means of financing local attempts to further Labour's modern, socialist aims when out of government.

There was a meeting point between the two seemingly conflicted tenures of owner-occupation and public housing: namely, the sale of council houses to sitting tenants. Though this was largely anathema to Labour principles – and since the 'Right to Buy' scheme of Margaret Thatcher in the 1980s has been solely associated with Tory ideology – Labour did allow for occasional council house sales by local authorities throughout the post-war period. Council house sales had been permitted through the 1936 Housing Act, with ministerial consent required. Under the Attlee government, the minister responsible was Aneurin Bevan, who unsurprisingly refused to countenance sales on the grounds that it would intensify the existing crisis in rented accommodation.[273] From 1951 to 1964, despite activist pressure, the Conservative government showed relatively little inclination to increase owner-occupation through the sale of council housing.[274] It was, however, still possible for Labour to attack 'rushed' Tory plans to sell off council houses as early as December 1951, although the party suggested it was due to a tight-fisted desire to avoid paying out housing subsidies rather than an intellectual project of home ownership.[275] A similar claim of penny-pinching from an opposing angle was used in a 1965 pamphlet, which drew attention to an 'amazing demonstration of wilful prejudice' against an attempt by the Labour-controlled Portland council in Dorset to build seventy houses for sale.[276] Equally, there were some instances of active 'privatisation' of council estates. Ben Jones has described the systematic selling off of council houses in Brighton by the Conservative council from 1952, although sales were not significant until 1959 and a Conservative policy of sales was retained in Bristol when the council was won back by Labour in 1963.[277]

Nonetheless, council house sales were not a major topic of discussion until Labour had returned to government in 1964. Following local election gains in 1966, a number of Tory councils engaged in what Aled Davies has described as 'sales activism': an attempt to promote council house sales through simultaneous rent increases and discounts for buyers.[278] 'I did not become Minister of Housing to preside over the squandering of public assets', declared Anthony Greenwood in a 1967 party conference speech backing a ban on council house sales, 'and this is what the sale of council houses means'.[279] In a further attack piece Labour referred to the Tory proposal as a 'monstrous electioneering gimmick', claiming that sales put pressure on waiting lists and reduced the numbers of three-bedroom houses available.[280] *Labour's Northern Voice* put 'A Total Ban on All Council House Sales' at the top of their December 1969 proposals to make 'housing a social service'.[281] Setting out the difference between the party and the Tory-controlled Birmingham City Council in a 1967 local election flyer, Birmingham Labour Party asserted 'Labour helps home ownership – but not at the expense of the 38,000 still waiting to rent'.[282] Though Greenwood was able to block sales, Conservative 'sales activism' weakened Labour considerably amongst those tenants keen to buy by the early 1970s.[283] Whilst the ease by which the Tories could outflank Labour on council house sales exposed some rigidity in Labour's position, 'sales activism' demonstrated ideological obstinacy for the Conservative part. Frank Allaun noted in a 1968 *Tribune* piece that 'local authorities will receive far less from the sale of council houses than they will have to spend on building new ones'.[284] There was no logic in this, unless the party in question was committed to creating owner-occupiers by any means necessary. In contrast, the Labour view was that council houses could sometimes be sold, but only under the right conditions and sales could be stopped at any moment.

'If the property is well distributed', argued Crosland in 1962, 'a property-owning democracy is a socialist rather than a conservative ideal'.[285] Jackson has argued that the 'egalitarian strategy' pursued by those such as Crosland, on the revisionist right of Labour, was aimed at freeing the people from 'economic and political domination of a wealthy minority'.[286] *Signposts for the Sixties* was indicative of this viewpoint, claiming that the fact that the Conservatives represented 'the top one per cent [owning] nearly half the nation's private wealth and property' meant that they could not deliver a 'property-owning democracy'.[287] In this light, Labour could pose as a more reasonable agent for would-be buyers. Writing in 1961, Douglas Houghton, MP for Sowerby, cautioned readers of *Labour Woman* that 'more and more house-hunters are being forced to buy', due to long council house waiting lists.[288] Surprisingly, Houghton claimed that far from being 'grinding money-lenders', the building societies were 'performing a public service and conduct themselves accordingly'.[289] Even if building societies were not the scoundrels that Munby had claimed them to be, it is unlikely that they were altruistic. In a 1963 *Socialist Commentary* piece, Roy Hattersley – then Chairman of the Sheffield Council Housing Committee, later MP for Birmingham Sparkbrook as well as Labour Deputy Leader – went so far to suggest that 'owner-occupation remains in many ways the ideal housing pattern', though he acknowledged that those who struggled to pay council rents would be unlikely to be able to afford, or be granted, mortgages.[290] The housing academic Barry Cullingworth argued that this was precisely the case, with families being forced to buy substandard dwellings due to their inability to raise loans.[291] Donnison noted in 1967 that one-fifth of house buyers would actually prefer to rent if they could find accommodation at reasonable cost.[292] The fact that Labour seemingly intended individuals to pay fully for the costs of housing meant that the poorest still lost out. Cullingworth recommended a household subsidy for all who might need it, 'irrespective of the character of their tenure'.[293] Though Labour introduced the 'option mortgage' in 1968, a subsidy to mortgage lenders to encourage them to charge low-income borrowers a lower interest rate, this was not the same as giving a subsidy direct to the low-income owner-occupier.[294] As we have seen, similar issues of inequality persisted throughout the period in both the public and private rented sectors.

With owner-occupation close to tenurial dominance, the issue was perhaps that Labour had begun to indulge in what MacColl had described as 'me-too-ism'. 'The parrot-cry has always been that Labour is anti-owner-occupier but the facts show how false this is', asserted the triumphant report of the NEC Housing Policy Study Group in 1969, pointing to increases of private sector building over previous Conservative totals.[295] It was true that private sector building was required to meet the enormous target of 500,000 houses per annum that the party had set itself, though total completions fell well short of this.[296] Although the 1967 LPRD policy review had noted that 'most people in the Party now accept that adequate provision for owner-occupation must be included in any future housing plan', some party members in the latter part of the 1960s seemed concerned that Labour had followed a Conservative lead.[297] One of the Housing Policy Study Group members, William Hilton, criticised in a memorandum higher rents for council tenants without penalties for owner-occupiers, rubbishing the idea that the private owner was 'an independent character satisfying his housing needs without state help or other advantage'.[298] While 'the average net tax relief for the owner-occupier is around £31 per annum', Hilton argued, 'the average subsidy for council tenants – from Exchequer funds – is £19 per annum'.[299] Daunton has described mortgage tax relief as an implicitly political policy: effectively a means of making a 'property owning democracy' significantly more attractive from a tax-beneficial perspective.[300] As is evident from the previous discussion on council housing, Labour had done little to reduce this disparity whilst in government, and by 1970 found themselves having to defend 'high subsidised' public housing from Conservative attacks. Responding to these charges in a discussion booklet for speakers, Labour asserted that 'nobody would argue that tax relief should be withdrawn from owner-occupiers even though it frequently goes to those on high incomes. However, the Tories have never mentioned this aspect and have confined their attacks of wasted money solely to the council sector'.[301]

Writing on this theme for *Tribune* after the general election defeat, Anthony Judge suggested that the answer was for Labour-controlled councils to actively build houses for sale in order to cross-subsidise council housing under threat of sharp rent rises.[302] Responding to Judge in the following issue, Reg Holmes of Doncaster remarked that in an era of high mortgages, the impact of his proposals 'will be mainly limited to the middle-class and the highly-paid worker'.[303] Rather more forcefully, Tom Braddock argued that building costs would rise if councils built homes for sale. His solution was municipalisation for all: proposing that all homes should be rented from a public authority at a percentage of the property value.[304] While Braddock's sympathies undoubtedly lay further left than most within Labour, one wonders whether greater state control over the private market as a whole may have appealed to a broad range of activists.

'There is not and cannot be a free market in housing', Crosland declared in 1971. His words epitomised the Labour conception of owner-occupation.[305] An absolute free market was anathema to Labour's socialist, modern vision: wide disparities in property had, in the view of Labour actors, created the slums and would do so again. Labour therefore aimed at extending state control over the housing system, and in their reading of what needed to be done, state housing had to take precedence in Britain's urban future. 'It is a requisite of social stability that one type of property should dominate', wrote Bevan in *In Place of Fear*, 'in the society of the future it should be public property'.[306] Uncontrolled, uninhibited owner-occupation did not serve the interests of those Labour saw as being in most need. Equally, the party focus on the provision of rented housing could often translate into a message of outright hostility towards owner-occupation. This could work both ways, given Tory hostility towards council housing. A 1950 *Town Crier* piece by a 'middle class' Labour voter and home owner had ridiculed the 'property owning democracy' desires of their 'Tory friends', who failed in the view of the author to see that the '£5 a week man' could not afford to buy a house, nor pay off a mortgage.[307] Indeed, it would ultimately require the fire sale of council housing through the 'Right to Buy' provisions of the Housing Act 1980 to create the property-owning democracy: as great an 'offloading of public capital' as the privatisation of British Telecom or Gas.[308] We have a tendency to see the ideological fault lines around housing in a particular light, given the effective political victory of the 'property-owning democracy'. The alternative conception of Labour in the modern moment – that of 'housing as a social service' – conceptualised owner-occupation as a choice some might make rather than a natural inclination encoded into the human psyche.

'To stand still is to decline': The failure of housing as a social service

In a 2014 piece for the *London Review of Books*, the journalist James Meek questioned the assumptions many of us have made about council housing in present-day Britain, stating he did not 'expect to find myself living in a council house in the traditional sense – that is, a household dwelling owned and run by the state – any time soon. But that's more to do with the shortage of council houses, and the way they're run, than with any objection on principle, or a conviction that council houses are doomed to be ugly and uncomfortable'.[309] Meek's piece is revealing of both the status of public housing in the early twenty-first century, and the way in which housing tenure has changed in Britain over the last forty years. In 2011, for the first time since the early 1960s, the private rented sector overtook the social rented sector in size.[310] The political legacy of the public housing sector in twenty-first-century Britain is not an overwhelmingly positive one. Even with the omnipresent political grouping 'Generation Rent', confined to less-than-adequate, overpriced private rented accommodation – and the (ultimately unsuccessful) revival of left discourse on council housing during the Labour leadership of Jeremy Corbyn – there remains a powerful assumption (including within certain sections of Labour) that the failure of state intervention in housing is inevitable. This was patently not the attitude of Labour in the post-war period. 'A free market in housing is impossible to obtain', mused James MacColl in 1957, 'and if it were obtained it would not do the job set for it'.[311] MacColl's sentiment stands as an apt description of the Labour attitude towards housing. 'Free' markets were a damaging illusion, and 'housing as a social service' meant a firm state hand over the housing system. This was not solely a story of public housing. Labour's approach to the owner-occupied and privately rented sections of the housing system had a direct effect on the provision of public housing, as much as policy towards public housing affected the other two tenures. While the private rented sector had collapsed to 20 per cent of total households by 1971, the owner-occupied sector was nearing 50 per cent.[312] In spite of the interdependency of the housing system, Labour tended to deal with each tenure in isolation. A 'social service' fit for the modern moment in the sense of the National Health Service could not arise while the future for the council home, privately rented home and the owner-occupied home remained unclear or ill-defined.

In the early 1960s, Crosland stated that there could be a clear, socialist form of housing policy, which should '… reflect social decisions and not solely market valuations – if necessary, at some cost to economic growth'.[313] Private landlords – and tenants – also bore some of the cost. If one element of Labour's post-war plans for the housing system could be said to have almost succeeded, it was the attempted abolition of the private landlord. This stood to reason – throughout the mid-twentieth century, Labour actors caricatured the landlord as an effectively anti-modern figure. Alderman Bradbeer of Birmingham Labour Party claimed in 1945 that his Conservative counterparts derived their wealth from 'the landlordism of the slums, the exploitation of labour with low wages, long hours and sweated conditions, the fear of sickness, the scourge of unemployment and the dread of the workhouse'.³¹⁴ The supposedly clear link between urban deprivation, Victorian avarice and Tory doctrine would lose little of its potency for many Labour members throughout the period. In this regard, the travails of the private rented sector invite a greater consideration of the ends that political actors sought, rather than simply the means by which they went about it. Ultimately, Labour's actions were seen as overcoming, in Crosland's words, 'Conservative priorities'.³¹⁵ Tory faith in the market as a just provider of housing was, in Labour eyes, not simply wrong but an anachronism. Private landlordism was the most objectionable of the symbols of a past housing order.

Labour actors were far more willing to countenance an expansion of owner-occupation in addition to the public stock, but with considerable reservations from their grassroots and local councils. For some Labour members, there was an element of truth in Harry Dickens' claim that 'whatever they say, they don't *like* private property'.³¹⁶ Others were more sanguine about the prospect of wider owner-occupation: surprisingly, this included voices from the left, as attested to by the position of Victory for Socialism and contributors to *Tribune* and *Labour's Northern Voice*. Labour engagement with the 'property-owning democracy' appeared to be more than just a revisionist musing. In spite of this, Labour could only ever see private ownership as part of a balanced modern housing system, not as the primary tenure. The aggressive Conservative pursuit of the property-owning democracy via council house sales in the late 1960s proved to be the more durable political project, focused on a housing system in which only one tenure was king.

In 1962, the North Kensington Labour Party claimed that 'a man is entitled to an adequate house for himself and his family and the community should accept the responsibility of providing this as a social service'.³¹⁷ Quite apart from the patriarchal tone, the sentiment of North Kensington Labour neatly captures the reasoning behind Labour's drive to create swathes of council homes. Housing would, in this view, take its place as one of the modern social services, with the slum merely a bad memory. However, Labour proved incapable of deciding whether public housing should have low rents for all or to utilise the subsidy principally for those most in need. The economist and Labour activist Silvan Jones expressed the former view in a 1960 letter to *Socialist Commentary*, remarking that 'tenants already pay according to their "ability", only indirectly through the tax system'.³¹⁸ However, whilst Jones' view was certainly shared by plenty of Labour members, the party were unable to make the according shift in the way in which housing was financed, through much greater subsidies and taxation (both local and national).

Housing was central to Labour's political culture and the modern moment offered the opportunity to go further as well as faster. To return to Meek's article, he comments that 'the slum-to-council-house journey was a one-off, exclusively for two past generations.'[319] Setting aside the assumptions inherent in Meek's observation, it historicises post-war housing policy as something with which we can have little connection. However, the built environment is not something that can be wholly confined to the past: much of the product of post-war housing policy still stands around us and is lived in. Although those generations who did gain council houses did so because of particular governmental choices in policy, it is equally important not to dismiss post-war housing policy as a historical quirk. Labour's contribution to the reshaping of the post-war housing system was predicated on an attempt to bring socialism – in a particular, welfarist form – to all. The modern moment allowed for added velocity: as *Signposts for the Sixties* put it, 'to stand still is to decline'.[320] Whether in terms of 'Generation Rent', housing affordability or availability, the driving forces behind Labour housing policy in the post-war period are reflected in the early twenty-first century. If urban modernism was a historically contingent phenomenon, many of the issues it attempted to address were not.

4

Workers' cottages and tall towns

Class, community and the modern home

Writing in a 1955 edition of *Socialist Commentary*, the sociologist Michael Young claimed that for those trapped in decaying inner-city houses, modern living was symbolised by the new homes of their neighbours, with 'the steam hissing above the Ascot, the shiny new paint and the smoke rising from modern grates'.[1] Whilst the fittings might have changed over the period discussed in this book, Young's portrait of material modernity remained a steady feature of housing policy throughout the post-war era. Though the Conservatives consistently promised new homes in their appeals to the electorate, Labour placed an emphasis on not simply new but modern homes throughout the period, equipped with all the amenities of the atomic age. Given that the party had originally favoured 'workers' cottages' of the kind promoted by the Clydeside Labourite John Wheatley, exploring exactly why this close embrace of architectural modernism occurred across an often-parochial movement is key to any explanation of the built legacy of 1945–70.

However, as Young alluded to in his description, there were spatial barriers of place and class to be overcome in bringing about modern cities. As a party originating from working-class organisations, Labour had (and has) a clear affinity with the lower segments of the British class structure. In the course of his work on the 'residualization' – the conversion to a tenure of last resort – of council estates, Ben Jones has suggested the most controversial question throughout the inter-war period was 'who ought to live in council housing?'[2] This class-infused proposition remained still true after 1945, and with the perceived spread of affluence from the 1950s, a protracted social debate as to whether council housing should be universal, for the working classes alone, or for a vulnerable 'underclass' continued. Across the pages of Labour periodicals and in official publications, Labour politicians and activists expressed a variety of views on the subject, which had a subtle but clear effect on housing policy. Returning again to Young, the concept of 'community' was a crucial part of all discussion on housing in the period examined. Major recent works by Jon Lawrence and Lise Butler have reinforced the centrality of Young's work on the subject to popular preconceptions in Britain about the 'decline' of community in post-war Britain, and his contribution to myth-making about 'lost' ideal communities.[3] As a leading Labour-leaning intellectual, as well as a major figure in the field of sociology, Young was the most prominent but by no means the only social scientist to attempt to discern what people 'really wanted' from their living environment. There has been a tendency in British history to take the declinist narratives of the period – individualism triumphing over community – at face value without really understanding the debate beneath it.[4] This chapter explores how the streets, lifts, concrete exteriors and stainless-steel interiors of the housing underpinning Labour's futuristic vision fitted into wider debates over design, class and community.

When applied to Britain, and especially England, the question of aesthetic preference in housing has powerful cultural determinants. 'Britain is more obsessed than ever', wrote Owen Hatherley in 2012, 'with an imaginary rural Arcadia which bears less and less resemblance to the places where we actually live'.[5] This utopia has a distinguished pedigree. The Tudor Walters report of 1918 recommended an expressly 'vernacular, rural' cottage design for working-class housing, evoking a simple (if imagined) past, influenced in part by the presence on the report committee of Raymond Unwin of the Garden City Movement.[6] A Labour forerunner to this 'workers' cottage' was the inspiration of John Wheatley in his 1913 pamphlet *Eight-Pound Cottages for Glasgow Citizens*. Wheatley depicted a detached 'four-apartment house' of a distinctly rural style, though his point of reference may have been Ireland (his place of birth), with a section of the pamphlet noting successful government schemes to improve Irish cottages.[7] Whilst the recommendations of Tudor Walters were the genesis of inter-war council housing schemes – to the extent that those built by the LCC 'reflected a watered-down version of the garden suburb' – Wheatley's cottage could be said to be an archetype for those within Labour who believed houses for working people should reflect pre-Industrial Revolution parochial tastes.[8] The 'Bevan House', promoted as the epitome of the housing drive of the 1945–51 Labour government, took a 'bourgeois' and 'traditional' design.[9] By contrast, with the tradition of tenement living in Scotland, Scottish councils were quite content to build flats as suburban estates were constructed in England and Wales.[10]

On the whole, Labour were slow to come around to the flat, and other distinctively modern forms of housing. In a highly critical assessment of flat living published in 1974, Anthony Sutcliffe claimed that the popularity of modern flats amongst the middle classes in the inter-war period legitimised them for use by working-class council tenants. This said, Birmingham Labour Party cited this middle-class multi-storey lifestyle as a reason why flats were *not* appropriate for the working classes.[11] Conversely, the leading London Communist Ted Bramley used Berthold Lubetkin's 'Highpoint' luxury flats in Highgate as the basis for his arguments about flat desirability. Lubetkin had supposedly assured him that similar modern amenities, as well as spacious gardens, tennis courts and a children's paddling pool, would be a feature of most working-class flats.[12] Moreover, Alison Ravetz claimed in her study of inter-war flat construction that modernism '… reminded observers of international trends, symbolised progress and helped to establish flats as an indispensable ingredient of modern urban environments'.[13] There existed a powerful sense that modern design, and in particular flats, might provide the materially superior socialist future that many within Labour envisaged.

It would be difficult if not impossible to discuss the history of housing without reference to class. Far from a simple question of economic structures, class consciousness and identity are 'positional and relational', and as Stephen Brooke has remarked 'class identity is found … in a sense of the limits of urban space'.[14] Scholars such as Ben Jones, Clare Langhamer, Jon Lawrence and Sam Wetherell have sought to address the previously partial attention paid by historians to the spatial elements of class and social change as a result of slum clearance, council housing and affluence.[15] Above all others, the working classes have been the primary focus of discussions about council housing. This book adopts the politicised representations of the working classes as the bottom rung of a 'structural' hierarchy of economic power and as a heterogeneous group sharing a common 'culture', with the caveat that neither of these representations were stable or neutral.[16] The belief that those in the working class who adopted a suburban lifestyle became 'bourgeois' individualists, whilst those who remained in older areas retained their identity as workers have been effectively challenged by scholars. Jon Lawrence argues that there was '… no cataclysmic exodus from mutualistic communitarianism to atomized, materialist individualism', arguing that English culture in particular has always accommodated both individualist and communitarian desires.[17] Whether the responses of Labour activists to a perception of increased affluence and new living environments actually affected housing provision has been less thoroughly investigated.

Perhaps the most celebrated of Labour commentators on the affluent society, Anthony Crosland encapsulated revisionist impressions in 1959, arguing that 'the basic fact about our social situation today is not a Marxist-type economic class-struggle ... our social antagonisms now have much more subtle origins'.[18] Another revisionist MP writing after the general election defeat in 1959, Douglas Jay, suggested that Labour was 'in danger of fighting under a label of class that no longer exists'.[19] While both revisionists were especially forthright in their belief that Labour needed to change with the times – and their analysis would prove to be half-correct at best – their statements capture some of the uncertainties Labour believed they faced through a common increase in prosperity. If the working classes were supposedly becoming more 'bourgeois', would they still be the intended recipients of council housing? Lawrence Black has described how Labour councils attempted to act as a 'moral vanguard' in their management of estates, viewing their tenants as a sort of 'deserving poor'.[20] Affluence seemed to pose a challenge to Labour paternalism. Further to this, the broader technological and cultural changes taking place across the era studied clearly had a considerable effect on one's sense of identity. In her post-war study of Banbury, the social scientist Margaret Stacey observed that in the years prior to 1930 Banbury life would have been more recognisable 'to a man who had lived a hundred years earlier than to one living at the present day'.[21] Labour's ambitions to provide better housing throughout this period of sustained change were confronted by a shifting sense of identity in the class from which they drew their support.

'Community is a vague concept', wrote the sociologist Leo Kuper in his 1953 survey of a new council estate in Coventry, 'and difficult to use either in research or planning, since it describes a qualitative aspect of the cohesion of a group'.[22] Though Kuper raised a still-pertinent sociological point, his apprehension as to whether one could utilise such an amorphous notion was not shared by the majority of his peers in the social sciences, nor indeed by those across the political spectrum. Dominant questions in the social sciences of income, employment and housing prompted interest in new inter-war housing estates amongst researchers.[23] Social investigators such as Ruth Glass (then Durant), examining the LCC Watling estate in north-west London, were concerned with determining the strength of community in these new settlements. Glass asserted that a community was 'a territorial group of people with a common mode of living, striving for common objectives', a description not tremendously different from E. P. Thompson's later contention that class formation derived from 'common experience'.[24] Glass believed that the predominance of young families on the estate, and the move away from the 'old mean street' of working-class life, meant that Watling could only ever be an 'artificial community'. This claim was repeated by Rosamund Jevons and John Madge in their study of peripheral council estates in Bristol.[25] Whilst 'community' as a pivotal element of one's living environment has distant origins, Patricia Garside has remarked that throughout the nineteenth century, it was believed that 'the "highest sphere" of life was expressed through voluntary associations and the local community'.[26] It is likely that the Garden City Movement's focus on 'social cohesion' brought the idea to the fore in town planning during the inter-war period, being an organisation with a voluntarist ethos of the late-Victorian type.[27] For Labour, community was seen as something that could be both designed into housing development and inspired through a rich associative lifestyle, based in part on *fin-de-siècle* utopian socialist attempts to create alternative 'radical settlements'.[28] Existing communities were viewed as something to be improved upon: as the NEC Housing and Town Planning Sub-Committee suggested in 1942, 'The East End [of London] of the future should be as desirable a place to live as the West End'.[29]

After 1945, social investigators tended to follow Glass in contrasting newer housing estates negatively with established communities, while extolling the virtues of a participatory lifestyle.[30] Most influential in this line of thought was Michael Young, who actually conducted a restudy of Watling in 1947.[31] Secretary of the Labour Party Research Department between 1945 and 1950, as well as author of *Let Us Face The Future*, the 1945 party manifesto, Young continued to have a powerful intellectual influence on Labour. He was a friend of both his replacement as Research Department Secretary, Peter Shore, and of Anthony Crosland, as well as being a frequent contributor to the revisionist Labour journal *Socialist Commentary*. Through his foundation of the Institute of Community Studies in 1953, Young had intended to 'reform the Labour Party through sociology'.[32] The 1957 publication of *Family and Kinship in East London*, written jointly with frequent co-collaborator and Labourite Peter Willmott, was of seminal importance to popular understandings of post-war dispersal, and as it will be argued, to housing policy. *Family and Kinship* painted a world in which the dispersal of working-class families from the close-packed slums of Bethnal Green to suburban homes in Debden (then in Essex) broke family ties and mutual dependencies, failing to recreate 'community' in a meaningful way. Mike Savage has asserted that *Family and Kinship* marked a move away from 'observational' studies of localities to emphasising a 'historical, temporally embedded, character which endures in a changing environment', in this case the working-class family.[33] Unusually for a social scientist, Young enjoyed similar levels of public influence to figures such as the literary critics Richard Hoggart and Raymond Williams or the historian Eric Hobsbawm, at a time when the humanities were the dominant academic influence on social commentary.[34] While Labour would endorse later moves towards higher-density settlement – typified by the 'deck access' blocks of the Park Hill complex in Sheffield or Robin Hood Gardens in Poplar – as a means of maintaining or recreating community, the reification of working-class life 'as it was' by figures such as Young and Willmott contributed to a contorted understanding of community. This belief, both within and without Labour, has had lasting effects on the way that the urban landscape of Britain has been imagined, designed and built.

Getting rid of class barriers? Class, affluence and modern homes

'The slums are a symbol of the old world', wrote the socialist author Douglas Brown in 1945, 'and decent modern houses are a symbol of the new'.[35] With considerably more ambivalence, George Orwell suggested in *The Road to Wigan Pier* that the replacement of the 'smoke-dim slums' of the industrial north by council houses was a marked improvement, 'but only by a small margin'.[36] The belief that there was a teleological progression from slum to modern council flat has remained a powerful one in spite of the warnings of historians.[37] One reason may well be that, as the examples of Brown and Orwell show, this was how change was characterised by social commentators in the period. As the party of the working classes, Labour politicians certainly took the view that they were duty-bound to provide decent homes for 'their people'. Sue Goss described the Labour council in Southwark between 1945 and 1964 in these terms, suggesting that 'they reflected in many ways the close-knit, somewhat insular communities they represented, conservative in social policy, but with strongly held views on the loyalty and natural affiliations of the working man'.[38] Frank Mort has suggested that 'progressive paternalism' characterised the majority of state intervention into housing and urban planning throughout the period.[39] The rise of material prosperity amongst the working classes, together with the gradual change in traditional habits amongst a new generation, presented a clear challenge to the kind of understanding of the working class described by Goss. This would develop by the late 1950s into a sense that the working class was being 'unmade', which, if Labour was to continue to depend electorally on working-class votes, represented an existential threat to the party.[40] This belief in the conversion of the working class to a middle-class identity was not confined to Labour. The Conservative Research Department thought that *embourgeoisement* of the proletariat was underway to the benefit of Conservatism, John Turner having wryly described this belief as 'Friedrich Engels, eighty years too late'.[41] If in the era of 'affluence' the sense that the working class was not quite what Labour imagined it to be was widespread, it is a real question what impact Labour responses to increased working-class affluence had on housing policy. Was the council house an appropriate working-class home for a modern, affluent age?

Speaking in 1971, Anthony Crosland observed that 'we know surprisingly little about people's *aspirations* for different types and standards of housing'.[42] He went on to comment that the Labour government of 1945 had wanted council estates to be 'well balanced and socially mixed communities, enabling (for example) teachers, doctors, local authority employees and social workers to live in the communities which they served'.[43] Crosland's musing reveals a curious imbalance in Labour's approach to housing. Labour knew very little about the desires of those they built housing for, and yet intended for council housing to be a mixed-class tenure. While it is a truism that the provision of council housing was a top-down exercise and generally not consultative, it is nonetheless revealing that Labour operated according to a perception of what the inhabitants of modern council housing should look like.[44] By and large, council estates did not become the 'socially mixed' form championed by Crosland. This was partly due to rent rises, as described in Chapter 3, as well through the choice of the teachers and doctors Crosland described. Crucially, the rise of affluence destabilised the paternalistic council housing culture, giving rise to arguments both within and without Labour that it was inappropriate for 'affluent' or 'respectable' workers to be resident on council estates. Charting the 'residualization' of council housing in Brighton, Ben Jones notes that the local press began to argue that affluent tenants should not live in council homes from as early as the 1930s.[45] The shift from 'respectable' working-class to 'residualization' had given rise by the 1970s to two opposing myths: 'failed community' council estates set against the idealised neighbourhoods of the pre-council housed past.[46] These two pictures of working-class life were given additional weight by the findings of social scientists, who had a tendency to reify older, established communities and critique the shortcomings of new estates. Prior to this, it is important to question why residualisation occurred, and why 'affluence' represented such a threat to Labour visions of modernity. Who, ultimately, was council housing for?

Since the Addison Act of 1919, local authorities had been required to build housing 'for the working classes'.[47] Labour resented this specificity as it restrained the ambition of the party to provide housing for all, with council housing tied explicitly to slum clearance in the 1935 Housing Act.[48] However, during the Attlee administration, Labour were able to begin to build council homes on a universal basis. Local authorities were now 'catering for general needs', observed a 1948 pamphlet, 'not for that indefinable category "the working classes".'[49] Symbolically, the 1949 Housing Act removed the restriction on building 'for the working classes'.[50] However, the ejection of the Labour government from power in October 1951 presented new questions about what should be prioritised once Labour regained power, as it might have assumed to after a short period of Conservative government.

In a lecture given in central London in November 1951, the editor of the *New Statesman* Kingsley Martin suggested that Labour had lost as the party leadership 'did not know where they were going' after creating the welfare state.[51] Though Martin might have been uncharitable, he made an interesting point. In terms of housing, although Labour's period in government had established council housing as a universal tenure in principle, councils largely continued to view their task as housing the 'working classes'. Critiquing this position, the left-wing activist and former MP Tom Braddock argued in 1952 that although 'housing, like everything else, is provided on a class basis and not on a basis of need', Labour could reject this course of action by turning housing into a genuine social service.[52] Returning to his lecture, Martin argued – in hindsight quite accurately – that the post-war welfare state reflected Scandinavian social democracy rather than socialism, and that there might yet remain wide inequalities within it.[53] Ross McKibbin cites Attlee's bizarre behaviour in organising the 1951 election – announcing the date to cabinet with only seven ministers present – as an example of Labour's inability to seriously think about how a social democratic or socialist state might look.[54] The difficulty Labour had in expanding upon the basic precepts of the Beveridgean welfare state – that all should receive the same uniform benefit – would become apparent in 1950s debates over housing.

Labour emphasised council housing as a superior alternative to the private rented sector, which was depicted as an obsolete leftover from the pre-atomic age. There was a powerful class element to this focus on council housing as a kind of vanguard tenure, which heightened as the Conservatives adopted a regressive approach to the tenure throughout the 1950s.[55] The Conservatives believed that the universal provision of welfare had been a temporary measure to deal with the after-effects of 1930s poverty and mass unemployment, and that full employment offered the opportunity to reintroduce means testing.[56] 'So long as we believe in mixed development and wish municipal estates to be representative of the whole community', argued James MacColl from an opposing perspective in 1954, 'we must avoid a covert means test by selecting only poorer families'.[57] Earlier that year, a *Socialist Commentary* article by Arthur Marsh suggested that housing policy was still based on a Victorian model: speculative building; slum clearance; and focused on housing the working classes.[58] 'If health is to be treated as a social service', considered Marsh, 'is it not anomalous to exclude housing, or to treat it piecemeal?'[59]

Intriguingly, it was the revisionist right of Labour that were most committed to housing as a universal social service. There was considerable resistance from the Labour left to anything that might seem to move the working classes from being first in the queue for council homes, often stereotyped as being a distraction from socialism.[60] The economist Denys Munby put forward the revisionist view in 1957, stating that the building of council housing for 'workers' by Labour councils was a 'counsel of despair', signalling that municipalities had given up on the idea of 'classless' communities.[61] Forming cohesive neighbourhoods of this kind was likely more an aspiration than a reality. Jon Lawrence writes that better-off households had 'no wish to be the unacknowledged agents of social improvement', citing the desire of skilled workers and the lower-middle classes to move off of overspill estates in 1960s Luton.[62] Even in an affluent era, Young and Willmott commented in a 1960 study of Woodford, 'Inside people's minds ... the boundaries of class are still closely drawn.'[63] Selina Todd suggests that the fact that inter-war social surveys saw the working classes as 'poverty-stricken unemployed in need of rescue, remedy or reform' had important effects on the provision of welfare post-war.[64] This perception of council housing as a 'poverty tenure' has been a lasting one, reaching a state of near-ubiquity in the present day. 'Snobbery is snobbery', argues the author Lynsey Hanley, claiming that 'council estates, no matter how pleasing they were to the eye, offended homeowners purely because they housed large numbers of poor people, and did so visibly'.[65] Council housing had certainly acquired an inter-war reputation as a 'poverty tenure', due to the relationship between the tenure and slum clearance, but Crosland remarked in *The Future of Socialism* that council homes had begun to lose these connotations.[66] The level of rents alone – as Chapter 3 discusses – would suggest that council housing was aimed at a better-off grade of worker.[67] Hanley's conflation of 'poor people' with the 'working classes' may in fact obscure more than it reveals.

In his 1956 study of the established working-class district of St Ebbes in Oxford, the sociologist John Mogey found that his interlocutors alternately claimed St Ebbes was both 'respectable' and 'rough'.[68] This contradictory description was not uncommon. In their study of council estates in 2000s Norwich, Ben Rogaly and Becky Taylor discuss the creation of status divisions by estate residents, different areas being considered 'rougher' or more snobbish.[69] Norbert Elias and John Scotson found a 'distinct form of social stratification' existing between an established working-class community and a newer working-class district in their study of the pseudonymous 'Winston Parva' near Leicester in the late 1950s and early 1960s.[70] In a similar sense, the sociologist Geoffrey Gibson remarked that during his observations of a New Town in 1959, one person claimed that 'we are all Elephant and Castle round here, but that street over there, they're Islington and Cricklewood. North Londoners – all stuck up and think they're so much better than us'.[71] Working-class experience was multifaceted. Quite apart from status distinctions north and south of the River Thames, there were of course considerable regional variations in income, which the affluence narrative obscured further.

The failure by Labour to win the 1959 general election – Labour's third successive defeat – was taken as evidence by many on the revisionist wing of the party that they had been appealing to a working-class formation that no longer existed. Revisionists tended to believe wholeheartedly that the working classes had entered a phase of *embourgeoisement*, with material luxuries such as the refrigerator, the motor car and suburban homes diminishing their proletarian sensibilities.[72] Sociologists largely joined in, with Robert Millar predicting the formation of a 'technicist' class melding the lower-middle and upper-working classes together.[73] The response of the Labour left was little better. In a 1959 essay, Crossman claimed that 'affluence' would be overtaken by Soviet progress, and moreover, that 'the luxuries, gadgets, entertainments and packaged foodstuffs' of the affluent society were 'irrelevant and even vulgar and immoral, compared with the solid respectability of the Communist way of life'.[74] There was little consideration by Crossman that an interest in futuristic-seeming consumer goods might have reflected a working-class adjusting to the atomic age.

Especially authoritative in setting the tone of the debate was the 1960 survey of voters by the political scientists Mark Abrams and Richard Rose, commissioned by *Socialist Commentary* and entitled *Must Labour Lose?*, in which they suggested that Labour was losing the allegiance of an 'affluent' working class.[75] Although Abrams and Rose actually acknowledged in their study a lack of evidence linking consumption patterns to voting habits, this did not diminish interest within the Labour Party on the subject.[76] Raphael Samuel, who had published in *New Left Review* his own investigation into working-class attitudes to Labour in Stevenage, believed that Abrams' survey was simply intended to confirm the revisionist position.[77] Abrams addressed the critique head on, claiming that prosperity did not convert the working classes into 'urban peasants determined to resist any party likely to threaten acquisitiveness'.[78] Abrams went on to state that his findings actually uncovered that ownership of consumer goods did not equate to voting Conservative: equal proportions of those owning washing machines or refrigerators voted Labour or Conservative.[79] Where there did appear to be a difference was in home ownership, with only 20 per cent of the voters in Abrams' survey who owned their own home voting Labour, contrasting with 46 per cent of those living in council housing who said they voted Labour.[80] A note by the Labour Party Research Department also picked out this point on differences in tenure, as well as remarking that Abrams did not appear to consider 'the (perhaps considerable) social and environmental pressures on [the voter's] political attitudes and loyalties'.[81] While owner-occupation seemed to frustrate Labour – as the Conservative adherents of the 'property-owning democracy' had intended – there were likely other cultural effects beyond asset ownership that cemented an anti-socialist vote. By contrast, the sample for Samuel's Stevenage investigation was nearly all council house tenants, revealing positive sentiments about the collective endeavour of forming a New Town community alongside ambitions to 'better' oneself.[82]

Labour activists were not averse to owner-occupation, but found it difficult to see working-class owner-occupation on equal terms with the expansion of council housing. The sense that suburban living in particular promoted Conservative habits would remain a constant fear in Labour circles, leading to a particular interest in controlling the built environment of new developments. In spite of these fears, a far-reaching investigation of workers in the boom town of Luton in the early 1960s, by a team of sociologists led by David Lockwood and John Goldthorpe, seemed to confirm that it was only the 'merest handful' of these affluent workers who chose by dint of their new circumstances to withdraw their support from Labour.[83] Rather, what seemed to be occurring in Luton was increasing working-class domesticity in an era of optimism about the future. Enjoying television within the household unit, or inviting friends over, could simply be the trappings of the 'modern' working classes rather than the atomisation Labour feared.[84]

Paradoxically, the crisis of 'too much affluence' was followed by one of poverty. The continued existence of poverty in the welfare state had not been overlooked, even if the hegemony of affluence was such that poverty had been largely 'forgotten'.[85] Not all lived in boom towns like Luton, and, as we have seen, conditions in the private rented sector remained poor. 'The parents with large families, the widows with children, the old people who object to having their rent paid by the Assistance Board, the men who often lose time through sickness, the workers in low-wage industries', listed Young in 1954, 'these are the people who suffer from poverty in the Welfare State'.[86] This was a clear indictment of the shortcomings of the welfare state, with its design focused on eliminating absolute destitution in uniform family units rather than being adaptive enough to deal with those on the margins. In her re-examination of a 1956 social survey conducted in Liverpool, Selina Todd asserted that the evidence suggested that most respondents were not 'affluent', many with unstable employment being vulnerable to periods of poverty.[87] Todd challenged the historiographical primacy of Brian Abel-Smith and Peter Townsend's 1965 *The Poor and the Poorest*. In an analysis of the Ministry of Labour's Family Expenditure Surveys of the early 1950s and early 1960s, Abel-Smith and Townsend suggested that poverty became concentrated within households with multiple children and elderly households in the 1950s and 1960s, to the extent that 'old age constituted the largest single cause of poverty in Britain at this time'.[88] Although Todd identified that working-class poverty was as much a feature of the 1950s and 1960s as working-class affluence, the fact that the old and those with difficulties of income or large families lived in the private rented sector was significant. Housing was 'inequality in its most visible form', as Abel-Smith put it in a 1963 Fabian pamphlet.[89]

The plight of the rather less affluent working classes 'trapped' in poor housing conditions in an advanced era was a regular theme. In a 1960 *Labour Woman* article, the author asked whether women's organisations should campaign for better accommodation for single persons. The author compared British housing programmes with those of the Netherlands, remarking that single persons' flatlets of 40 square metres were built in some Dutch developments, complete with living room with both a curtained off sleeping recess and dining recess.[90] A further *Labour Woman* piece later the same year noted the successful conversion of Victorian villas into flatlets for the elderly in Bedford, in an early recognition that turning 'old houses into new homes' whilst retaining housing standards was a real possibility.[91] The consequences of not providing suitable accommodation for single persons were explored in a 1964 *Socialist Commentary* article entitled 'Bed-sitter Land'. In the piece, bedsits were characterised by tyrannical landladies and poor living standards, with desperate bedsitters described as being anyone from the young to the very old.[92] The dereliction of the private rented sector represented a serious check to Labour visions of rising prosperity and modern housing for all.

Simply putting those deemed worthy into council housing was no sure way of reducing deprivation. Whilst depictions of marginalised groups in the 1960s have subsequently been highlighted as the flipside of affluence, Townsend in particular was well aware that the 'poor and poorest' were not simply the aged or the vulnerable. In a 1966 Fabian Society lecture, Townsend noted that many poorer people did not qualify for council homes at all, or had to leave it for 'far worse and usually more costly' private rented housing.[93] This inequality of place would, Townsend believed, only get worse, with those in areas of bad housing exemplifying a new strand of impoverished alongside the more recognisable 'underclass'.[94] He expanded on this theme further in a 1967 presentation to the NEC Social Services Committee, suggesting that 'by the standards of the past more are prosperous; by the standards of today more may be poorer'.[95] Townsend's comments reflected the difficulties posed by an era of relative rather than absolute poverty. The fact that the post-war welfare state retained the class-based, patriarchal design of preceding eras, based on male breadwinner families, meant more were excluded as household patterns began to change.[96] This was especially true of housing, with hardship hard to identify amongst those with access to council housing, and far more apparent among those shut out of the tenure altogether.

Perhaps most obviously, access to council housing was largely restricted to the white population. This was in spite of a steadily increasing non-white population, with large numbers of Commonwealth migrants finding themselves generally excluded from council housing on arriving in Britain in the 1950s and 1960s. Labour councils were generally complicit in this process of racialised selectivity. Immigrant families only gained access to council estates in the London borough of Southwark in the 1970s, despite arriving in substantial numbers from the early 1960s.[97] Council housing was provided near-exclusively to the existing white working class, the Labour council seeing council homes as a kind of collective good to be distributed amongst 'their people'.[98] Even the left-wing Labour MP Fenner Brockway, a staunch supporter of anti-discrimination measures, suggested in 1964 that he might be prepared to limit immigration until a major house-building programme had been completed.[99] As a consequence of being denied state help, as Chapter 1 details, Commonwealth immigrants often became concentrated in 'blighted' private rented housing scheduled for slum clearance. The localised character of council housing led the Wilson administration to initially hold off instructing local authorities to house immigrants, seeing it as a local matter.[100] A 1965 edition of the Labour councillors' newssheet *Partnership* reported on the manipulation of waiting lists to select tenants according to race, noting that 'many councils retain residential qualifications of up to seven years before a person's name is allowed to go on the waiting list'.[101] Labour sought to address this through a series of Race Relations Acts in 1965 and 1968, which made it illegal for councils to discriminate in housing on the grounds of race. As has been suggested, the close concentration of Commonwealth immigrants in inner city areas due to be demolished created a new form of visual poverty. In Birmingham, the numbers of immigrants moving into slum-clearance central areas were almost equal to the numbers of the white population moving out.[102] By the 1970 general election, awareness of this process was such that Labour's manifesto included as a priority that there 'must be decent housing for everyone ... immigrant ghettoes must not be allowed to develop'.[103] Whilst the conditions by which immigrant 'ghettoes' formed were complex and by no means limited to exclusion from council housing, separation from housing that was supposedly for 'the people' certainly played a part. In answering the question as to who council housing was for, it must be concluded that for many Labour councillors, activists and party members, it was clearly not overseas immigrants.

What was the class dynamic of council housing? In a 1966 debate in the House of Commons, William Molloy, Labour MP for Ealing North, objected to the caricaturing of 'affluent tenants', arguing that 'we want people to have welfare, not through a test, not through any examination, but because they are entitled to all the best their nation can give, simply because they are members of that nation, and for no other reason'.[104] The people to be gifted modernity in the form of council housing were the working classes, or, rather, Labour's perception of the working classes. This perception was a deserving, uniformly white, male grouping – and perhaps, most importantly, a stable formation. While it is possible to detect some sincerity in the egalitarian drive to a classless society, there seems little doubt that the working classes, or at least an imagined version of that formation, took priority in the minds of most within Labour.

'Insecurity and fluidity' described working-class experience best, according to late-1940s survey work conducted by the sociologist Ferdynand Zweig.[105] This notion that to be working class was to have a hard lot informed Labour attitudes and explains the confused attitude expressed by many in the party to working-class affluence where it emerged. Zweig commented that 'council houses ... are getting rid of the class barriers' and this was certainly true for at least a time, though the tenure would ultimately serve to reinforce class barriers.[106] It would be wrong to understate the extent of the change for those who did gain council homes or the significance attached to it. Judy Giles writes that for many this must have been seen as 'a long overdue recognition of their right to the benefit of progress'.[107] In spite of this, the pervasive understanding that council homes were for those less well-off became the defining feature of the tenure, undermining grander visions of classless estates. The selective character of Labour visions of modernity served to weaken a universal conception of welfare.

Designing modern communities: Labour and the social sciences

The reaction against 'Victorian' cities was based on the belief that stronger, healthier urban communities could be created through careful planning. Changing the urban living environment from the narrow confines of the slum to the open space and easy conviviality of modern estates was of paramount importance. Labour interest in 'community' as a concept paralleled and was influenced by the fascination of architects, planners and social scientists with the subject. Although Labour had tended to be suspicious of the Garden City Movement, the belief of Raymond Unwin that 'social cohesion … could be encouraged through the visual coherence of a place' had long-lasting effects on notions of how community might be designed, not least through Unwin's role on the Tudor Walters Committee.[108] Of course, Labour's own archetypal good community was in the first instance a working-class community. This assertion of a 'traditional' model of community sat uneasily with an enthusiasm for modernity. It is rather ironic, write Jeremy Seabrook and Trevor Blackwell, that 'the predominance of the concept of community arose at the very moment of the dissolution of certain aspects of its reality'.[109] Moreover, Labour aimed to build or consolidate 'political communities' as well as a physical communities: better societies that would reliably vote for them.[110] Conversely, post-war social scientists aimed to investigate how social change played out in particular localities, often recommending their own vision of a good society on the basis of their research. Though the work of certain social scientists, such as Young, had a considerable effect on Labour thought, much of the post-war community studies canon complicates or undermines Labour beliefs on how society could be formed. What did Labour consider to have made a good community? And what practical effect did this have on housing policy?

The physical space of a locality was of considerable significance to those wishing to create ideal communities. Between the wars, the extensive development of 'out-country' suburban estates in the areas surrounding London by the LCC, replicated in cities across Britain, was accompanied by limited multi-storey flat development in some cities. The most significant of the latter kind of developments was Quarry Hill in Leeds, built by the city's Labour council and opened in 1938, with a circular design based on the vast Karl-Marx Hof in Vienna.[111] Housing around 3,000 residents and originally planned to be complete with shops, a nursery and even gardens for cultivation, Quarry Hill was intended as a 'self-contained estate, as a self-conscious exercise in model housing and town planning'.[112] However, Charles Jenkinson, the Leeds Housing Committee Chair, saw the estate as a 'decanting centre' for people moving to cottage estates 'which he believed every right-minded person would prefer'.[113] Quarry Hill ran considerably over budget during construction, with the result that the nursery as well as additional features such as a concert hall and swimming pool were never built. Leeds, like most other 1930s councils – whether Labour-run or otherwise – therefore continued to build suburban council estates, with large-scale private 'ribbon development' constructed at a far greater rate. By the end of the 1930s, social scientists and planners had begun to question whether large-scale suburban estates had 'failed' as communities. Ruth Glass (then Durant) argued in her survey of Watling that the estate was little more than a 'colony', lacking community spirit, which she appeared to suggest could be measured by the success of the estate's community centre.[114] Equally, Rosamund Jevons and John Madge were critical of suburban council estates in Bristol and believed they had not been designed to encourage social cohesion.[115] Labour displayed an interest post-war in creating communities that seemingly redressed these issues of dislocation and disunity.

'Just what is a community?' asked an article in a 1952 edition of *People's Pictorial*. A host of 'characters' on an unnamed Midlands council estate were introduced: a parson; a gas worker; a schoolteacher; a carpenter's apprentice; an engine-driver; a bus driver; and an engineer.[116] Only three female voices were introduced: a hospital worker; a comptometer operator; and a 'housewife'. 'Don't just think the people who live on [the] estate are only a lot of discontented grumblers', cautioned the article, 'They're not. You see, every one of their grumbles is an individual part which fits into the jigsaw puzzle.'[117] Whilst Gari Phillips, the parson, wanted a greater public focus on family life, claiming that the 'bricks and mortar of their surroundings mould character', Tony Howard, the gas worker, wanted more shops, a technical college for adult learning, and football pitches as 'teams of local people playing on nearby pitches brings a great amount of community spirit to a neighbourhood'.[118]

The comments of each of the estate 'characters' are revealing of seemingly divergent attributes ascribed to community in the post-war era. On one level, as the parson suggested, community could involve turning inward to a more individualistic home-centred lifestyle. In contrast, the 'community spirit' that the gas worker desired appeared to involve a more performative type of community. Although, as Lawrence argues, individualism and communitarian impulses are not mutually exclusive, there are tensions between them.[119] Labour activists were generally suspicious of individualist desires, believing a lack of communitarianism to weaken the solidaristic ties necessary for their movement to succeed. Closely related to this belief, but distinct, was what might be described as the post-war 'social science' view of community, with the left version of it characterised best by Michael Young. Young argued that as well as active citizenship, preserving and replicating family or kinship-based community was of utmost importance.[120] Where the two lines of thought tended to coalesce was in the belief that 'withdrawing' from the community into the home indicated a less successful community. This supposition would have far-reaching effects on housing policy.

Investigations into new estates drew particular attention to the new forms of living that the shift to modern housing offered. Privacy was the theme of Leo Kuper's 1953 study of a suburban council estate in Coventry. The estate comprised a mixture of low-rise 1930s council housing and newer factory-produced steel prefabs set in a 'neighbourhood unit', arranged in cul-de-sacs with houses facing one another.[121] Due to the novelty of the prefabs, Kuper mainly interviewed residents from one prefab cul-de-sac, Braydon Road, finding that 'inability to control noises within the house' as a consequence of thin partition walls could cause anxiety or irritation between neighbours. Examples of noises included 'bronchial coughs, babies crying at night, or a Welsh husband who joins in with singing on the wireless'.[122] The cul-de-sac design and large windows of prefab houses meant that 'for a person sensitive to neighbours' reactions the effect may be rather like the telescreen described by Orwell in his novel *Nineteen-Eighty-Four*'.[123] Kuper did acknowledge that some residents of Braydon Road were not bothered by the fact that people could see into their gardens, remarking that 'people vary in their requirements for privacy', and it is probable that for most residents a prefab was a considerable advance on their previous circumstances in Coventry.[124]

John Mogey was similarly critical of the 1930s council estate layout of Barton, in Oxford, commenting that the 'unimaginative [cottage] layout ... has an unintended result in dividing the area into several sections'.[125] Mogey was a Labour activist and was, like Young, a contributor to *Socialist Commentary*. He contrasted the absence of corner shops, cafes or fish-and-chip shops on the estate where casual contact between neighbours could be made, in contrast to the older Oxford district of St Ebbes, from which a large number of Barton residents had been rehoused.[126] Perhaps tellingly, Mogey found that 'the housing-estate family developed a much more critical attitude to their much superior house', but 70 per cent of those who criticised their council house did not wish to return to St Ebbe's.[127] Contrary to Mogey's expectations, though St Ebbe's was presumed to be friendlier 'its inhabitants keep themselves aloof from neighbourly contact', whilst at Barton, 'most people know their immediate neighbours'.[128] Nevertheless, following the tone of much sociological investigation in the 1950s, Mogey claimed that Barton lacked 'social cohesion' due to its 'middle class' design.[129] This dismissive attitude was partly a critique of the suburban lifestyle and partly based on a monolithic conception of class-based community. Labour activists were drawn to both of these critiques, fearful as they were of the supposedly bourgeois characteristics of suburbs, and accommodating of a belief that Labour was fundamentally a working-class movement.

Throughout the 1950s, Labour internally reassessed their housing policy, gradually pushing for a much wider extension of council housing via the policy of municipalisation, as we have seen in earlier chapters. Local authority programmes of urban slum clearance in large cities – a number of which were run by Labour councils – offered the opportunity to address perceived issues with housing development. 'Community spirit suffer[ed]' on new housing estates, claimed Young in a 1954 *Socialist Commentary* piece.[130] He went on to claim that community spirit was relational, suggesting that people in the same streets 'adjust themselves to each other like plants in a garden'.[131] In this regard, Young cautioned that though community spirit would return over time, it took a generation or more to do so, meaning that uprooting established communities for new estates was a risky endeavour. Young had initially registered his unease with large-scale housing projects in his 1949 Labour pamphlet *Small Man, Big World*.[132] 'We once thought that the town planner and the architect had the magic wands in their hands', he wrote in a 1956 reappraisal of that pamphlet for *Socialist Commentary* in the 'different mental climate' of the 1950s, going on to claim that new settlements were 'the most dreary places in the world, lacking individuality or character'.[133]

Young and his co-collaborator Willmott would go on to expand on this in *Family and Kinship* when it was published in 1957, claiming that the strength of working-class community was dependent on tradition and close contact between relatives. However, though Young and Willmott recognised the desire of people in Bethnal Green to have a 'home of one's own', those who had obtained one in the new council estate of Debden in outer London were believed to, or accused others of, 'keeping themselves to themselves'.[134] In fact, as Lawrence has recently emphasised in his re-analysis of the surviving field notes from *Family and Kinship*, Bethnal Green inhabitants were (unsurprisingly) just as variable in their willingness to engage with their neighbours or relatives.[135] Importantly, the research contrasted significantly with the findings of a 1940s study of Bermondsey led by Raymond Firth, whose team were rather more willing to confront their findings of isolated nuclear families, and a seemingly contradictory range of individualist and communitarian responses.[136] Young and Willmott characterised Debden as lacking 'the sociable squash of people and houses, workshops and lorries' that they had found in Bethnal Green.[137] Without the presence of kin to serve as a bridge to meeting and interacting with others – Debden being primarily composed of younger families – Young and Willmott asserted that it would never become a community as robust as Bethnal Green.[138] *Family and Kinship* was well received by the revisionist left, with a 1957 *Socialist Commentary* review by the Labour council grandee Peggy Jay, in which she was evidently surprised by Young and Willmott's recounting that some Debden residents wished to return to 'the grime, the noise and the overcrowding' of Bethnal Green.[139] Whilst Jay felt that the authors should give 'credit where credit's due' to the material quality of council housing, she agreed with Young and Willmott that 'skilful architecture and designs cannot create a community'.[140]

Young and Willmott's belief in the importance of family and community was outlined further in their later survey of the middle-class suburb of Woodford, published as *Family and Class in a London Suburb* in 1960. Woodford was, of course, not 'designed' as a mixed-class community in the same manner as a council estate or a New Town, but Young and Willmott utilised it to re-emphasise the benefits (as they saw it) of 'traditional' working-class communities. In Woodford – a primarily middle-class area but with the working-class residents numbering around a third of the population – Young and Willmott observed that 'the move outwards is also a move upwards'.[141] Far from creating a 'mixed-class' community, class differences were accentuated in Woodford. One such example was the comment of a Woodford resident that '... some of them [East-Enders] are, well, without being snobby, they seem to me to be just a little bit lower'.[142] This said, Young and Willmott reported positively, that people believed that they belonged to a friendly community 'almost as unanimously as the people of Bethnal Green'.[143] There remained, nonetheless, the judgement that the one-class, closely packed Bethnal Green was a more effective community than the suburb or council estate, due to the supposed communitarian conviviality it contained. Reviewing *Family and Class* for *Socialist Commentary* in 1961, Tosco R. Fyvel agreed on this point, wondering whether new suburbs produced 'greater superficiality and guardedness in personal relations'.[144] Similarly, Leah Manning felt in her *Labour Woman* review that 'snobbish beyond belief' Woodford compared poorly to 'whole-hearted Bethnal Green': which would of course have been Young and Willmott's intention.[145] From the left, Elizabeth Thomas argued in *Tribune* that the book emphasised the 'futility' of the 'Crosland-Jay-Morrison doctrine of watering down our principles to appeal to the middle classes i.e. the inhabitants of Woodford.'[146] If suburbia produced and reproduced Tory snobbery, then there was little point in creating more of it.

What was needed was not a 'middle-class' way of living but modern, 'socialist' housing. 'Social services ... are valuable political tools for remodelling our society', John Mogey claimed in a 1958 *Socialist Commentary* piece, 'so that socialist principles of equality, dignity and brotherhood can be more fully realized.'[147] Some elements of Labour saw these principles as being best realised by tenant democracy on council estates. 'Housing to us is not only an exercise in planning and building techniques', asserted a 1959 Co-operative Party pamphlet, 'it is an exercise in democracy – in government *by* as well as *for* the people.'[148] James MacColl had warned in 1954 that tenants did not take kindly to 'fussy paternalism' in council estate management, and that they may find it difficult living under 'even a benevolent Leviathan'.[149] By the close of the 1950s, Labour activists were increasingly sceptical of the ability of suburban to promote 'socialist principles'. Writing the lead article for a 1959 edition of *Socialist Commentary*, the magazine's editor Rita Hinden contended that 'present-day apathy' could be attributed to 'the degeneration of proud local communities into amorphous, anonymous suburbs in which no one counts, and almost no one belongs'.[150] The sociologist Geoffrey Gibson went still further, claiming that the greatest expression of popular feeling was a 'common hostility' towards development corporation officers trying to foster community spirit.[151] In contrast to Mogey – and prefiguring left arguments in the 1970s – Gibson argued that the best government could do to 'plan' community would be to leave people to it.[152] This was not a common interpretation within Labour. More prominent by the early 1960s was what Glendinning and Muthesius describe as the 'belief that the modern block of flats ... can generate community feelings'.[153] The issue was that the Labour vision of communitarian socialism invoked an immutable vision of what 'community' was, and should be – which was to prove inflexible when it did not come to pass.

The interpretation of community offered to Labour by Young and Willmott did not go uncontested. 'One of the fashions now current in British Sociology, and more particularly among the left of the Labour Party', claimed the sociologist Hannah Gavron in 1962, 'is to sentimentalize working-class life'.[154] Gavron went on to claim that this tendency to romanticise the pre-affluent (or modern) had resulted in the creation of 'Hoggartsville' – a wry reference to Richard Hoggart's fond portrayal of his working-class upbringing – which was 'a world brimming over with extended family life, warmth and neighbourliness'.[155] Labour's understanding of modernity drew its strength from the conviction that the solidarity of the working classes could be transposed without significant change to futuristic new landscapes. This rested on the assumption that social scientists like Young and Willmott – and the sentimental like Hoggart – were correct, and that 'community' in the manner described by their writings was a genuine alternative to the perceived inadequacies of the suburb or the council estate. It required, as Gavron perceived, some high-handed dismissal of the benefits of progress. 'Admittedly, the lavatory must be shared with others, there are no bathrooms, the walls are damp, the children all sleep in one room with their parents, and the women are all old and tired before they are thirty', Gavron observed, 'but then Man does not live by bread alone'.[156] Through the study of Young and Willmott's field notes for *Family and Kinship*, Lawrence argues that 'if *Family and Kinship* was powerful politics, it was poor sociology', finding numerous instances of respondents far less positive about the extended family (and Bethnal Green at large) that the authors deemed so necessary to their interpretation of community.[157] Young and Willmott's work sits more easily as part of the anti-planning canon, prefiguring Jane Jacobs's influential arguments about high-density street life as the most favourable.[158]

As the examples of Gavron and Raymond Firth illustrate, not all social scientists were committed to 'Hoggartsville'. Examining a 'blighted and partly blitzed' area of inner-city Liverpool in the mid-1950s, a team led by Charles Vereker, claimed that 'a point which the sociologist is able to clarify for the town planner' is that long-standing communities did not necessarily want to stay put, their findings being that most residents of longer-term communities also were the most desirous of moving.[159] The discovery that recent arrivals were the least willing to move prompted Vereker and his colleagues to warn against assessing a community purely on 'the firmness of its roots', given that the inhabitants might have 'different aspirations' for the future.[160] Considering Vereker's survey, as well as a 1960s study of the council estate to which some of the inner-city Liverpudlians were relocated, Selina Todd noted that the experience of class-conscious community was not specific to a fixed location, with people continuing to identify as working class.[161] In a study of the giant Becontree estate in Dagenham forty years after its creation, Peter Willmott was surprised to find that it had taken on an 'East End' character, noting that 'most people are still unmistakeably cockneys'.[162] While the estate planners had not accounted for population increase, meaning that some of the second generation had to move away, Willmott concluded that Dagenham maintained 'a way of life ... that satisfies most people'.[163] Mark Clapson opines that 'suburban sociability and community life was and remains nuanced', maintaining that it was principally the anti-suburban trend in intellectual circles that prompted new developments to be labelled un-neighbourly.[164]

One interesting example of anti-suburban thought can be seen in the intellectual perception of pubs. Social scientists seemed to have a particular fascination with pubs as a reflection of community vitality, which may have reflected their own choice of leisure time after a day of fieldwork. It is true that Labour councils often had something of a 'Victorian philanthropic impulse' to control working-class habits – often in opposition to popular preferences – and refused to build pubs on estates such as Wythenshawe in Manchester.[165] This said, Clare Langhamer argues that 'the nature of housing provision did not directly cause a shift towards homecentred leisure but it reflected, reinforced and enabled developing trends to reach fruition'.[166] In effect, popular preferences were moving away from pub life, new homes or not. Social investigators often found this difficult to grasp. 'Pubs, which I have always regarded as a fairly reliable barometer of community spirit', exclaimed Gibson in 1958, 'are, in the New Towns, unfriendly, "chromium-plated", and empty'.[167] One has to question how reliable Gibson's barometer truly was, and how much it might have been based on an assumption of working-class habits. In a similar vein, Young and Willmott lamented that the pubs of Woodford were 'not small cosy bars of the Bethnal Green type, filled with the cheerful jangle of a honky-tonk piano or a twanging juke-box'.[168] As early as 1952, Ferdynand Zweig claimed that for London workers 'the pub life of Britain is definitely on the decline', but attributed this as much to the development of working men's clubs with a wider range of entertainment as to the popularity of cinemas, sports and the 'high price of beer and spirits'.[169] Kuper had made a similar observation in Coventry, one of his respondents asserting that 'the [working men's] club is not a low dump like the local pub ... we like a drink, but not that boozy atmosphere'.[170] It may have instead been the case that an over-focus on the pub as an instrument of community cohesion reflected instead a limited cultural conception of working-class life.

Somewhat ironically, the more strikingly modern, high-density developments aimed at solving the supposed issues of suburbia ultimately became labelled as the most socially problematic. Though later waves of high-density estates such as Park Hill in Sheffield actively aimed to recreate the 'warmth of the slum', to the extent that old street names were retained for the estate decks, most were more straightforward affairs.[171] Investigating the creation of a multi-storey council estate on the older working-class area of Barton Hill in Bristol with blocks up to fifteen storeys high – created in order to reduce the numbers relocated to an 'overspill estate' – Hilda Jennings claimed that the new flats were considered 'unnatural' to 'apparently the great majority'.[172] She did, however, acknowledge that 'the separate storeys in many cases soon became units of social life'.[173] Jennings' belief that the old Barton Hill had been 'an associative type of society' led her to conclude that a better means of facilitating contacts between neighbours should be established, as she claimed that residents of the tower blocks wanted the 'non-material satisfactions associated with the old areas'.[174] Similarly, in his defence of an area of Sunderland faced with redevelopment by high-rise flats, Norman Dennis claimed that 'informants feared the loss of a neighbourhood in which all families embraced a similar style of life'.[175] However, there were few comprehensive studies of modern, high-rise housing actually conducted during this period. Instead, most social scientists tended to report anecdotal dislike for flats, much as they did for suburban homes.

The most far-reaching of these was Pearl Jephcott's study *Homes in High Flats*, which explored five high-rise estates in Glasgow. Conducted between 1967 and 1969, Jephcott's analysis ranged from the large Castlemilk estate, with a population of 40,000 and nearly five miles from the Glasgow city centre, to the iconic Red Road Estate, closer to the centre but 'curiously cut off from the main stream of city life', to the architecturally intriguing Hutcheson C blocks on concrete stilts with shared verandas.[176] Jephcott took considerable interest in the community life of the high-rise estates. A tenants' association on one estate replicated the 'welfare' activities of the old street, including organised bus trips to Saturday morning cinema matinees for children ('to give mothers time to shop'), outings for the elderly and 'a steamer trip to Arran'.[177] In spite of this dynamism, organised groups were limited by 'a lack of suitable places in which to meet', with some attempting to use lift halls, and, in one case, 'a tiny, cold, unventilated caretaker's storeroom'.[178] Although Jephcott was certainly of the view that flats inhibited community life and conducted her study on those lines, in a recent re-analysis of her transcripts, Ade Kearns et al. suggest that the type of community life desired varied considerably among tenants. 'In a multistorey flat … one only sees whom one chooses to see', remarked one Castlemilk man, 'it gives you superiority that you would never otherwise have unless you owned your own house'.[179] Equally,

Kearns and her co-researchers conducted a number of oral history interviews with former residents, which also revealed that in some cases the patterns of tenement conviviality so eulogised by those committed to Hoggartsville did in fact carry over to new high-density estates.[180] Jephcott's study provides a useful epilogue for the post-war debate around 'community' on new estates. Though Labour activists adapted to sociological assumptions that suburban life had 'failed' to recreate community by promoting the need to keep communities together in developments of increasingly high density, this was still found insufficient. Notwithstanding the shortcomings of high-density accommodation, which will be explored in the next section, 'community' as understood by Labour could not be located as it had never existed in the first place.

Considering the post-war disruption of working-class life in relocation to council estates, suburbs or new towns, the academic Raymond Williams cautioned that 'we cannot be sure exactly what will happen, but it would be rash to assume that all former patterns are permanently gone'.[181] Nonetheless, this was precisely the point at which both Labour and most social scientists investigating community started. Informed by a belief that post-war prosperity had decisively shifted working-class behaviour away from an idealised norm, as well as by the notion that the physical space of new housing developments inhibited community formation, most accounts expressed a sense of futility. This was a misplaced sense of pessimism. Ben Jones has discussed how social networks were largely reconstituted in suburban housing estates, with a 'subtle shift' towards the home.[182] For many working-class families, this was a welcome shift. 'Home may be private', Hoggart had recalled of Hunslet, 'but the front door opens out of the living room on to the street'.[183] Private life was not necessarily a threat to a communitarian ethos. 'Past gains need not be sacrificed wholesale to supposed future trends', commented Vereker and his co-researchers in a prescient observation, 'nor must the warmth and intimacy of certain families' lives prevent a determined effort to refurbish the physical environment'.[184]

The politics of progressive design: Modern architecture and socialism

Concluding *The Future of Socialism*, Tony Crosland sounded a call for socialists to throw their weight behind building sophisticated communities imbued with a sort of *joie de vivre*. Britain, he wrote, needed a greater sense of culture and gaiety, with

... more open-air cafes, brighter and gayer streets at night, later closing-hours for public houses ... more murals and pictures in public places, better designs for furniture and pottery and women's clothes, statues in the centre of new housing-estates ...[185]

Crosland fundamentally implied a collective vision of a newly affluent society: people had more money to spend, but they would joyously spend their income in public places. Whether this inspiring notion of a truly collective society could come to pass in housing policy – or indeed, was in any sense realistic – was another matter entirely. At the same time as conjuring up a vision of Europeanised congeniality, Crosland also pointed to an aesthetically distinct modern utopia. This would most often take the form of a modern flat of rationalised design, sometimes a house, presented as a solution to the problems of the age. The modern flat was believed to be able to satisfy, as Langhamer puts it, 'a cross-class dream of attaining a "home of one's own".[186] Though politicians from across the spectrum were entranced by the possibilities of modernism, Labour were especially susceptible to what Finnimore characterises a 'tendency to eulogise non-traditional housing and, by implication, draw attention to the progressiveness of social policy.[187] Reflecting on the previous discussion, higher densities were also believed to be most effective in encouraging the sort of community life Labour believed to be a part of a good society. In effect, the modern flat attempted to do two things: firstly, to distribute the trappings of modern homes that Labour believed the working classes deserved; and secondly, to serve as an active demonstration of or propaganda piece for the modern future, encouraging the citizenry to embrace a distinctly socialist utopia.

We must appreciate the context in which modern housing became seen as the answer to the issues thrown up by urban transformation. It may be best summarised as one in which 'the ruling aesthetic' was 'light and space'.[188] In an early appraisal of the multi-storey boom in 1974, E. W. Cooney stated that this ideological attachment almost certainly pushed architectural development beyond relatively modest four-storey tenements to grander modern projects.[189] Conversely, in the same volume Anthony Sutcliffe struggled to make sense of the popularity of the flat form, claiming that 'the standard of accommodation offered by the English flat has always been markedly inferior to the separate cottage or villa'.[190] Glendinning and Muthesius have pointed out that 'it became necessary to attribute to the flat some specific, desirable characteristics' in order to move beyond arguments about whether flats or houses were better.[191] One of these characteristics was the idea that flats could provide 'modern amenities' more effectively than traditional houses. Intriguingly, when interviewed by

John Gold in the late 1980s, the architect-planner Arthur Ling – responsible for the Lansbury Estate in Poplar as well as the later stages of the modernist redevelopment of Coventry – claimed that he 'had reservations about the over-reliance on high flats ... as opposed to a balanced mix of residential types'. Ling went on to emphasise the context of the modern moment, in that there was 'a New Jerusalem to build, if you like', to explain why flats became the preeminent form, in popular terms if not in actual numbers.[192] Ruth Oldenziel and Karin Zachmann have focused their attention on the significance of the modern kitchen, noting that it 'was a key modernist indicator for society's civilization in the twentieth century'.[193] The material design of the home was characterised as simplifying housework for the housewife, offering the possibility of empowerment. Labour took on this rhetoric and fitted it into a wider dialogue of a modern, socialist future. More than anything else, for Labour housing was 'the gateway to health, education, higher domestic standards'.[194] In this regard, the modern flat was understood by Labour activists as the harbinger of the socialist mission to replace the iniquities of 'then' with the social equilibrium of 'now'.

Labour adherents were not wholly entranced by the modern flat during the Second World War and its immediate aftermath. In a 1943 pamphlet expounding their post-war programme, Birmingham Labour Party came out against the flat explicitly, arguing that 'flats are generally unsatisfactory from the point of view of the happy family life, especially where there are young children'.[195] It is likely that Birmingham Labour were thinking in particular of tenements, but concerns over the suitability of flats for children would repeatedly occur in sociological studies of flat life. 'Well-built houses of bricks and mortar' were, according to Birmingham Labour, 'best suited to the English climate and the English way of living'.[196] This patriotic invocation was echoed in a paper presented to Clapham Labour Party in 1944, in which the speaker suggested that the 'ideal' home was a three-bedroom detached house, complete with 'rusticated brick facings, perhaps half weather tiled, with a well-made and substantial oak front door and crazy paving to the forecourt path and garage entrance'.[197] Other elements of the British left were less conservative in their tastes. The Communist Party of Great Britain claimed in 1944 that the supposedly high figures in favour of a house with a garden were 'a good deal of unreal nonsense'.[198] It was 'the barrack-like tenements with which [the working classes] are familiar' that had stoked popular fears, according to the Communists.[199]

'A society which does not bequeath any architectural monuments to posterity', argued the socialist author Douglas Brown, 'will be a dull, uncreative, unpleasant one in which to live!'[200] Across several photographic panels in his

1945 pamphlet *An Englishman's Home*, Brown contrasted the filthy slum kitchen with a gleaming modern one, articulating his desire that 'the housewife must have a constant supply of hot and cold running water, a deep sink with working space on either side, stainless rails for pots and pans, a plate-rack, a working table with cupboards and doors, a well ventilated food cupboard'.[201] 'Newness' was also a feature of civic propaganda, Charlotte Wildman observing that Manchester City Council's 1947 film *A City Speaks* compared the decrepit slums of Hulme with the brand-new bathrooms, kitchens and inside toilets of houses in the Wythenshawe council estate.[202] While modern design was portrayed as signs of advanced socialism, there nevertheless remained within many local Labour parties a desire for the cottage aesthetic of the inter-war period, albeit with all the interior 'newness' available.

In a 1950 edition of *Labour Woman*, an article lambasted the fact that women were still forced to use old methods on 'washing day', referencing a recent report on domestic home water supply that exposed the large numbers of homes reliant on water heated in a kettle or pan.[203] As the article put it, this was 'just like great-grandmother in 1850!', before going on to wonder, in a pointed riposte to gendered design attitudes, 'how many men working on farms, or in factories, are obliged to use exactly the same tools and equipment as their great-grandfathers in the same trades!'[204] The feeling that in spite of the great leap forward after 1945, living standards for many had remained relatively stagnant began to drive Labour discussion towards the need for conspicuously modern amenities. A further *Labour Woman* piece of 1950 by Muriel Nichol, former MP for Bradford North, reported on a travelling exhibition of 'good and bad design in the home' by the Council of Industrial Design, which had a discussion forum for housewives. Nichol noted of the exchange: 'It is evident that women have strong views on an age which has explored the secrets of atomic energy and built aeroplanes which can travel at the speed of sound, yet cannot apparently make a tomato sauce bottle which will let out the tomato sauce.'[205] The need for progress in the context of the Cold War was further enhanced by what Susan Reid describes as the domestic confrontation between socialism and capitalism, who offered 'competing images of modernity and the good life'.[206]

Even if Labour were aligned with the 'capitalist' side, the party did on occasion look wistfully behind the Iron Curtain. In 1953, the Labour newspaper *Forward* published an article on 'Fine Flats and Crowded Shops in Stalin Allee', reporting on the developments in East Berlin.[207] The correspondent, the Labour MP for South Ayrshire, Emrys Hughes, had visited a flat on the grand boulevard, noting that 'it was a large, roomy comfortable flat with higher ceilings than we have in most of our municipal flats in Britain'.²⁰⁸ Hughes was especially impressed by 'a good, spotlessly clean bathroom and a modern scullery and an arrangement by which rubbish disappeared down a chute'.²⁰⁹ Similarly, Betty Hodgson, a delegate for Leeds Trades Council as part of a British-Soviet Friendship Society trip to the USSR in 1952, wrote approvingly of dinner at a dock engineer's 'comfortable and attractively furnished' flat in Odessa.²¹⁰ The wonder of modern amenities remained a steady feature of the flat's appeal, with even the sceptical Jephcott reporting in 1971 that modern flats were 'delightfully easy to run' for the housewife.²¹¹

There nonetheless remained in Labour ranks those less convinced of the modern flat. In a colour party publication commemorating the 1951 Festival of Britain, some reticence was evident in an article on the Lansbury Estate in Poplar, which took centre stage as the architecture exhibition at the Festival.²¹² Although photographs portrayed the six- and three-storey blocks of flats, the publication nonetheless assured the reader that 'there are houses in Lansbury as well, for not everyone likes flats. But houses or flats, they provide grand homes for the families who move in'.²¹³ Such qualified support was far from uncommon, but in the circumstances of poor post-war housing conditions, Labour activists began to see modern flats as an effective way to deliver higher living standards.

Throughout the 1950s, the party magazine *Labour Woman* devoted columns to modernity and affluent living abroad, which gives some sense of how international progress was drawn upon in the pursuit of modern amenities. In a July 1950 article entitled 'The Housewife in Labour Sweden', T. H. Goff of the TUC wrote with fascination of homes equipped with automatic lighting, refrigerators, stainless steel kitchen-fittings, built-in furniture, electric cookers and double-glazed windows.²¹⁴ Social Democratic Sweden was a 'housewife's paradise', due to the existence of labour-saving devices freeing women from drudgery. 'The housewife's lot in this country of cleanliness is a relatively easy one', Goff went on, 'her home is built around her needs especially to save her work'.²¹⁵ This theme continued in a 1956 feature entitled 'Meet Fru Larsen of Copenhagen', which observed that Fru Larsen did not 'want life to be all house-cleaning, there must be time to live, to cultivate one's interests, to play with the children'.²¹⁶ An earlier article discussing Copenhagen in 1952 had also been impressed by Danish homeliness, with the approving detail that 'blocks of flats have tremendous windows which let in plenty of light and air, and many have balconies screened at the side so that no-one is overlooked by his neighbours'.²¹⁷

A 1956 piece by Anna Rudling, a Social Democrat activist, focused on Fru Anderson of Sweden, returned to the kitchen to highlight the standardisation of Swedish kitchens, based on a scientific survey of housewives' working conditions. 'Nothing has been arranged at random in Fru Anderson's modern kitchen', Rudling wrote admiringly.[218] As well as providing a recipe for Swedish meatballs, Rudling excitedly described that 'her sink is covered by stainless steel. Her stove is electrical. All the floors in her little flat are covered by easily cleaned linoleum. She has a rubbish chute and vacuum cleaner, and the opportunity of using a wonderfully equipped laundry'.[219] Ironically, communal laundries were one modern amenity actually losing dynamism in this period. By 1957, 40 per cent of all households in Britain had private washing machines.[220]

Labour Woman features outside of Scandinavia were occasionally more critical. A 1956 piece by Bettina Hirsch – a writer for *Die Frau*, the Austrian Social Democratic Party equivalent of *Labour Woman* – was quite taken with Frau Schmidt's modern fourth-floor flat in Vienna, especially a tree-lined grass court below it with fountains and sculptures by female Viennese artists.[221] Despite such acclaim, estate sculptures were not always well received when transferred to Britain. A *Tribune* article of 1956 reported how tenants of the South Kilburn estate in Willesden were 'disgusted' by nude statues on their estate. 'They do not want art', reported *Tribune* of the tenant response, 'they want something useful.'[222] Frau Schneider in West Germany elicited more sympathy than praise in an article by the Social Democratic Party activist Kathë Bonnesen, given that her flat was just 36 square metres in size. Bonnesen observed that this was 'not a lot of room for four persons and is not very practical to boot'.[223] Frau Schneider also had little in the way of modern amenities, being unable to afford a refrigerator.[224] Nevertheless, the modernity of European home life is demonstrative of the modern future Labour hoped to build: functionally crafted, technologically advanced and centred on the family home.

Labour councils across Britain had by the early 1960s began to build high-density housing in large volumes. The London County Council made a 'clear union' between Brutalist architecture and concrete, with their Morris Walk estate in Woolwich a triumphal example of modernism.[225] It is important to note that Labour councils were operating within a favourable context. As detailed by Otto Saumarez Smith, 'an almost unquestioned use of a modernist idiom' in political discussion of urban design had seen the Conservatives embrace the basic tenets of modernism by the early 1960s.[226] Although their recommendations were not adopted until 1967, the 1961 report of the Parker Morris Committee on space standards in the home was one such representation of this 'modernist idiom'.[227] Equally, as we have discussed, subsidies did play a part in stimulating high-rise building, though they were not wholly responsible for sustaining it. Even with central government approval of modern housing, this did not stifle debate within Labour locally. In a 1962 debate within the pages of West Ham's Labour newspaper, points for and against the construction of a sixteen-storey block of flats were put forward. Opposing, Councillor T. C. McMillan claimed that 'it would be out of keeping with the small houses in the area'.[228] McMillan did not appear to object to flats entirely, arguing that the construction of a single block without a surrounding 'mixed' estate of houses was 'bad planning of the type strongly condemned by the LCC town planning department'.[229] In the other corner, under the heading 'Common Sense', the West Ham Housing Committee Chairman E. Kebbell proposed that 'to go up in the air is plain, down-to-earth common sense when land is scarce'.[230] 'Tall point blocks, with only four to six flats to a floor, give more privacy than the lower slab blocks', Kebbell claiming, noting that in the latter 'access to a flat is gained by passing other people's doors'.[231] He may have been correct in terms of tenant views. Jephcott suggested in her 1971 study that most residents believed the high flat offered increased privacy.[232]

The physically poor state of much of urban Britain had by the early 1960s converted many sceptics to the flat, with flats now 'represented as the *sine qua non* of rapid slum clearance' by the once-suspicious Birmingham Labour Party.[233] Labour's re-entry into government in October 1964 drove this impulse still further. 'It is only lack of planning which has made tall towns a practical impossibility', a Labour Party Research Department memorandum in March 1964 had stated, 'and there is no reason why we should not be able to enjoy the spice of intensely urban living'.[234] The memorandum went on: 'Much of our resistance to living in tall buildings comes from outdated habits, and the fact we have neglected urban services and amenities that should have been provided long ago.'[235] In spite of this strident tone, earlier chapters have discussed the conservationist trend set by the 1963 policy publication *Labour's Plan for Old Houses*, which recommended renovation rather than reconstruction.[236] This said, the 'tall towns' that the research department spoke of were becoming a reality in many British cities, from the 'dazzling vision of Worstedopolis' envisaged by Bradford's city planners, to the 'British Brasilia' of Newcastle.[237]

A key element of reaction to modern flats centred around potential issues for families with young children. High flats were near-universally thought to be 'nae use for the bairns', in Jephcott's Glasgow study.[238] The demographic profile of new housing estates, usually principally composed of young families, made this an especially pressing point. A *Labour Woman* article of 1961 by the MP for East

Flint, Eirene White, looked at a new survey, *Two to Five in High Flats*, on play spaces in high-rise developments.[239] White had sat on a committee investigating the matter, which also included the former editor of *Labour Woman*, Mary Sutherland, and Margaret Thatcher. The survey, sponsored by Joan Maizels and financed by the Joseph Rowntree Trust, had covered eighty tower blocks across eighteen LCC or borough council estates and found that only three estate had play areas for small children, with half having no enclosed space at all.[240] *Two to Five in High Flats* found that two-thirds of mothers living above the fifth floor worried about the safety of young children, to the extent that toddlers were rarely let out to play. Comments such as 'balcony worries me to death – I don't let them out of my sight' characterised the study.[241] White concluded her *Labour Woman* piece by remarking that the 'contrast with Stockholm and Copenhagen, where they have had high flats with proper playgrounds and play-leaders for years, is disturbing, to say the least'.[242]

The points raised by the study found further expression in 1965, when *Labour Woman* reported on the attempt by the National Joint Committee of Working Women's Organisations to have better play spaces built into high flat developments.[243] A deputation met the representative of the Ministry of Housing and Local Government, James MacColl, and made it clear that they were committed to obtaining a 'firm promise at that all new high-storey flats should include, as part of the building, space for the provision of some desirable form of social amenity'.[244] It was evidently not thought possible or desirable to create playgroups for existing developments such as the blocks studied by Jephcott, as she found that play spaces were sparse, with most young children limited to playing within the flat.[245] Jephcott was herself an action research practitioner, actively engaged in setting up playgroups for the benefit of her research subjects.[246] Interestingly, she suggested that the deck access 'streets in the sky' of Park Hill in Sheffield was considered a 'socially successful' example of a modern flat development. It would be precisely this later wave of developments that would be most condemned, with Park Hill tenants believed 'incapable of grasping the benefits that planners sought to provide them with'.[247]

Retracing Orwell's steps for a 1970 *Socialist Commentary* piece entitled 'The Motor-Road to Wigan Pier', Stanley Reynolds focused his fire on 'those grey concrete horrors' that had replaced the 'mean little streets' of Orwell's visit.[248] 'There is none of the grime of a century or better on them, they do not have damp or teeming walls', commented Reynolds, 'but they are prison architecture just the same'. More reasonable was his observation that, in contrast to 'cottage' estates, high blocks were rarely planned as 'self-sufficient villages'.[249] Coming just two years after the 1968 collapse of the Ronan Point block in Newham, Reynold's comments certainly reflected the mood of the time. Though Ronan Point, crucially, represented the end of the dominance of the high flat rather than urban modernism – the 1970s seeing extensive construction of lower-rise estates – the reaction against slum clearance examined in the previous chapter had made many Labour activists far less keen on 'tall towns' as an improved alternative.

Labour's 1970 manifesto, *Now Britain's Strong Let's Make It Great to Live In*, had implied a job as yet unfinished. It was strongly assertive of the need to build still further, claiming that Britain was divided between the luxuries of the suburbs and the deprivation of the inner city.[250] Yet urban modernism had begun to run out of steam. The decline of the high flat was emphatic of the 'aging and partial decay of the interwar architectural culture'.[251] It is difficult to argue against the notion that modernism had peaked by the latter half of the 1960s, though Burnett's claim that the flat was an 'incident' is rather more questionable.[252] His assertion that 'the individual house in a garden has survived as the ideal of the majority of English people' may have some truth to it, but the fact that the built elements of his 'incident' are still lived in by large numbers of people would make it something considerably more than that.[253] The rise of modern housing had an important political component to it: Labour were serious in their desire to deliver the 'modern amenities' of the future to all. The contested aesthetic associations of modern council housing, supposedly evocative of 'Victorian rookeries' in some readings, should not blind scholars to the aims of the modernist project.[254] The initially positive reception of modern housing was not simply a socialist conceit. As the *Labour Woman* discussions of modern life across Europe indicate, modern dwellings with electric lighting and linoleum floors were an exciting prospect in the years after the Second World War. Where problems arose, it was often to do with a lack of consultation and continued social problems, as well as too much of an assumption that tenants would be as beguiled by the architectural wonder of modern developments as some within Labour were. Most significantly, the end of modernism without did not mean the end of modernism within – Samuel has described how a turn to conservation of 'period' dwellings in the early 1970s was actually 'modernization in disguise, a continuation and extension of the 1950s ideals of open plan living, rather than a reversal of them'.[255] Modernity was undoubtedly part of an architectural, political and cultural 'moment' in history – but a 'moment' that is still present in the built landscape of twenty-first-century Britain.

'Our new homes are a model to the world'

The debates within Labour on modern homes – and who should live in them – of this chapter exemplify the intricate character of post-war urban transformation. Far from being simply a question of ministerial discussions and houses built accordingly, modern housing was representative of a particular historical moment with political characteristics. While the Conservatives did briefly embrace architectural modernism, Labour activists approached modernity with significantly more enthusiasm. Considerations of class and community in addition to the more familiar subject of design contributed to the overall conception of the modern home in Labour visions. 'Our new homes are a model to the world', stated the party magazine issued with the Festival of Britain in 1951, 'The new towns and the Lansbury scheme and other schemes like it point the way to the kind of world that Labour is starting to build in Britain.'[256]

Class and community were of pivotal concern in how Labour conceived of modern homes. This chapter has discussed how Labour struggled to determine whether, in the context of rising living standards and apparent affluence, the working classes were suited to the council home. The problem was fundamentally with who Labour imagined the working classes to be – their top-down appeal principally pitched at a male-breadwinner nuclear family archetype – which would also determine approaches to design and community in the provision of housing. A large number of local Labour parties, such as the Southwark party described by Sue Goss, were parochial in character and believed themselves to be the authentic voice of the working classes.[257] This tendency to see the beneficiaries of council housing as passive recipients had an important role in defining the modern council home as precisely what Labour did not want it to be: a tenure for an updated version of the nineteenth-century 'deserving poor'. In a similar manner, the acceptance by many within Labour of the Hoggartian maxim that working-class life '[centred] on … groups of known streets' led the party to suspect council estates of weakening solidaristic class ties.[258] Sociologists increasingly cleaved to a nostalgic view of 'traditional' working-class community, and the Labour movement's own sentimental habits meant that they were acquiescent in this powerful narrative. There were certainly some solidaristic ties in the life of the street, but the flaw in Labour thinking was to believe that privacy was anathema to socialism.

It is perhaps fitting to summarise Labour thinking on the modern home with an epilogue to modern housing. Urban modernism has come to be described by prominent historians such as Kenneth Morgan as consisting of 'impersonal tower blocks, often badly designed ghettos of violence and fear'.[259] Though hyperbolic, Morgan's view of modern housing as little more than a concrete mistake has reinforced a 'common sense' that the modern moment was pointless and even malicious. The implication of this view is that high-rise, and perhaps modern estates as a whole, could not be pleasant living environments simply because of what they were. Labour believed near-exactly the opposite throughout the post-war period. Whilst the unwillingness of Labour activists to consult prospective tenants or the issues caused by poor construction in some developments should not be trivialised, those same activists believed that monumental architecture and modern amenities would create a new world. In essence, the reaction against modernity – which encompassed a cultural sense that the aesthetic had run its course and a political belief that large-scale urban transformation was no longer an effective means of solving urban deprivation – has translated into a unifying logic that the negative picture of modern council housing in twenty-first-century Britain was somehow inevitable.

Afterword

Gazing over the city of Bristol in 1958 from the fifteen-storey Barton House block, Tony Benn was moved to recount in his diary that 'to see the bright airy rooms with the superb view and to contrast them with the poky slum dwellings of Barton Hill below was to get all the reward one wants from politics'.[1] Benn's confidence that the view from the top of a modern, high-rise block represented a political creed in practice could be said to epitomise post-war modernity as Labour saw it: bringing a socialist future within reach through good housing. 'If every family were properly housed', asserted a 1950 *Labour Woman* editorial sagely, 'we would need fewer hospitals'.[2] Benn himself in some ways personified this future-chasing outlook, becoming Minister of Technology in the Wilson government. Perhaps an even more telling indication of the long-term effectiveness of urban transformation as a purported means of securing socialism was the following note by Benn in that day's entry, in which he asserted that 'the people were happy, despite the grumbles about detail'.[3] Yet 'grumbles about detail' would prove significant.

Some twelve years later in May 1970 – one month before Labour's general election defeat – Frank Allaun sounded a more sombre note in *Labour's Northern Voice*. Why, he asked his readers, would his constituency advice bureau be especially busy on a Sunday morning after a wet week? 'Because of tenants with rain pouring through the roof and soaking the bedding', he explained, adding that it was 'the devil's own job to get the landlord to do the repairs'.[4] After six years of Labour government, with housing given a relatively high priority even in the face of financial constraints, it might be asked why squalor – in this case leaking roofs and parsimonious landlords – had still not been displaced. The effect of this faltering journey to a socialist utopia was to unsettle the belief of Labour activists that constant progress – represented by new housing, new hospitals, new schools amongst others – was achievable. We might consider Drucker's point that Labour 'exists, as a result of certain remembered past actions, to do a particular job now and in the future'.[5] The 'particular job', in housing terms, was to sweep away the built legacy of the Industrial Revolution, creating in place the homes that Labour believed to be a necessary step in their vision of socialist progress. In this Labour activists were influenced by a modern impulse common to the period. Considering modernity as a cultural moment with political expressions, rather than simply a form of architecture, allows us to understand further why urban transformations in the post-war period were characterised by a boundless sense of optimism, as well as the sincere belief on the part of political actors that they were accelerating into the future.

Writing in the pages of the Birmingham Labour Party newspaper *Town Crier* ahead of municipal elections in 1945, Councillor Albert Bradbeer claimed that his Conservative opponents 'consist[ed] of men and women whose ideas date back to the reign of Queen Victoria'.[6] By contrast, Labour candidates had 'their feet firmly planted in the 20th century', aiming to 'translate into reality the modern conceptions of a society which will ensure a fuller, healthier, happier and more kindly life for all'.[7] The shift away from such political positive thinking over the post-war period can be illustrated by a 1970 *Socialist Commentary* editorial (uncredited but presumably by the editor, Rita Hinden), following the election defeat of that year. 'Before 1945 there was an optimistic belief in the inevitability of gradualness', stated the editorial, 'that public opinion and socialist objectives were essentially at one with another'. Similarly, the editorial went on, 1964 was marked by a belief that 'socialism, through pushing through the technological revolution, would once again solve all our social problems'.[8] Remarking that 'our optimistic dreams have again eluded us', the editorial was clear that the political logic – and popular spirit – of the post-war era had ended. Notably, this self-criticism came from the 'modernising' revisionist wing of the party, who had exerted considerable influence over the leadership of the party since the early 1950s. Even activists on the Labour left, who largely interpreted election defeat as a signal to redouble the party commitment to socialism, identified a loss of confidence as central to the defeat. In a post-election analysis, Richard Clements, editor of *Tribune*, argued that the economic retrenchment of the late 1960s had 'characterised the prospects of future Labour Governments as bleak indeed'.[9] Grim determination, rather than an assumption in the inevitability of progress, would characterise the radical expansion of the welfare state in the 1970s. It is no coincidence that confidence in modernist urban transformation faltered at a similar moment. In early 1973, the architect Sir Hugh Casson claimed in an article for *The Times* that growing disenchantment with modernist architecture was tantamount to 'a paralysis of the nation's cultural nerve'.[10]

Disenchantment was twofold, consisting of a popular reaction to comprehensive redevelopment schemes (often aided by left activists) and a 'heritage' turn in which older housing benefitted from a cultural reassessment. Notably, as Saumarez Smith argues, modernist architecture (and by extension thoroughgoing urban transformation) 'often served as a proxy for the whole gamut of state-led, top-down progressivism' and was particularly targeted by the New Right as the 1970s went on.[11] The 'optimistic dreams' of urban transformation advanced by Labour activists in the post-war period had real consequences. It is for this very reason that this book has sought to recover this ideology through avoiding contemporary derision, taking the views of Labour activists as genuine.[12]

Writing in 1962, Tony Crosland argued that although he believed that Labour and Conservative had intermingled on many subjects of policy, they did not share the same objectives. He described this crossover as a case of 'new moods, old problems': the style of Labour arguments might have changed, but the concerns of socialism remained in his view broadly the same.[13] Perhaps more than any other figure, Crosland embodied the meeting point between the modern impulse and the future-orientated socialism of the post-war Labour Party. This book has explored this coalescence as a means of deepening our understanding the momentous changes in Britain's urban environment between 1945 and 1970. There exist strong contemporary presumptions as to why British cities were radically transformed in that period, with relatively little interrogation of the political rationale behind those changes. *In Place of Squalor* has sought to address this gap, situating post-war Labour thought as essentially neoteric, party activists being committed to 'building socialism' – in literal terms – through new homes and new cities. The book has drawn attention to the temporal limitations of Labour's vision and how declining optimism about the ability of the party to build the future closely followed the diminished standing of modernism. Without a clear comprehension of why, despite the 'new moods', the 'old problems' retained their salience, significant gaps will remain in the study of urban Britain in the mid-twentieth century.

The modernist writer Marshall Berman acknowledged that the rise of anti-development movements headed by figures such as Jane Jacobs in New York had heralded the end of urban modernism, but he noted that these critiques were based on equally flawed assumptions. He asserted that Jacobs' account of the city, focused on the counter-culturalism of Greenwich Village, contained 'positively pastoral' visions of vibrant neighbourhoods without crime, and suggested that there was some irony in the contemporary 1970s obsession over vanished 'homes, the families and neighbourhoods' that many attacking modernism had 'left in order to be modern in the modes of the 1950s and 1960s'.[14] Berman's frustration at the popular disavowal of modernity in favour of a logic that he believed was poorer in ambition still forms one side of the argument about the urban modern moment in the twentieth century. The other side is provided by critics such as the intellectual historian Jackson Lears. In a review of Robert Caro's far-reaching biography of the 'modernist pharaoh' of New York, Robert Moses, he argued that any attempt to see the modernism that Moses' projects embodied as anything more than 'smashing up people's homes' was simply a '[fantasy] of urban liberation'.[15] In Lears' view, the destruction of old neighbourhoods was a catalyst for the shift to contemporary urban capitalism – the inner areas of London, New York, Paris and other Western cities becoming the centres of a new urban elite rather than the homes of ordinary people. Although Lears acknowledged that the endpoint of urban renewal promulgated by Jane Jacobs and others had had a role in this – namely, through 'gentrification' – his counter-argument sounded suspiciously like Michael Young's advocacy of an imagined, vigorously working-class Bethnal Green as the epicentre of community. The politics of urban transformation remain vibrant, and the past remains a contested space.

In depicting Labour thought in the course of urban policy, this book has shown in a practical sense how the more abstract elements of Labour's vision of socialist progress were actually realised (or not). Equally, this investigation allows a closer look at Labour's intentions versus the outcomes of the policies they pursued. Tracing the reasoning behind particular urban policies can put political ideas into their contemporary place, rather than seeing them as oddities or aberrations in the present day. The popular resonance of Labour's basic message – better housing, an end to slums – did not diminish over the period, even if the increasingly infinite timeframe of the policies that the party began to pursue did not endear them to the electorate. This sense of radical change worked on two levels: within the context of modernity, a cultural phenomenon that can be historicised, and Labour's socialist self-regard as a party of progress.

Embracing the more abstract aspects of political discourse in this fashion could well make for innovative political and urban histories. It has long been apparent that the dominant tendency across historical scholarship in both urban and political fields is to omit the influence of ideology in favour of rational, governmental policymaking, in an almost ironic return to older historiographical high political traditions. This book argues that political parties had distinct ideological objectives that we should engage with seriously, noting the contention of Daunton that we should avoid viewing the past 'as if the end result were obvious'.[16] In this respect, I hope to encourage urban historians to take greater notice of political thought and reasoning when analysing the process of change to the built environment. Since the 2008 financial crash, the cost of renting or buying a home, the poor quality of accommodation, lack of state alternatives to private provision and reconstruction of urban communities have combined to cement housing in place as a core political issue. Housing had a high profile at the 2019 general election, with the Conservatives committing to a substantial reform of the private rented sector – that tenure being the effective linchpin of contemporary housing discourse – the need for which only strengthened during the subsequent Covid-19 pandemic.[17] Popular interest in housing histories has correspondingly deepened, albeit still with a tendency to elide the post-war era in favour of the earlier part of the twentieth century.[18] At the same time, the value of the built legacy of the mid-twentieth century remains highly disputed. In a grim twist of fate, the tower block of 1960s vintage has assumed the place of the Victorian workers' cottage, stereotyped as a space of poor public health, stymied aspiration and aesthetic blight. This prejudice was given tragic emphasis with the 2017 Grenfell Tower fire in a twenty-four-storey council block in North Kensington, with the successive inquiry drawing attention to narrow public assumptions about post-war housing (and post-war council estates in particular).[19] Paying attention to the influence (or echoes) of the past on the present shape of the urban environment – whether the belief that people should own their own home, that a state alternative to private landlords is a prerequisite for a civilised society or that the Georgian villa represents the pinnacle of architectural development – will enable a more fruitful approach to the controversies of the early twenty-first century.

Notes

Introduction

1 The GLC was the overarching local government body for planning and coordinating housing provision within London, having replaced the earlier London County Council (LCC) in 1965, though individual London boroughs continued to produce their own plans. Initially controlled by the Labour Party, they were displaced by the Conservatives in the 1967 local elections.
2 London Metropolitan Archives (hereafter LMA), Greater London Council, *Somewhere Decent to Live* (1967), https://www.youtube.com/watch?v=1A2wa9yeAKk (accessed 6 February 2016).
3 LMA, GLC, *Somewhere Decent to Live* (1967).
4 Aneurin Bevan, *In Place of Fear* (London: William Heinemann, 1952), p.118.
5 *BBC News* (14 April 2015), http://www.bbc.co.uk/news/uk-14380936 (accessed 6 February 2016).
6 For a comprehensive survey of major local authority projects, see Miles Glendinning and Stefan Muthesius, *Tower Block: Modern Public Housing in England, Scotland, Wales and Northern Ireland* (New Haven: Yale University Press, 1994).
7 Important exceptions are: Peter Mandler, 'New Towns for Old', in Becky Conekin, Frank Mort and Chris Waters (eds), *Moments of Modernity: Reconstructing Britain, 1945–1964* (London: River Oram, 1999), pp.208–27; Otto Saumarez Smith, *Boom Cities: Architect Planners and the Politics of Radical Urban Renewal in 1960s Britain* (Oxford: Oxford University Press, 2019); and Guy Ortalano, 'Planning the Urban Future in 1960s Britain', *The Historical Journal*, 54 (2011), 477–507.
8 Marshall Berman, *All That Is Solid Melts into Air: The Experience of Modernity* (London: Verso, 1983), First published 1982, p.33.
9 *Ibid.*, p.16.
10 *Ibid.*
11 Martin Daunton and Bernhard Rieger, 'Introduction', in Martin Daunton and Bernard Rieger (eds), *Meanings of Modernity: Britain from the Late-Victorian Era to World War II* (Oxford: Oxford University Press, 2001), pp.1–24 at p.5.
12 Thomas Linehan, *Modernism and British Socialism* (Basingstoke: Palgrave Macmillan, 2012), p.49.
13 *Ibid.*, p.57.

14 Bruno Latour (translated by Catherine Porter), *We Have Never Been Modern* (Cambridge, MA: Harvard University Press, 1993), p.102.
15 John R. Gold, *The Practice of Modernism: Modern Architects and Urban Transformation 1954–1972* (Oxford: Routledge, 2007), p.13.
16 See, in particular, John R. Gold, *Experience of Modernism, Modern Architects and the Future City* (Oxford: Routledge, 1997); Gold, *The Practice of Modernism* (Oxford: Routledge, 2007); Alan Powers, *Britain: Modern Architectures in History* (London: Reaktion, 2007). Two works that do address the political elements of modernism and the subsequent conservation movement are: Patrick Wright, *On Living in an Old Country: The National Past in Contemporary Britain* (Oxford: Oxford University Press, 2009), First published 1985; Raphael Samuel, *Theatres of Memory Volume 1: Past and Present in Contemporary Culture* (London: Verso, 1994).
17 H. M. Drucker, *Doctrine and Ethos in the Labour Party* (London: Allen and Unwin, 1979), p.18.
18 Martin Francis, *Ideas and Policies under Labour, 1945–51: Building a new Britain* (Manchester: Manchester University Press, 1997), p.5.
19 C. A. R. Crosland, *The Future of Socialism* (New York: Schocken, 1967), First published 1956, p.61.
20 Jeremy Nuttall, *Psychological Socialism: The Labour Party and Qualities of Mind and Character, 1931 to the Present* (Manchester: Manchester University Press, 2006), p.70.
21 Ross McKibbin, *Parties and People: England 1914–1951* (Oxford: Oxford University Press, 2010), p.152.
22 Ralph Miliband, *Parliamentary Socialism: Study in the Politics of Labour*, 2nd edition (London: Merlin Press, 1975), First published 1961, p.274.
23 *Ibid.*, p.16.
24 Ben Jackson, *Equality and the British Left* (Manchester: Manchester University Press, 2007), p.173.
25 Lawrence Black, *The Political Culture of the Left in Affluent Britain, 1951-64: Old Labour, New Britain?* (Basingstoke: Palgrave Macmillan, 2003), p.15.
26 C. A. R. Crosland, *The Conservative Enemy: A Programme of Radical Reform for the 1960s* (London: Jonathan Cape, 1962), p.195.
27 It is important to note that Crosland was regarded with a degree of suspicion by the left and the older right, due to his 'revisionist' credentials (although he had achieved some sort of balance by the time of his death in 1977). However, *The Future of Socialism* was without question the most influential socialist text of the 1950s – provoking serious debate from all quarters.
28 Working Class Movement Library, Salford (hereafter WMCL), Allaun Papers, *Labour's Northern Voice* (June 1953), p.3.
29 *Ibid.*

30 Latour, *We Have Never Been Modern*, p.60.
31 Labour History Archive, Manchester (hereafter LHA), *Talking Points*, 18 September 1948, p.8.
32 LHA, LP/329.12, Ritchie Calder, *Science and Socialism*, 1948, p.3.
33 *Ibid.*, p.5.
34 Linehan, *Modernism and British Socialism*, p.137.
35 John Gyford, *The Politics of Local Socialism* (London: Allen and Unwin, 1985), pp.6–7.
36 Jeremy Nuttall, 'Pluralism, the People, and Time in Labour Party History, 1931–1964', *The Historical Journal*, 56:3 (2013), 731. Works on Labour's engagement with temporality in general are relatively thin on the ground, with notable exceptions including: Richard Jobson, *Nostalgia and the Post-war Labour Party: Prisoners of the Past* (Manchester: Manchester University Press, 2018); and Nuttall, 'Pluralism, the People, and Time in Labour Party History, 1931–1964', 729–56.
37 Samuel, *Theatres of Memory*, p.163.
38 Examples of this writing include: John Burnett, *A Social History of Housing 1815–1970* (Newton Abbot: David Charles, 1978); Michael Harloe, *The People's Home? Social Rented Housing in Europe and America* (Oxford: Oxford University Press, 1995); Rodney Lowe, *The Welfare State in Britain since 1945* (Basingstoke: Palgrave Macmillan, 1993); Peter Malpass, *Housing and the Welfare State: The Development of Housing Policy in Britain* (Basingstoke: Palgrave Macmillan, 2005); Stephen Merett, *State Housing in Britain* (London: Routledge and Kegan Paul, 1979); Alison Ravetz, *Council Housing and Culture: The History of a Social Experiment* (London: Routledge, 2001); Peter Malpass, 'The Wobbly Pillar? Housing and the British Postwar Welfare State', *Journal of Social Policy*, 32:4 (2003), 589–606.
39 See for examples of this kind of social history: Joanna Bourke, *Working-Class Cultures in Britain 1890–1960: Gender, Class and Ethnicity* (London: Routledge, 1994); Stephen Brooke, '"Slumming in Swinging London?" Class, Gender and the Post-War City in Nell Dunn's *Up the Junction* (1963)', *Cultural and Social History*, 9:3 (2012), 429–49; Mark Clapson, *Invincible Green Suburbs, Brave New Towns: Social Change and Urban Dispersal in Postwar England* (Manchester: Manchester University Press, 1998); Judy Giles, *The Parlour and the Suburb: Domestic Identities, Class, Femininity and Modernity* (Oxford: Berg, 2004); Claire Langhamer, 'The Meanings of Home in Postwar Britain', *Journal of Contemporary History*, 40:2 (2005), 341–62; Jon Lawrence, 'Class, Affluence and the Study of Everyday Life in Britain, c.1930–64', *Cultural and Social History*, 10:2 (2013), 273–299; Ben Jones, *The Working Class in Mid-Twentieth-Century England* (Manchester: Manchester University Press, 2012); Ross McKibbin, *Classes and Cultures: England, 1918–51* (Oxford: Oxford University Press, 1998); Ben Rogaly and Becky Taylor, *Moving Histories of Class and Community: Identity, Place and Belonging in Contemporary*

England (Basingstoke: Palgrave Macmillan, 2009); Simon Szreter, 'Health, Class, Place and Politics: Social Capital and Collective Provision in Britain', *Contemporary British History*, 16:3 (2002), 27–57; Selina Todd, 'Affluence, Class and Crown Street: Reinvestigating the Post-War Working Class', *Contemporary British History*, 22:4 (2008), 501–18.

40 See for examples of local case studies: Harold Carter, 'Building the Divided City: Race, Class and Social Housing in Southwark 1945–1995', *The London Journal*, 33:2 (July 2008), 155–85; Zoe Doye, 'The Labour Party and Public Housing, 1951–64: An Examination of National Policy and Its Implementation in London' (PhD thesis, Birkbeck University of London, 2004); Sue Goss, *Local Labour and Local Government: A Study of Changing Interests, Politics and Policy in Southwark from 1919 to 1982* (Edinburgh: Edinburgh University Press, 1988); Gyford, *The Politics of Local Socialism*; Matthew Hollow, 'Governmentality on the Park Hill Estate: The Rationality of Public Housing', *Urban History*, 37:1 (2010), 117–35; Nick Tiratsoo, *Reconstruction, Affluence and Labour Politics: Coventry, 1945–1960* (London: Routledge, 1990).

41 See for Labour views: Ben Jackson, 'Revisionism Reconsidered: "Property-Owning Democracy" and Egalitarian Strategy in Post-War Britain', *Twentieth Century British History*, 16:4 (2005), 416–40; Glen O'Hara, *Governing Post-War Britain: The Paradoxes of Progress, 1951–73* (Basingstoke: Palgrave Macmillan, 2012); Peter Weiler, 'Labour and the Land: From Municipalization to the Land Commission, 1951–1971', *Twentieth Century British History*, 19:3 (2008), 314–43. See for Conservative views: Alan G. V. Simmonds, 'Conservative Governments and the New Town Housing Question in the 1950s', *Urban History*, 28:1 (2001), 65–83; Alan G. V. Simmonds, 'Raising Rachman: The Origins of the Rent Act, 1957', *The Historical Journal*, 45:4 (2002), 843–68; Peter Weiler, 'The Conservatives' Search for a Middle Way in Housing, 1951–64', *Twentieth Century British History*, 14:4 (2003), 360–90; Aled Davies, '"Right to Buy": The Development of a Conservative Housing Policy, 1945–1980', *Contemporary British History*, 27:4 (2013), 421–44.

42 See for examples of the 'new urban social history': Simon Gunn, 'The Rise and Fall of British Urban Modernism: Planning Bradford, circa 1945–70', *Journal of British Studies*, 49:4 (2010), 849–69 and 'The Buchanan Report, Environment and the Problem of Traffic in 1960s Britain', *Twentieth Century British History*, 22:4 (2011), 521–42; Erika Hanna, *Modern Dublin, Urban Change and the Irish Past* (Oxford, 2013); Ortalano, 'Planning the Urban Future in 1960s Britain', and Ortalano, *Thatcher's Progress: From Social Democracy to Market Liberalism through an English New Town* (Cambridge: Cambridge University Press, 2019); Sam Wetherell, 'Freedom Planned: The Enterprise Zone and Urban Non-Planning in Post-War Britain', *Twentieth Century British History*, 27:2 (2016), and Wetherell, *Foundations: How the Built Environment Made Twentieth-Century Britain* (Princeton: Princeton

University Press, 2020); Alistair Kefford, 'Housing the Citizen-Consumer in Post-War Britain: The Parker Morris Report, Affluence and the Even Briefer Life of Social Democracy', *Twentieth Century British History*, 29:2 (2017), 225–8; Jesse Meredith, 'Decolonizing the New Town: Roy Gazzard and the Making of Killingworth Township', *Journal of British Studies*, 57 (2018), 333–62; Sarah Mass, 'Commercial Heritage as Democratic Action: Historicizing the "Save the Market" Campaigns in Bradford and Chesterfield, 1969–76', *Twentieth Century British History*, 29:3 (2017), 459–84; Saumarez Smith, *Boom Cities*. For an examination of housing as an agent of modernity in a French context, see Kenny Cupers, *The Social Project: Housing Postwar France* (Minneapolis: University of Minnesota Press, 2014).

43 One further, if less ambitious, book could be added to this list: Catherine Flinn, *Rebuilding Britain's Blitzed Cities: Hopeful Dreams, Stark Realities* (London: Bloomsbury, 2019). Flinn is interested in reconstruction from the perspective of planning, both expert and popular, and gives an in-depth account of how grand plans reshaped specific blitzed cities. She does not, however, engage with the political side of post-war urban transformation.

44 James Greenhalgh, *Reconstructing Modernity: Space, Power and Governance in Mid-Twentieth Century British Cities* (Manchester: Manchester University Press, 2018), p.66.

45 Gøsta Esping-Andersen, *The Three Worlds of Welfare Capitalism* (Princeton: Princeton University Press, 1990).

46 Glendinning and Muthesius, *Tower Block*, p.285.

47 *BBC News* 'England "Needs Millions of Homes to Solve Housing Crisis"' (8 January 2019), https://www.bbc.co.uk/news/uk-england-46788530 (accessed 24 March 2022).

48 Tom de Castella, 'Why Can't the UK Build 240,000 Houses a Year?', *BBC News* (13 January 2015), http://www.bbc.co.uk/news/magazine-30776306 (accessed online 6 February 2016). Oliver Wainwright, 'Homes Sweet Homes: A Brick by Brick Breakdown of Housing Manifestos', *The Guardian* (31 May 2017), https://www.theguardian.com/artanddesign/2017/may/31/housing-manifestos-conservatives-labour-lib-dems-homes (accessed online 10 February 2019).

49 Wainwright, 'Homes Sweet Homes'.

50 Steve Akehurst, 'Housing and the 2017 Election: What the Numbers Say', Shelter Blog, https://blog.shelter.org.uk/2017/06/housing-and-the-2017-election-what-the-numbers-say/ (accessed 24 March 2022). Cassie Barton, 'GE2019: How Did Demographics Affect the Result?' House of Commons Library (21 February 2020), https://commonslibrary.parliament.uk/ge2019-how-did-demographics-affect-the-result/ (accessed 27 February 2022).

51 See Phil Child, 'Labour's Radical Renting History', *Tribune* (8 July 2020), https://tribunemag.co.uk/2020/07/labours-radical-renting-history (accessed 18 March 2023).

52 There are numerous examples of this, but most notably: the film *Harry Brown* (2009), set on an ultra-violent London housing estate; episodes of the popular BBC police drama *The Bill* (1984–2010) made conspicuously heavy use of modern housing estates, including the blocks of the High Path estate in South Wimbledon; and the novel *High Rise* (1975) by J. G. Ballard describes a dystopian tower block where, in an inversion of the usual theme, the opulence of the aesthetic surroundings causes the inhabitants to descend into a near-feral state. The latter was adapted to film in 2015, with considerable media discussion of the aesthetics of high rise accompanying the film's release.

53 Peter Hennessy, *Having It So Good: Britain in the Fifties* (London: Penguin, 2006), p.493. Similar sentiments are contained within the other major popular histories of the period, especially Dominic Sandbrook, *Never Had It So Good: A History of Britain from Suez to the Beatles* (London: Abacus, 2006) and *White Heat: A History of Britain in the Swinging Sixties* (London: Abacus, 2006). David Kynaston is more balanced, but still rather pessimistic: *Austerity Britain, 1945–51* (London: Bloomsbury, 2007); *Family Britain, 1951–57* (London: Bloomsbury, 2010); *Modernity Britain: Opening the Box 1957–59* (London: Bloomsbury, 2013); *Modernity Britain: A Shake of the Dice 1959–62* (London: Bloomsbury, 2015).

54 BBC, *Further Abroad: Get High* (1994).

55 Christopher Beanland, *Concrete Concept: Brutalist Buildings Around the World* (London: Frances Lincoln, 2016); Danny Dorling, *All That Is Solid: The Great Housing Disaster* (London: Allen Lane, 2014); John Grindrod, *Concretopia* (London: Old Street, 2014); Lynsey Hanley, *Estates: An Intimate History* (London: Granta, 2007); Owen Hatherley, *Militant Modernism* (London: Zero, 2009); Hatherley, *A Guide to the New Ruins of Great Britain* (London: Verso, 2010); Hatherley, *A New Kind of Bleak: Journeys through Urban Britain* (London: Verso, 2012).

56 Dorling, *All That Is Solid*, p.154.

57 *Mining Review*, 15:5 (1962), https://www.youtube.com/watch?v=uc_jnGcEc00 (accessed 27 February 2016).

58 After being rebuffed, Lubetkin went to his pig farm in Gloucestershire, before being commissioned to build the Cranbrook, Dorset and Lakeview council estates in Bethnal Green.

59 BBC, 'Where We Live Now: New Town, Home Town' (1979), http://www.bbc.co.uk/iplayer/episode/p01rk56y/where-we-live-now-3-new-town-home-town (accessed online 27 February 2016).

60 Raymond Williams, *The Long Revolution* (London: Chatto and Windus, 1961), p.359.

61 *Ibid.*

Chapter 1

1. LHA, LP/362.5/318, Douglas Brown, *An Englishman's Home* (1945), p.5.
2. *Ibid.*
3. *Ibid.*, pp.4–6.
4. Drucker, *Doctrine and Ethos*, p.25.
5. See Christopher Klemek, *The Transatlantic Collapse of Urban Renewal: Postwar Urbanism from New York to Berlin* (Chicago: University of Chicago Press, 2012).
6. George Orwell, *The Road to Wigan Pier* (London: Penguin, 2001), First published 1937, p.46.
7. Walter Greenwood, *Love on the Dole* (London: Vintage, 1993), First published 1933, p.11.
8. Jim Yelling, 'Incidence of Slum Clearance', *Urban History*, 27:2 (2000), 234–54 at 243. Manchester had the highest extra-London total, at 73,536. In spite of the existence of a large proportion of poor-quality housing, Wales did not undergo slum clearance to any high degree, with Cardiff only clearing 4,408 houses between 1955 and 1985. Scotland and Northern Ireland were subject to different housing laws and their story of slum clearance is not told in depth here.
9. Yelling, 'Incidence of Slum Clearance', 235.
10. Herbert Tout, *The Standard of Living in Bristol: A Preliminary Report of the Work of the University of Bristol Social Survey* (Bristol: Arrowsmith, 1938), p.11.
11. Harloe, *The People's Home?*, p.147.
12. Szreter, 'Health, Class, Place and Politics', 32.
13. Malpass, *Housing and the Welfare State*, p.42.
14. Martin Daunton, *A Property-Owning Democracy? Housing in Britain* (London: Faber, 1987), p.63.
15. Birmingham City Archives, Birmingham (hereafter BCA), B363.10942, Socialist Medical Association, 'Defeat Tuberculosis Now! Report of the National Tuberculosis Conference', 1952, pp.3–4.
16. LHA, *Labour Woman*, November 1964, p.170.
17. LHA, LP/GS/8, *Town Crier*, 17 March 1945, p.8.
18. Stefan Muthesius, *The English Terraced House* (New Haven: Yale University Press, 1982), p.117.
19. Alison Ravetz, 'Housing the People', in Jim Fyrth (ed.), *Labour's Promised Land: Culture and Society in Labour Britain 1945–51* (London: Lawrence and Wishart, 1995), p.149.
20. LHA, LP/362.5/319, Tom Braddock, *Houses, Rents and the Building Trade*, 1953, p.14.
21. Francis, *Ideas and Policies under Labour*, p.125.
22. LHA, Brown, *An Englishman's Home*, p.7.

23 LHA, Labour Party, LP/GS/362.5/319, *A Guide to Post-War Housing Policy*, 1948, pp.9–10.
24 Ravetz, 'Housing the People', p.151.
25 Ben Jones, 'Slum Clearance, Privatization and Residualization: The Practices and Politics of Council Housing in Mid-Twentieth-Century England', *Twentieth Century British History*, 21:4 (2010), 510–39 at 512; Peter Shapely, Duncan Tanner and Andrew Walling, 'Civic Culture and Housing Policy in Manchester, 1945–79', *Twentieth Century British History*, 15:4 (2004), 410–34 at 418.
26 Jim Yelling, 'Public Policy, Urban Renewal and Property Ownership, 1945–55', *Urban History*, 22:1 (1995), 48–62 at 53–4.
27 *Ibid.*, 54.
28 LHA, *Talking Points*, 21 January 1951, p.6.
29 Malpass, *Housing and the Welfare State*, p.82.
30 Peter Weiler, 'The Rise and Fall of the Conservatives' "Grand Design for Housing", 1951–64', *Contemporary British History*, 14:1 (2000), 122–50 at 123–4.
31 Weiler, 'The Conservatives' Search for a Middle Way in Housing', 362–3.
32 *Ibid.*, 363.
33 Yelling, 'Public Policy, Urban Renewal and Property Ownership', 56–7.
34 LHA, *Socialist Commentary*, January 1954, p.8.
35 John English, Ruth Madigan and Peter Norman, *Slum Clearance: The Social and Administrative Context in England and Wales* (London: Croom Helm, 1976), p.25.
36 Housing Repairs and Rent Act 1954, p.9, http://www.legislation.gov.uk/ukpga/Eliz2/2-3/53/contents (accessed 8 May 2016).
37 Norman Dennis, *People and Planning: The Sociology of Housing in Sunderland* (London: Faber, 1970), p.123.
38 Merrett, *State Housing in Britain*, p.121.
39 WCML, Allaun Papers, *Labour's Northern Voice*, October 1956, p.4.
40 LHA, *Talking Points*, 16 January 1954, p.5.
41 LHA, *Socialist Commentary*, June 1955, p.169.
42 *Ibid.*, p.170.
43 LHA, *Socialist Commentary*, November 1954, p.311.
44 LHA, *Talking Points*, 21 January 1956, p.13.
45 LHA, LP/GS/362.5/319, Labour Party, *Homes for the Future*, 1956, p.6.
46 LHA, *Labour Woman*, September 1956, p.169.
47 Samuel, *Theatres of Memory*, p.58.
48 LHA, LP/GS/8, *Baron's Court Citizen*, June 1963, p.7.
49 *Ibid.*
50 Muthesius, *English Terraced House*, p.36.
51 *Ibid.*
52 WCML, Allaun Papers, *Labour's Northern Voice*, January 1957, p.8.

53 LHA, LPRD Re/13, James Vickers, 'Slum Clearance', December 1959.
54 Dennis, *People and Planning*, p.213.
55 Hilda Jennings, *Societies in the Making: A Study of Development and Redevelopment within a County Borough* (London: Routledge and Kegan Paul, 1962), p.26.
56 LHA, *Labour Woman*, January 1964, p.15.
57 *Ibid.*
58 LHA, *Socialist Commentary*, February 1961, p.18.
59 *Ibid.*, p.17.
60 LHA, LP/GS/362.52/318, CPGB, Reuben Falber, *Beware Sharks: Tory Rent & Housing Policy Exposed*, 1960, p.11.
61 LHA, *Socialist Commentary*, March 1961, p.16.
62 *Ibid.* Arthur Street was off Leith Walk, towards the old port of Leith.
63 LHA, *Socialist Commentary*, March 1961, p.17.
64 Goss, *Local Labour and Local Government*, p.72.
65 LHA, LP/GS/8, *West Ham South Citizen*, June 1962, p.2.
66 LHA, LPRD Re/330, 'Labour's Plan for Private Rented Houses', September 1962, p.2.
67 *Ibid.*, pp.3–6.
68 *Ibid.*, p.7.
69 David John Ellis, 'Pavement Politics: Community Action in Leeds, c. 1960–1990' (PhD thesis, University of York, 2015), pp.77–8.
70 LHA, *Labour Woman*, December 1963, p.9.
71 Enda Delaney, *The Irish in Post-War Britain* (Oxford: Oxford University Press, 2007), p.87.
72 Kennetta Hammond Perry, *London Is the Place for Me: Black Britons, Citizenship and the Politics of Race* (Oxford: Oxford University Press, 2016), p.58.
73 Paul Gilroy, *Ain't No Black in the Union Jack: The Cultural Politics of Race and Nation* (London: Routledge, 1992), First published 1987, pp.96–7.
74 Gavin Schaffer and Saima Nasar, 'The White Essential Subject: Race, Ethnicity, and the Irish in Post-War Britain', *Contemporary British History*, 32:2 (2018), 209–30 at 215.
75 Delaney, *The Irish in Post-War Britain*, p.102.
76 Anthony H. Richmond, *Migration and Race Relations in an English City: A Study in Bristol* (London: Oxford University Press for the Institute of Race Relations, 1973), pp.46–9. Harold Carter describes similar conditions in his historical study of Southwark: Carter, 'Building the Divided City', 155–85.
77 *Ibid.*, p.48.
78 Hammond Perry, *London Is the Place for Me*, p.85.
79 John Davis, 'Rents and Race in 1960s London: New Light on Rachmanism', *Twentieth Century British History*, 12 (2001), 69–92 at 80.

80 Gilroy, *Ain't No Black*, pp.97–8.
81 Ben Jones and Camilla Schofield, '"Whatever Community Is, This Is Not It": Notting Hill and the Reconstruction of "Race" in Britain after 1958', *Journal of British Studies*, 58 (2019), 142–73 at 152.
82 *Ibid.*, 157–9.
83 Gilroy, *Ain't No Black*, p.100.
84 LHA, *Socialist Commentary*, December 1964, p.5.
85 Elizabeth Buettner, 'This Is Staffordshire Not Alabama: Racial Geographies of Commonwealth Immigration in Early 1960s Britain', *The Journal of Imperial and Commonwealth History*, 42:4 (2014), 710–40 at 716.
86 *Ibid.*, 717.
87 Rachel Yemm, 'Immigration, Race and Local Media: Smethwick and the 1964 General Election', *Contemporary British History*, 33:1 (2019), 98–122 at 100.
88 *Tribune* (20 October 1964), p.8.
89 *Ibid.*, p.9.
90 Hammond Perry, *London Is the Place for Me*, p.194. Unfortunately, this was not the end of Griffiths' career. He went on to write a book on the 'connection' between immigration and disease, and served as MP for Portsmouth North from 1979 to 1997.
91 MACE Archive, ATV, Midland News, 7 December 1964.
92 Hammond Perry, *London Is the Place for Me*, p.194.
93 Buettner, 'This Is Staffordshire Not Alabama', 716.
94 Hammond Perry, *London Is the Place for Me*, p.298.
95 Camilla Schofield, *Enoch Powell and the Making of Postcolonial Britain* (Cambridge: Cambridge University Press, 2013), p.209.
96 'Was Powell Speech Just a River of Lies?', *Express and Star* (16 March 2008), https://www.expressandstar.com/news/2008/03/16/was-powell-speech-just-a-river-of-lies/ (accessed 28 July 2021).
97 Shirin Hirsch, *In the Shadow of Enoch Powell: Race, Locality and Resistance* (Manchester: Manchester, 2018), p.55.
98 *Tribune* (10 May 1964), p.5.
99 LHA, *Socialist Commentary* (July 1968), p.7.
100 *Tribune* (20 December 1968), p.5.
101 WCML, 'Notting Hill: A National Disgrace', *Labour's Voice* (June 1969).
102 *Ibid.*
103 Jones and Schofield, '"Whatever Community Is, This Is Not It"', 173.
104 Frank Allaun, *No Place Like Home: Britain's Housing Tragedy* (London: Andre Deutsch, 1972), p.110.
105 *Ibid.*
106 LHA, LP/GS/362.5/319, Labour Party, *Labour's Plan for Old Houses* (1963), p.4.

107 Allaun, *No Place Like Home*, p.197.
108 LHA, LP/GS/362.5/319, Labour Party, *Let's Go with Labour for the New Britain* (1964), p.15.
109 Office for National Statistics, 'UK House Building: Permanent Dwellings Started and Completed', March 2021, https://www.ons.gov.uk/peoplepopulationandcommunity/housing/datasets/ukhousebuildingpermanentdwellingsstartedandcompleted (accessed 25 March 2022).
110 Yelling, 'Incidence of Slum Clearance', 236.
111 Dunleavy, *The Politics of Mass Housing*, p.72.
112 Richard Crossman, *The Diaries of a Cabinet Minister: Volume I* (Worcester: Ebenezer Baylis, 1976), First published 1975, p.127.
113 *Ibid.*
114 Yelling, 'Incidence of Slum Clearance', 244.
115 *Ibid.*, 245.
116 LHA, Labour Party, LP/GS/362.5/319, *Facts on Housing* (March 1965), p.6.
117 English et al., *Slum Clearance*, p.31.
118 *Ibid.*, p.32.
119 Yelling, 'Incidence of Slum Clearance', 245.
120 David Donnison, *The Government of Housing* (London: Penguin, 1967), p.288.
121 Davis, 'Rents and Race in 1960s London', 71.
122 *Report of the Committee on Housing in Greater London* (Cmd. 2605) (London: Her Majesty's Stationery Office, 1965), p.120.
123 *Ibid.*, p.121.
124 *Ibid.*, p.112.
125 *Ibid.*, pp.122–3.
126 *Tribune* (19 March 1965), p.9.
127 *Tribune* (2 April 1965), p.7.
128 Brian Abel Smith and Peter Townsend, *The Poor and the Poorest: A New Analysis of the Ministry of Labour's Family Expenditure Surveys of 1953–54 and 1960* (Andover: Chapel River Press, 1969), First published 1965, p.62.
129 LHA, Labour Party Research Department Re/124, 'Housing Policies: A Review', April 1967, p.8.
130 WCML, Frank Allaun, 'Labour Need Extra Aid to Build More Houses at Reasonable Rents', *Labour's Northern Voice* (February 1966), p.1.
131 Peter Malpass, Stephen Merrett and Peter Shapely have all advanced a version of this argument.
132 English et al., *Slum Clearance*, pp.33–4.
133 Gyford, *The Politics of Local Socialism*, p.34.
134 LHA, LP/362.5/319, Labour Party, *Housing: Report of the Housing Policy Study Group* (1969), p.4.

135 *Ibid.*, p.9.
136 *Ibid.*
137 Glendinning and Muthesius, *Tower Block*, p.326.
138 Chris Hamnett, 'Gentrification and the Middle-Class Remaking of Inner London, 1961–2001', *Urban Studies*, 40:12 (2003), 2401–26 at 2402.
139 LHA, *Socialist Commentary* (November 1954), 311.
140 Ruth Glass, *London: Aspects of Change* (London: Cox and Wyman, 1964), p.xvii.
141 Phil Child, 'Slum Clearance and Attitudes towards Social Housing in Cambridge, 1950–75' (MPhil dissertation, University of Cambridge, 2012), p.66; Joe Moran, 'Early Cultures of Gentrification in London, 1955–1980', *Journal of Urban History*, 34:1 (2007), 101–201 at 105.
142 Crossman, *Diaries: Vol. I*, p.450.
143 H. Brack, 'A Difference in Subsidies', *The Times* (4 January 1965), p.9; 'Minister's Letters Go to Council', *The Times* (16 February 1966), p.6.
144 Moran, 'Early Cultures of Gentrification', 102.
145 Samuel, *Theatres of Memory*, p.70; Sophie Andreae, 'From Comprehensive Development to Conservation Areas', in Michael Hunter (ed.), *Preserving the Past: The Rise of Heritage in Modern Britain* (Stroud: Alan Sutton, 1996), p.140.
146 For examples of these campaigns in Leeds, Manchester, Sunderland and Nottingham, see Ellis, 'Pavement Politics' (PhD thesis, University of York, 2015); Shapely, *The Politics of Housing*; Norman Dennis; Ray Gosling, 'St Ann's, Nottingham', in Anne Lapping (ed.), *Community Action* (London, 1970), pp.22–7.
147 James Kincaid, Raphael Samuel and Elizabeth Slater, 'But Nothing Happens', *New Left Review* (January–April 1962), pp.13–14.
148 Gyford, *Politics of Local Socialism*, p.34.
149 Ken Coates and Richard Silburn, *Poverty: The Forgotten Englishmen* (Harmondsworth: Penguin, 1976), First published 1970, p.103.
150 LHA, LP/362.5/320, Anthony Crosland, *Towards a Labour Housing Policy* (1971), p.4.
151 LHA, Labour Party Research Department Re/208, A. Crosland, 'Towards a Labour Housing Policy', December 1971, p.3.
152 Yelling, 'Incidence of Slum Clearance', 254.
153 Hatherley, *Guide to the New Ruins*, xxiv.

Chapter 2

1 Hansard, Debates, Commons, vol.432, col.1154 (30 January 1947), http://hansard.millbanksystems.com/commons/1947/jan/30/town-and-country-planning-bill (accessed 14 June 2016).

2   *Ibid.*
3   Richard Hoggart, *The Uses of Literacy* (London: Penguin, 1992), First published 1957, p.59. Hunslet was a central district of Leeds in which Hoggart spent his formative years.
4   Frank Mort, 'Fantasies of Metropolitan Life: Planning London in the 1940s', *The Journal of British Studies*, 43:1 (2004), 120–51 at 122–3.
5   Gold, *The Practice of Modernism*, p.12.
6   Glendinning and Muthesius, *Tower Block*, p.325.
7   Otto Saumarez Smith, 'Graeme Shankland: A Sixties Architect-Planner and the Political Culture of the British Left', *Architectural History*, 57 (2014), 393–422 at 395.
8   LHA, Labour Party, *Towns for Our Times* (1961), p.19.
9   LHA, Labour Party, *Leisure for Living* (1958), p.17.
10 *Ibid.*
11 Berman, *All That Is Solid*, p.310.
12 J. B. Priestley, *English Journey* (London: Great Northern Books, 2009), First published 1934, pp.335–8.
13 Eve Blau, 'From Red Superblock to Green Megastructure: Municipal Socialism as a Model and Challenge', in Mark Swenarton, Tom Avermaete and Dirk van den Heuvel (eds), *Architecture and the Welfare State* (Routledge: Abingdon, 2015), p.38.
14 Abigail Beach and Nick Tiratsoo, 'The Planners and the Public', in Martin Daunton (ed.), *The Cambridge Urban History of Britain. Vol. 3, 1840–1950* (Cambridge: Cambridge University Press, 2000), p.525.
15 James C. Scott, *Seeing Like a State: How Certain Schemes to Improve the Human Condition Have Failed* (Yale University Press: New Haven, 1998), p.346.
16 See for one such example: Ade Kearns, Valerie Wright, Lynn Abrams and Barry Hazley, 'Slum Clearance and Relocation: A Reassessment of Social Outcomes Combining Short-Term and Long-Term Perspectives', *Housing Studies*, 34:2 (2017), 201–25.
17 Glendinning and Muthesius, *Tower Block*, p.97.
18 Peter Hall, *Cities of Tomorrow: An Intellectual History of Urban Planning and Design in the Twentieth Century* (Oxford: Blackwell, 1988), p.93.
19 Jane Jacobs, *The Death and Life of Great American Cities* (London: Jonathan Cape, 1962), p.289.
20 Glendinning and Muthesius, *Tower Block*, p.325.
21 Dennis Hardy, *Utopian England: Community Experiments 1900–1945* (London: Routledge, 2000), p.81.
22 Patricia L. Garside, 'Politics, Ideology and the Issue of Open Space in London, 1939–2000', in Peter Clark (ed.), *The European City and Green Space: London, Stockholm, Helsinki and St Petersburg 1850–2000* (Ashgate: Aldershot, 2006), p.73.

23 Hall, *Cities of Tomorrow*, pp.108–9.
24 Patrick Geddes, *Cities in Evolution* (London: Williams and Norgate, 1949), First published 1915, pp.1–2.
25 Lewis Mumford, *The Culture of Cities* (London: Secker and Warburg, 1940), p.493.
26 Tiratsoo, *Reconstruction, Affluence and Labour Politics*, p.9.
27 LHA, LP/362.5/319, Tom Braddock, *Houses, Rents and the Building Trade* (1953), p.16.
28 Linehan, *Modernism and British Socialism*, pp.94–5.
29 LHA, LP/GS/8, Labour Party, *Festival* (1951), p.7.
30 McKibbin, *Parties and People*, p.144.
31 Malpass, *Housing and the Welfare State*, p.56.
32 *Ibid.*, p.58.
33 Alison Ravetz, *The Government of Space: Town Planning in Modern Society* (London: Faber, 1986), p.32.
34 Stephen Brooke, *Labour's War: The Labour Party during the Second World War* (Oxford: Clarendon, 1992), p.108.
35 LHA, Labour Party Research Department Re/14, Housing and Town Planning Sub-Committee, 'Memorandum on Some of the Problems of Post-War Reconstruction and Suggested Methods for Their Solution', 14 October 1941, p.1; LHA, Labour Party Research Department Re/55, Housing and Town Planning Sub-Committee, 'Preliminary Report', January 1942, p.1.
36 Ravetz, *Government of Space*, pp.77–85.
37 LHA, LP/362.5.53/319, Ted Bramley, *The New London* (1938), p.7.
38 Mort, 'Fantasies of Metropolitan Life', 128–9.
39 Patrick Abercrombie and J. H. Forshaw, *County of London Plan* (London: Macmillan, 1943), p.8.
40 LHA, LP/362.5/318, Birmingham Labour Party, *Homes for the People* (1943), p.7 and p.13.
41 LHA, LP/362.5/318, Labour Party, *Housing and Planning after the War: The Labour Party's Post-War Policy* (1944), p.11.
42 LHA, LP/362.5/318, Communist Party of Great Britain, *Memorandum on Housing* (1944), p.23.
43 Roger Smith, 'Multi-Dwelling Building in Scotland 1750–1970: A Study Based on Housing in the Clyde Valley', in Anthony Sutcliffe (ed.), *Multi-Storey Living: The British Working-Class Experience* (London: Croom Helm, 1974), p.223.
44 LSE Archives (hereafter LSEA), Beveridge Papers, BEVERIDGE/7/2, Lecture by Lord Beveridge to TCPA, 2 October 1959.
45 Ortalano, 'Planning the Urban Future', 481. The first thirteen were: Stevenage, Crawley, Hemel Hempstead, Harlow, Newton Aycliffe, Peterlee, Welwyn Garden City, Hatfield, Basildon, Bracknell and Corby. From 1961: Skelmersdale, Dawley

(redesignated in 1968 as Telford), Redditch, Runcorn, Washington, Milton Keynes, Peterborough, Northampton, Warrington and Central Lancashire.

46 See Mark Clapson, 'The Suburban Aspiration in England Since 1919', *Contemporary British History*, 14:1 (2000), 151–74 at 156; Alan G. V. Simmonds, 'Conservative Governments and the New Town Housing Question in the 1950s', *Urban History*, 28:1 (2001), 65–83 at 82; and Guy Ortalano, *Thatcher's Progress: From Social Democracy to Market Liberalism through an English New Town* (Cambridge: Cambridge University Press, 2019), p.128.
47 Ortalano, *Thatcher's Progress*, p.198.
48 Dunleavy, *The Politics of Mass Housing*, p.70.
49 Shapely, *Politics of Housing*, p.134.
50 LHA, *Socialist Commentary* (September 1958), p.4.
51 LHA, LP/362.5.53, Norman Mackenzie, *New Towns: The Success of Social Planning* (1955), p.1.
52 Clapson, 'The Suburban Aspiration', 156.
53 Ortalano, *Thatcher's Progress*, p.106.
54 LHA, *Labour Woman* (May 1951), pp.104–5.
55 Ravetz, *Government of Space*, pp.71–2.
56 LHA, *Socialist Commentary* (September 1954), p.251.
57 *Ibid.*, p.253.
58 *Ibid.*, p.255. Taylor had been MP for Barnet 1945–50.
59 *Ibid.*, p.254.
60 Stephen Taylor, 'The Suburban Neurosis', *The Lancet* (26 March 1938), p.759.
61 Black, *Political Culture of the Left*, p.127.
62 Ian Nairn, 'Outrage: The Birth of Subtopia Will Be the Death of Us', *Architectural Review* (1 June 1955).
63 Philip Bagwell and Peter Lyth, *Transport in Britain: From Canal Lock to Gridlock* (London: Hambledon, 2002), pp.127–8.
64 LSEA, Shore Papers, SHORE/5/7, National Council of Social Service, *Size and Social Structure of a Town* (1943), p.11.
65 LHA, *Socialist Commentary* (September 1954), p.254.
66 LHA, *Socialist Commentary* (October 1954), p.289.
67 LHA, LP/362.5/318, John Wheatley, *Eight-Pound Cottages* (1915), p.6.
68 *Ibid.*
69 Simon T. Abernethy, 'Opening Up the Suburbs: Workmen's Trains in London 1860–1914', *Urban History*, 42:1 (2015), 70–88.
70 Hall, *Cities of Tomorrow*, p.68.
71 Andrzej Olechnowicz, *Working-Class Housing in England between the Wars: The Becontree Estate* (Oxford: Oxford University Press, 1997), pp.22–3.

72　Colin G. Pooley and Jean Turnbull, 'Commuting, Transport and Urban Form: Manchester and Glasgow in the Mid-Twentieth Century', *Urban History*, 27:3 (2010), 360–83. Pooley and Turnbull note that trams remained prominent in Glasgow for far longer than elsewhere, due to consistent corporation investment in the service, as well as due to popularity amongst commuters.

73　Bagwell and Lyth, *Transport in Britain*, p.109. Morrison's bill was carried into effect by the National Government in 1933, and Morrison, as leader of the LCC Labour group, was able to make full use of it when Labour won control of the LCC in 1934.

74　Olechnowicz, *Working-Class Housing*, p.2.

75　Rosamond Jevons and John Madge, *Housing Estates: A Study of Bristol Corporation Policy and Practice between the Wars* (Bristol, 1946); Ruth Durant, *Watling: A Social Survey* (London, 1939).

76　Jevons and Madge, *Housing Estates*, p.89.

77　LHA, LP/362.5/319, Ted Bramley, *The New London* (1938), p.27.

78　LHA, LP/362.5/319, Ted Bramley, *Lights on London: The Battle for Homes* (1945), pp.50–1.

79　George Orwell, 'The Lion and the Unicorn: Socialism and the English Genius', in George Orwell, *Essays* (London: Penguin, 2000), First published 1941, p.158.

80　Pooley and Turnbull, 'Commuting, Transport and Urban Form', p.366.

81　LHA, *Labour Woman* (August 1956), p.118.

82　Simon Gunn, 'People and the Car: The Expansion of Automobility in Urban Britain, c.1955–70', *Social History*, 38:2 (2013), 220–37 at 224.

83　Hoggart, *Uses of Literacy*, pp.120–1.

84　LHA, LP/362/319, J. B. Cullingworth, *Restraining Urban Growth: The Problem of Overspill* (1960), p.15.

85　*Ibid.*, p.30.

86　WCML, Allaun Papers, *Labour's Voice* (November 1959), p.7.

87　*Tribune* (31 August 1956), p.6.

88　*Ibid.*

89　LHA, Labour Party, *Towns for Our Times* (1960), p.14.

90　N. L. Tranter, *British Population in the Twentieth Century* (Basingstoke: Palgrave Macmillan, 1996), p.59.

91　LHA, Labour Party, *Signposts for the Sixties* (1961), p.23.

92　LHA, Labour Party Research Department Re/103, Home Policy Sub-Committee, 'Planning and the Community Draft Pamphlet', January 1961, p.13.

93　Saumarez Smith, *Boom Cities*, pp.96–7.

94　*Ibid.*, p.95.

95　LHA, Labour Party, *Towns for Our Times* (1960), pp.26–7.

96　LSEA, Shore Papers, SHORE 3/9, Paul Thompson, *Architecture: Art or Social Service?* (1963), p.20.

97 LHA, *Socialist Commentary*, 'Face of Britain' (September 1961), xi. Other contributors included: Ron Bryant; David Eversley; the economist Robin Marris; D. L. Munby; the architect-planner Graeme Shankland; and the noted architects Alison and Peter Smithson, later famous for the brutalist Robin Hood Gardens estate in East London.
98 *Ibid.*, p.3.
99 Jacobs, *Death and Life*, p.338.
100 *Ibid.*, p.339.
101 LHA, Labour Party Research Department Re/103, Home Policy Sub-Committee, 'Planning and the Community Draft Pamphlet', January 1961, p.10.
102 *Ibid.*, p.27.
103 LHA, *Socialist Commentary*, 'Face of Britain' (September 1961), ii.
104 *Ibid.*, vii and xiii.
105 Gunn, 'The Buchanan Report', 530–1.
106 *Ibid.*, 534.
107 Gunn, 'Rise and Fall of British Urban Modernism', 858.
108 LHA, *Socialist Commentary* (June 1959), p.6.
109 LHA, *Socialist Commentary* (September 1961), p.5.
110 LHA, *Socialist Commentary*, 'Face of Britain' (September 1961), vi.
111 *Ibid.*, ii and viii.
112 Glendinning and Muthesius, *Tower Block*, p.42.
113 Owen Hatherley, *Red Metropolis: Socialism and the Government of London* (London: Repeater Books, 2020), p.69.
114 Alison Ravetz, 'From Working Class Tenement to Modern Flat: Local Authorities and Multi-Storey Housing between the Wars', in Anthony Sutcliffe (ed.), *Multi-Storey Living: The British Working-Class Experience* (London: Croom Helm, 1974), p.146. Simon Parker has discussed the LCC's use of flats at the Woodberry Down estate in North London, which built upon an inter-war development in 'From the Slums to the Suburbs: Labour Party Policy, the LCC and the Woodberry Down Estate, Stoke Newington 1934-1961', *London Journal*, 24:2 (1999), 51–69.
115 LHA, LP/362.5/318, Birmingham Labour Party, *Homes for the People* (1943), p.10.
116 Hall, *Cities of Tomorrow*, p.220.
117 LHA, LP/362.5/318, Communist Party of Great Britain, *Memorandum on Housing* (1944), p.22.
118 *Ibid.* The Conservative Secretary of State for Levelling Up, Housing and Communities, Michael Gove, has become an unlikely champion of urban densification, drawing on contemporary urban theory in a 2023 speech setting out government urban priorities: https://www.gov.uk/government/speeches/long-term-plan-for-housing-secretary-of-states-speech (accessed 9 August 2023).
119 Mass-Observation Online, Mass-Observation, 'An Enquiry into People's Homes', 1943, pp.221–3.

120 BCA, AF.32994249, Birmingham Trades Council, 'Observation by Trades Council Delegates of the Housing Plan: Housing for the People!', 23 October 1944. One signatory was George Corbyn Barrow, a left-wing lawyer from the Cadbury family of confectioners.
121 LHA, *Socialist Commentary* (June 1955), p.169.
122 LHA, Labour Party, *Homes for the Future* (1956), p.38.
123 LHA, Labour Party Research Department Re/62, Home Policy Sub-Committee, 'Housing: Looking Ahead', June 1960.
124 LHA, Labour Party, *Towns for Our Times* (1961), p.19.
125 LHA, Labour Party Research Department Rd/748, 'The Quality of Living', May 1964, p.2.
126 *Ibid.*, p.12.
127 Mark Swenarton, 'Developing a New Format for Urban Housing: Neave Brown and the Design of Camden's Fleet Road Estate', *The Journal of Architecture*, 17:6 (2012), 973–1007.
128 Finnimore, *Houses from the Factory*, p.63.
129 LHA, LP/329.12, Ritchie Calder, *Science and Socialism* (1948), p.3.
130 *Ibid.*, p.8.
131 LHA, LP/380.3, British Workers' Delegation, *Russia with Our Own Eyes* (1950), p.72.
132 LHA, LP/380.3, British Workers' Delegation, *What We Saw in Russia* (1952), p.4.
133 Stephen V. Ward, 'Soviet Communism and the British Planning Movement: Rational Learning or Utopian Imagining?', *Planning Perspectives*, 27:4 (2012), 499–524 at 503.
134 LHA, LP/380.3, British Workers' Delegation, *Russia with Our Own Eyes* (1950), p.72.
135 LHA, LP/380.3, British Workers' Delegation, *What We Saw in Russia* (1952), p.26.
136 *Ibid.*, p.24.
137 Kevin Morgan, 'The Problem of the Epoch? Labour and Housing, 1918–51', *Twentieth Century British History*, 16:3 (2005), 227–5 at 233.
138 LHA, LP/328.231, Harry Barham, *Building as a Public Service: A Plan for Reconstruction* (1945), pp.6–9.
139 *Ibid.*, p.10.
140 Glendinning and Muthesius, *Tower Block*, p.190.
141 LHA, Labour Party, *Guide to Post-War Housing Policy* (1948), p.26.
142 *Labour Party Annual Conference Report* (hereafter LPACR) (1950), pp.157-62; LPACR (1953), pp.205–6.
143 *LPACR* (1953), pp.205–6.
144 *LPACR* (1950), pp.157–62. The NFBTO would voluntarily dissolve in 1971 on the mass merger of building unions to form UCATT.
145 Finnimore, *Houses from the Factory*, p.110.

146 Charlie McGuire, Linda Clarke and Christine Wall, '"Through Trade Unionism You Felt a Belonging – You Belonged": Collectivism and the Self-Representation of Building Workers in Stevenage New Town', *Labour History Review*, 81:3 (2016), 211–36 at 218.
147 WCML, Allaun Papers, *Labour's Voice* (December 1956), p.5.
148 LHA, LP/328.231, Sir Richard Coppock, *Eye to the Future* (July 1961), p.7.
149 Glendinning and Muthesius, *Tower Block*, p.216.
150 *Ibid.*, p.318.
151 *Ibid.*, p.217.
152 *Tribune* (29 October 1965), p.7.
153 WCML, Allaun Papers, *Labour's Voice* (July–August 1959), p.3.
154 Shapely, Tanner and Walling, 'Civic Culture and Housing Policy', 419.
155 McGuire, Clarke and Wall, 'Through Trade Unionism You Felt a Belonging – You Belonged', 221.
156 LHA, *Talking Points* (14 October 1966), p.5.
157 *Tribune* (8 August 1969), p.5.
158 Shapely, Tanner and Walling, 'Civic Culture and Housing Policy', 421.
159 Harloe, *The People's Home*, pp.264–5.
160 Gold, *The Practice of Modernism*, p.169.
161 LHA, LP/GS/1, Labour Party, *Let's Go with Labour for the New Britain* (1964), p.15.
162 Glendinning and Muthesius, *Tower Block*, p.216.
163 LHA, *Labour Woman* (January 1966), p.4.
164 Crossman, *Diaries: Vol. I*, p.461.
165 *Ibid.*, pp.535–6.
166 Gold, *The Practice of Modernism*, p.169.
167 Finnimore, *Houses from the Factory*, p.110.
168 *Tribune* (7 November 1969), p.1.
169 Glendinning and Muthesius, *Tower Block*, p.313; Davies, 'Right to Buy', 429.
170 Gyford, *The Politics of Local Socialism*, p.25.
171 Dunleavy, *The Politics of Mass Housing*, p.37.
172 Gold, *The Practice of Modernism*, p.170.
173 Saumarez Smith, 'Central Government and Town-Centre Redevelopment in Britain', 219.
174 Finnimore, *Houses from the Factory*, p.181; Glendinning and Muthesius, *Tower Block*, p.164.
175 Glendinning and Muthesius, *Tower Block*, p.175.
176 LHA, LPRD Re/442, Home Policy Committee, 'The Present Level of New House Building', April 1969, p.2.
177 *Ibid.*
178 *Ibid.*, p.3.

179 Nicholas Bullock, 'West Ham and the Welfare State 1945–70: A Suitable Case for Treatment?', in Mark Swenarton, Tom Avermaete and Dirk van den Heuvel (eds), *Architecture and the Welfare State* (Abingdon: Routledge, 2015), pp.103–5.
180 Glendinning and Muthesius, *Tower Block*, p.313.
181 *Ibid.*
182 Peter Shapely, 'Introduction', in *People and Planning: Report of the Committee on Public Participation in Planning (The Skeffington Report)* (Abingdon: Routledge, 2014), p.viii.
183 Gyford, *Politics of Local Socialism*, p.26.
184 Dennis, *People and Planning*, p.3.
185 Gyford, *Politics of Local Socialism*, p.9.
186 *Tribune* (15 August 1969), p.8.
187 *Tribune* (4 June 1971), p.3.
188 Andreae, 'From Comprehensive Development to Conservation Areas', p.141.
189 Dennis, *People and Planning*, p.47.
190 LHA, *Socialist Commentary*, 'Face of Britain' (September 1961), xix.
191 Clare Griffiths, 'Socialism and the Land Question: Public Ownership and Control in Labour Party Policy, 1918–1950s', in Matthew Cragoe and Paul Readman (eds), *The Land Question in Britain, 1750–1950* (Basingstoke: Palgrave Macmillan, 2010), pp.240–1.
192 *Ibid.*, p.247.
193 Michael Tichelar, 'The Conflict over Property Rights during the Second World War: The Labour Party's Abandonment of Land Nationalization', *Twentieth Century British History*, 14:2 (2003), 165–88 at 167.
194 LHA, Labour Party, *Let Us Face the Future* (1945), p.9.
195 Griffiths, 'Socialism and the Land Question', p.252.
196 Weiler, 'Labour and the Land', 343.
197 O'Hara, *Governing Post-War Britain*, p.139.
198 *Ibid.*
199 Crosland, *The Conservative Enemy*, p.183.
200 Matthew Cragoe and Paul Readman, 'Introduction', in Matthew Cragoe and Paul Readman (eds), *The Land Question in Britain* (Basingstoke, 2010), p.3.
201 *Ibid*, pp.12–13.
202 Michael Tichelar, 'The Labour Party and Land Reform in the Inter-War Period', *Rural History*, 13:1 (2002), 85–101 at 85.
203 *Ibid.*, 87.
204 LHA, John Wheatley, *Eight-Pound Cottages*, p.6.
205 Tichelar, 'The Labour Party and Land Reform', 85.
206 *Ibid.*, 89–91.
207 Griffiths, 'Socialism and the Land Question', 241.

208 *Ibid.*, 246.
209 Tichelar, 'The Labour Party and Land Reform', 92.
210 Roy Douglas, *Land, People and Politics: A History of the Land Question in the United Kingdom 1878–1952* (London: Allison and Busby, 1976), pp.210–11.
211 Griffiths, 'Socialism and the Land Question', 250.
212 LHA, Labour Party Research Department Rd/55, Housing and Town Planning Sub-Committee, 'Preliminary Report', January 1942, p.3.
213 *Ibid.*, p.8.
214 Tichelar, 'The Conflict over Property Rights during the Second World War'.
215 LHA, Labour Party Research Department Rd/55, Housing and Town Planning Sub-Committee, 'Preliminary Report', January 1942, pp.8–9.
216 Tichelar, 'The Conflict over Property Rights', 188.
217 *Ibid.*, 175.
218 Davis, 'Macmillan's Martyr', 130.
219 *Ibid.*
220 LHA, LP/362.5/318, Douglas Brown, *An Englishman's Home* (1945), p.16.
221 Davis, 'Macmillan's Martyr', 134.
222 LHA, Labour Party Research Department Rd/220, Social Services Sub-Committee, 'Town and Country Planning', February 1948, p.1.
223 *Ibid.*
224 Richard Crossman, *The Backbench Diaries of Richard Crossman* (London: Hamish Hamilton, 1981), p.225.
225 Tichelar, 'The Labour Party and Land Reform', 94.
226 LHA, LP/GS/8, *Forward* (29 August 1953), p.1.
227 *Ibid.*
228 Tichelar, 'The Conflict over Property Rights', 175.
229 LHA, LP/GS/8, *Forward* (29 August 1953), p.4.
230 LHA, LP/GS/8, *Forward* (12 September 1953); LHA, LP/GS/8, *Forward* (5 September 1953), 8.
231 Davis, 'Macmillan's Martyr', 139.
232 WCML, Allaun Papers, *Labour's Voice* (September 1960), p.3.
233 *Ibid.*
234 O'Hara, *Governing Post-War Britain*, p.135.
235 *Ibid.*
236 Alison Ravetz, *Remaking Cities* (London, 1980), pp.81–2.
237 *Ibid.*, p.81.
238 LHA, Labour Party, *Towns for Our Times* (1961), p.24.
239 LHA, LP/362.5/319, Frank Allaun, *Britain's Housing Tragedy – And How to End It* (1962), p.7.
240 *Ibid.*
241 LHA, Labour Party, *Signposts for the Sixties* (1960), p.20.

242 Weiler, 'Labour and the Land', 330.
243 LHA, Labour Party, *Signposts for the Sixties* (1960), p.21.
244 *Ibid.*
245 O'Hara, *Governing Post-War Britain*, pp.139–40.
246 LHA, *Socialist Commentary*, 'Face of Britain' (September 1961), x–xx.
247 *Tribune* (30 June 1961), p.3.
248 LHA, *Socialist Commentary*, 'Face of Britain' (September 1961), xxi.
249 *Ibid.*, xxii.
250 Crosland, *The Conservative Enemy*, p.194.
251 LHA, Labour Party Research Department Rd/189, 'The *Socialist Commentary* Land Ownership Proposals: A Comparison with Labour's Scheme', December 1961, p.1.
252 *Ibid.*
253 Other Group members included James MacColl, Arnold Goodman, Michael Stewart, Peter Shore and Prof. Dennis Lloyd.
254 LHA, Labour Party Research Department Rd/244, Study Group on Land Problems, 'Memorandum by the Rt. Hon Lord Silkin, P.C.', April 1962.
255 LHA, Labour Party Research Department Rd/203, North Kensington Labour Party, 'Conclusions of a Study Group on Housing', January 1962.
256 LHA, Labour Party Research Department Rd/230, 'The Labour Party's Policy on Land Ownership', March 1962.
257 Weiler, 'Labour and the Land', 333.
258 WCML, Allaun Papers, *Labour's Northern Voice* (January 1962), p.1.
259 O'Hara, *Governing Post-War Britain*, p.141.
260 *Ibid.*, p.142.
261 Crossman, *Diaries: Vol. I*, p.101.
262 Weiler, 'Labour and the Land', 336.
263 *Ibid.*, 338–9.
264 Davis, 'Macmillan's Martyr', 140.
265 O'Hara, *Governing Post-War Britain*, 142.
266 LHA, Labour Party, *Report of the Housing Policy Study Group* (August 1969), p.24.
267 *Ibid.*
268 *Ibid.*
269 LHA, *Labour Woman* (May 1967), p.87.
270 O'Hara, *Governing Post-War Britain*, p.142; Weiler, 'Labour and the Land', 341.
271 Ravetz, *Remaking Cities*, pp.88–9.
272 Peter Weiler, 'Labour and the Land: The Making of the Community Land Act, 1976', *Contemporary British History*, 27:4 (2013), 389–420 at 407.
273 Labour Party, *It's Time for Real Change* (2019), p.78.
274 Ravetz, *Council Housing and Culture*, p.4.
275 Drucker, *Doctrine and Ethos*, pp.82–3.

Chapter 3

1. LHA, LP/362.5/319, Labour Party, *A Guide to Post-War Housing Policy* (1948), p.18.
2. Francis, *Ideas and Policies under Labour*, p.130.
3. LHA, Labour Party, *A Guide to Post-War Housing Policy* (1948), p.18.
4. LHA, Labour Party Research Department, *Partnership* (October 1965), p.1.
5. A. E. Holmans, *Historical Statistics of Housing in Britain* (2005). This figure is drawn from official Ministry of Housing data, with the author calculating that in 1971 the tenurial mix by households was as follows: 50.7 per cent owner-occupied; 28.2 per cent local authority; 0.9 per cent housing associations; 11 per cent private rented.
6. Dorling, *All That Is Solid*, p.14.
7. Daunton, *Property-Owning Democracy*, p.4.
8. Tony Crook and Peter A. Kemp, *Transforming Private Landlords: Housing, Markets & Public Policy* (Oxford: Oxford University Press, 2011), p.54.
9. Notable exceptions to this rule include, on the private landlord, Shapely, *Politics of Housing* and Weiler, 'Labour and the Land'. On owner-occupation: Jackson, 'Revisionism Reconsidered'; and Black, *Political Culture of the Left*.
10. Malpass, *Housing and the Welfare State*, p.139.
11. Crosland, *The Conservative Enemy*, pp.189–90.
12. Owen Jones, *Chavs: The Demonization of the Working Class* (London: Verso, 2011), p.60.
13. Ross McKibbin, 'A Brief Supremacy: The Fragmentation of the Two-Party System in British Politics, c. 1950–2015', *Twentieth Century British History*, 27:3 (2016), 450–69 at 463.
14. Szreter, 'Health, Class, Place and Politics', 48.
15. See Ravetz, *Council Housing and Culture*; Malpass, *Housing and the Welfare State*; Shapely, *Politics of Housing*; Harloe, *The People's Home*. There has been a popular resurgence of the 'working-class triumph' interpretation, see especially John Boughton, *Municipal Dreams: The Rise and Fall of Council Housing* (London: Verso, 2018).
16. LHA, *Talking Points* (5 March 1955), p.32.
17. Hansard, Debates, Commons, vol.426, col.870 (30 July 1946), http://hansard.millbanksystems.com/commons/1946/jul/30/housing (accessed 14 June 2016).
18. *Ibid.*
19. Ravetz, 'From Working Class Tenement to Modern Flat', p.130.
20. Brooke, *Labour's War*, p.315.
21. Malpass, *Housing and the Welfare State*, p.67.
22. Nicklaus Thomas-Symonds, *Nye: The Political Life of Aneurin Bevan* (London: IB Tauris, 2016), p.152.

23 Malpass, *Housing and the Welfare State*, p.68.
24 *Ibid.*, p.65.
25 Francis, *Ideas and Policies under Labour*, p.124.
26 *Ibid.*, pp.72–3.
27 LHA, LP/GS/8, *People's Pictorial*, Vol. 2 (1952), p.14.
28 Malpass, *Housing and the Welfare State*, p.87.
29 LHA, *Socialist Commentary* (May 1950), p.106. Crane would also be a founding member of Amnesty International in 1961.
30 *Ibid.*
31 Harloe, *The People's Home*, p.184.
32 LHA, *Socialist Commentary* (May 1950), pp.106–7.
33 LHA, LPRD Rd/345, 'Differential Rents, Pooled Rents, Rent Rebates', February 1950, p.1.
34 *Ibid.*, pp.2–3.
35 *Ibid.*, pp.10–11.
36 *Ibid.*, p.10.
37 LHA, LP/380.3, British Workers' Delegation to the USSR, *Russia with Our Own Eyes* (1950), p.105.
38 LHA, LP/380.3, British Workers' Delegation to the USSR, *What We Saw in Russia* (1952), p.24.
39 LHA, *Labour Woman* (June 1954), p.129.
40 *Ibid.*
41 LHA, *Labour Woman* (April 1954), p.78.
42 *Ibid.*
43 Malpass, *Housing and the Welfare State*, p.87.
44 LHA, LP/362.5/319, James MacColl, *Policy for Housing* (1954), p.19.
45 LHA, LP/362.5/319, David Eversley, *Rents and Social Policy* (1955), p.24.
46 *Ibid.*, p.30.
47 LHA, *Socialist Commentary* (February 1954), p.52.
48 *Ibid.*
49 LHA, LP/362.5/319, David Eversley, *Rents and Social Policy* (1955), p.34.
50 Crosland, *Future of Socialism*, p.145.
51 Peter Baldwin, *The Politics of Social Solidarity: Class Bases of the European Welfare State 1875–1975* (Cambridge: Cambridge University Press, 1990), pp.290–3.
52 Crosland, *Future of Socialism*, p.143.
53 Baldwin, *Politics of Social Solidarity*, p.112.
54 WCML, Allaun Papers, *Labour's Northern Voice* (June 1955), p.5.
55 *Ibid.*
56 WCML, Allaun Papers, *Labour's Northern Voice* (July 1955), p.2. Dell would later become MP for Birkenhead from 1964 to 1974, joining the SDP when it formed.

57 Zoe Doye, 'The Labour Party and Public Housing, 1951–64: An Examination of National Policy and Its Implementation in London' (PhD thesis, Birkbeck College University of London, 2004), p.94.
58 LHA, *Labour Woman* (August 1955), p.127.
59 LHA, *Labour Woman* (October 1955), p.155.
60 *Tribune* (10 February 1956), p.9.
61 *Tribune* (17 February 1956), p.1.
62 *Ibid.*
63 Peggy Duff, *Left, Left, Left: A Personal Account of Six Protest Campaigns, 1945–65* (London: Allison and Busby, 1971), p.90.
64 LHA, Local Government Box, Letter from Watford Borough Council Labour Group to Local Government Officer, 7 January 1961.
65 LHA, Local Government Box, Letter from Local Government Officer to Watford Borough Council Labour Group, 11 January 1961.
66 *Ibid.*
67 LHA, Local Government Box, Letter from Local Government Officer to W.B. Powell, 15 October 1962.
68 Shapely, *Politics of Housing*, p.166.
69 *Tribune* (17 February 1956), p.10.
70 Duff, *Left, Left, Left*, p.93.
71 *Ibid.*, p.96.
72 *Ibid.*
73 Donnison, *The Government of Housing*, p.256.
74 *Ibid.*, p.268.
75 LHA, Labour Party Research Department Re/124, 'Housing Policies: A Review', April 1967.
76 WCML, Allaun Papers, *Labour's Northern Voice* (December 1963), p.4.
77 *Ibid.*
78 Harloe, *The People's Home*, p.287; Jones, 'Slum Clearance, Privatization and Residualization', p.528.
79 LHA, *Talking Points* (31 July 1970), p.2.
80 Donnison, pp.192–3.
81 *Daily Mirror* (7 February 1966), p.2.
82 Crossman, *Diaries: Vol. I*, p.449.
83 *Tribune* (11 February 1966), p.8.
84 LHA, Labour Party Research Department Re/399, James MacColl, 'A Rent Policy', January 1969, p.1.
85 *Ibid.*
86 *Ibid.*, p.2.
87 LHA, Labour Party Research Department Re/400, W. S. Hilton, 'Comments on Re/369', January 1969, p.1.

88 LHA, Labour Party Research Department Re/486, Housing Policy Study Group, 'Report of the Housing Policy Study Group', June 1969, p.9.
89 Ibid.
90 Baldwin, *The Politics of Social Solidarity*, pp.156–7.
91 LHA, *Talking Points* (1970), p.1.
92 Malpass, *Housing and the Welfare State*, pp.97–8.
93 Ibid., p.99.
94 Allaun, *No Place Like Home*, p.169.
95 Shapely, *The Politics of Housing*, p.44.
96 *The Times* (25 September 1958), p.6.
97 Charles Dickens, *Bleak House* (London: Penguin, 1994), First published 1852, p.202.
98 *The Times* (25 September 1958), p.6.
99 Ibid.
100 Malpass, *Housing and the Welfare State*, p.2.
101 Crook and Kemp, *Transforming Private Landlords*, p.54.
102 Ibid., p.8. The only figures obtainable pre-1979 are for England and Wales rather than UK-wide.
103 Davis, 'Rents and Race in 1960s London'; Alan G. V. Simmonds, 'Raising Rachman: The Origins of the Rent Act, 1957', *The Historical Journal*, 45:4 (2002), 843–68; Weiler, 'Labour and the Land.' I am grateful to *Twentieth Century British History* for allowing me to reproduce in this chapter much of: Phil Child, 'Landlordism, Rent Regulation and the Labour Party in Mid-Twentieth Century Britain, 1950–64', *Twentieth Century British History*, 29:1 (2018), 79–103.
104 Crosland, *The Conservative Enemy*, p.190.
105 LHA, LP/362.5/318, John Wheatley, *Eight-Pound Cottages for Glasgow Citizens* (1913), p.4.
106 J. J. Smyth, *Labour in Glasgow, 1896–1936: Socialism, Suffrage, Sectarianism* (East Linton: Tuckwell Press, 2000), p.69.
107 Shapely, *The Politics of Housing*, p.33.
108 LHA, LP/GS/8, *Town Crier* (17 March 1945), p.8.
109 Francis, *Ideas and Policies under Labour*, p.130.
110 Malpass, *Housing and the Welfare State*, p.65.
111 Carter, 'Building the Divided City',162–3.
112 Yelling, 'Public Policy, Urban Renewal and Property Ownership', 51–4.
113 LHA, LP/GS/8, *Town Crier* (17 March 1945), p.8.
114 Simmonds, 'Raising Rachman', 853.
115 Ibid., 849.
116 Davis, 'Rents and Race in 1960s London', 74.
117 Simmonds, 'Raising Rachman', 848.
118 Shapely, *The Politics of Housing*, p.38.

119 LHA, LP/362.52/319, D. L. Munby, *The Rent Problem* (1952), p.15.
120 *Ibid.*, p.20.
121 LHA, LP/GS/8, *Forward* (June, 1953), p.4.
122 Housing Repairs and Rent Act 1954, p.9, http://www.legislation.gov.uk/ukpga/Eliz2/2-3/53/contents (accessed 8 May 2016).
123 WCML, Allaun Papers, *Labour's Northern Voice* (December 1953), p.1.
124 *Ibid.*
125 LHA, LP/GS/1, Labour Party, *Challenge to Britain* (1953), p.28.
126 Anthony Sutcliffe and Roger Smith, *History of Birmingham, Volume III: Birmingham 1939–1970* (London: Oxford University Press, 1974), p.230.
127 WCML, Allaun Papers, *Labour's Northern Voice* (June 1953), p.3.
128 *LPACR* (1954), pp.109–111.
129 Hansard, Debates, Commons, vol.526, col.1066 (13 April 1954), http://hansard.millbanksystems.com/commons/1954/apr/13/housing-repairs-and-rents-bill#S5CV0526P0_19540413_HOC_458 (accessed online 14 June 2016).
130 LHA, LP/362.5/319, James MacColl, *Policy for Housing* (1954), pp.3–4.
131 *Ibid.*, p.24.
132 Weiler, 'Labour and the Land', 323.
133 LHA, Labour Party Research Department Rd/491, Social Services Sub-Committee, Michael Young and Peter Willmott, 'Seven Million Bathrooms: Interim Report to Labour Party NEC', March 1955, p.1. It is possible that Young and Willmott arrived at the figure of 7 million by counting all rented properties.
134 *Ibid.*, p.3.
135 LHA, LP/362.52/319, David Eversley, *Rents and Social Policy* (1955), p.13.
136 LHA, Labour Party Research Department Rd/491, Social Services Sub-Committee, Michael Young and Peter Willmott, 'Seven Million Bathrooms: Interim Report to Labour Party NEC', March 1955, pp.3–4.
137 LHA, LP/362.52/319, David Eversley, *Rents and Social Policy* (1955), pp.14–15.
138 *Daily Mail* (29 April 1955), p.1.
139 LHA, *Talking Points* (1956).
140 Weiler, 'Labour and the Land', p.324.
141 LHA, Labour Party Research Department Re/54, Housing Study Group, 'Discussion of Synopsis for the Research Project on Housing', 2 February 1956.
142 LHA, Labour Party Research Department HF/421, Labour Party, *Homes for the Future* (1956), p.15.
143 *Tribune* (29 June 1956), p.3. Bromo-seltzer was a brand of anti-acid, used as a hangover cure.
144 Crosland, *The Future of Socialism*, p.144.
145 LHA, LP/362.5/319, James MacColl, *Plan for Rented Houses* (1957), p.1.
146 Simmonds, 'Raising Rachman', 852.

147 Davis, 'Rents and Race in 1960s London', 75.
148 *Ibid.*, 74.
149 *Ibid.*, 76.
150 *Tribune* (9 February 1957), p.9.
151 *Ibid.*
152 Crook and Kemp, *Transforming Private Landlords*, p.16.
153 *Ibid.*, pp.16-7.
154 *Tribune* (9 July 1957), p.5.
155 *LPACR* (1957), pp.98–104.
156 LHA, *Labour Organiser* (March 1957), p.58.
157 WCML, Allaun Papers, *Labour's Northern Voice* (October 1957), p.4.
158 LHA, LP/362.52/319, Labour Research Department, *Tenant's Guide to the 1957 Rent Act* (1957).
159 WCML, Allaun Papers, *Labour's Northern Voice* (October 1957), p.4.
160 Weiler, 'Labour and the Land', 326.
161 *Tribune* (12 July 1957), p.1.
162 *Daily Mail* (13 November 1958), p.1.
163 *Daily Mail* (6 November 1958), p.9; *Daily Mail* (13 November 1958), p.1.
164 LHA, Local Government Box, Correspondence between Uxbridge CLP and Labour Party Research Department, 7 April 1959.
165 LSEA, MacColl Papers, MACCOLL/266, Harry Dickens, *Whose Home?* (1958), pp.7-8.
166 *The Manchester Guardian* (25 September 1958), p.8.
167 *Daily Mail* (25 September 1958), p.6.
168 *The Manchester Guardian* (25 September 1958), p.8.
169 LHA, LP/362.5/319, James MacColl, *Plan for Rented Houses* (1957), p.20.
170 LSEA, MacColl Papers, MACCOLL/266, Harry Dickens, *Whose Home?* (1958), p.22.
171 LHA, LP/362.5/319, Labour Party, *100 Questions Asked and Answered on Labour's Housing Policy* (1958), p.17.
172 Weiler, 'Labour and the Land', 327.
173 *Ibid.*
174 LHA, LP/GS/3, Campaign Committee, 'Draft Letter from Morgan Phillips to *The Times* on Labour Housing Policy', 16 December 1958.
175 WCML, Allaun Papers, *Labour's Northern Voice* (September 1958), p.5.
176 LHA, LP/362.5/319, James MacColl, *Plan for Rented Houses* (1957), p.7.
177 LSEA, MacColl Papers, MACCOLL/259, LPRD comments to *Plan for Rented Houses* (July 1957), 4.
178 LHA, LP/362.5/319, Labour Party, *100 Questions Asked and Answered on Labour's Housing Policy* (1958), p.16.

179 M. J. Barnett, *The Politics of Legislation: The Rent Act 1957* (London: Littlehampton Book Services, 1969), p.235.
180 *Ibid.*
181 Labour Party, 'Britain Belongs to You', 1 (1959), https://www.youtube.com/watch?v=dEEwn21Ip_k&t=185s (accessed 26 March 2022).
182 Barnett, *The Politics of Legislation*, p.235.
183 LHA, Labour Party Research Department Re/272, Local Government Sub-Committee, 'Note by Ian Mikardo MP on cost of municipalising houses', January 1958.
184 LHA, LP/362.5/319, Labour Party, *100 Questions Asked and Answered on Labour's Housing Policy* (1958) p.17.
185 LHA, Labour Party Research Department Re/272, Local Government Sub-Committee, 'Note by Ian Mikardo MP on Cost of Municipalising Houses', January 1958.
186 LHA, Local Government Box, Correspondence between Uxbridge CLP and Labour Party Research Department, 7 April 1959.
187 WCML, Allaun Papers, *Labour's Northern Voice* (November 1960), p.3.
188 *Ibid.*
189 WCML, Allaun Papers, *Labour's Northern Voice* (March 1961), p.7.
190 LHA, Labour Party Research Department Rd/297, Local Government Sub-Committee 'Municipalisation: Defining Our New Approach', July 1962.
191 Weiler, 'Labour and the Land', 334.
192 Shapely, *The Politics of Housing*, p.39.
193 LHA, Labour Party Research Department Rd/297, Local Government Sub-Committee 'Municipalisation: defining our new approach', July 1962.
194 LHA, Local Government Box, 'Letter from J. G. Davies, Swansea East Labour Association to Labour Party Research Department', 16 October 1961.
195 *Ibid.*
196 LHA, Local Government Box, 'Letter from Labour Party Research Department to J. G. Davies, Swansea East Labour Association', 18 October 1961.
197 *Ibid.*
198 LHA, LP/362.52/319, Labour Party, *Labour's Plan for Old Houses* (1963), p.5.
199 Myra Woolf, *The Housing Survey 1964 in England and Wales* (London: Her Majesty's Stationery Office, 1967), p.78.
200 LHA, LP/362.52/319, Labour Party, *Labour's Plan for Old Houses* (1963), p.7.
201 Davis, 'Rents and Race in 1960s London', 1–2.
202 *Ibid.*, p.77.
203 LHA, *Labour Woman* (September 1963), p.3.
204 *Tribune* (6 September 1963), p.5.
205 LHA, LP/GS/8, *Baron's Court Citizen* (June 1963), p.7.

206 LHA, Local Government Box, 'Letter from Mrs R Chambers to Harold Wilson', 23 February 1963.
207 *Ibid.*
208 *Ibid.*
209 LHA, Local Government Box, 'Letter from Local Government Officer to Mrs R Chambers', 11 March 1963.
210 LHA, *Socialist Commentary* (March 1965), p.11. Richard would later become a European Commissioner, and has sat as a Labour peer since 1989.
211 *Ibid.*, p.13.
212 Malpass, *Housing and the Welfare State*, p.92.
213 Daunton, *Property-Owning Democracy*, p.65.
214 Crossman, *Diaries: Vol. I*, p.389.
215 Malpass, *Housing and the Welfare State*, p.93.
216 Hansard, Debates, Commons, vol.710, col.80 (5 April 1965), https://api.parliament.uk/historic-hansard/commons/1965/apr/05/rent-bill#S5CV0710P0_19650405_HOC_284 (accessed 26 March 2022).
217 LHA, Labour Party Research Department Re/124, 'Housing Policies: A Review', April 1967, p.7.
218 *Ibid.*, p.8.
219 Richard Crossman, *The Diaries of a Cabinet Minister: Volume II: 1966–68* (London: Hamish Hamilton, 1976), p.598.
220 LHA, *Socialist Commentary* (December 1968), pp.26–8.
221 LHA, Labour Party Research Department Re/349, Home Policy Sub-Committee, Frank Allaun MP, '*Old Houses into New Homes*: Rent Proposals', September 1968.
222 *Ibid.*
223 LHA, Labour Party Research Department Re/352, Home Policy Sub-Committee, Anthony Greenwood MP, '*Old Houses into New Homes*: Rent Proposals', September 1968.
224 *Ibid.*
225 LHA, *Labour Woman* (April 1969), p.64.
226 LHA, Labour Party Research Department Re/448, Housing Policy Study Group 'Housing: Report of the Housing Policy Study Group', June 1969, p.7.
227 *Ibid.*, p.8.
228 Crook and Kemp, *Transforming Private Landlords*, p.54.
229 LHA, LP/362.5/320, Fabian Society, *The End of the Private Landlord* (September 1973), p.1.
230 *Ibid.*, p.19; Crook and Kemp, *Transforming Private Landlords*, p.54.
231 LHA, *Socialist Commentary* (January 1956), p.16.
232 *Ibid.*, pp.16–17.

233 See: Weiler, 'Conservative's Search for a Middle Way in Housing' and Davies, '"Right to Buy"'.
234 See: Jackson, 'Revisionism Reconsidered'; Jackson, *Equality and the British Left*.
235 Jackson, 'Revisionism Reconsidered', 423.
236 Ortalano, *Thatcher's Progress*, p.224.
237 Malpass, *Housing and the Welfare State*, p.49.
238 Peter Scott, *The Making of the Modern British Home: The Suburban Semi and Family Life between the Wars* (Oxford: Oxford University Press, 2013), p.8.
239 George Orwell, *Coming Up for Air* (London: Penguin, 1990), First published 1939, p.9.
240 Davies, '"Right to Buy"', 424.
241 Weiler, 'Conservatives' Search for a Middle Way in Housing', 362.
242 Davis, 'Macmillan's Martyr', 140.
243 Malpass, *Housing and the Welfare State*, p.51.
244 John Campbell, *Nye Bevan and the Mirage of British Socialism* (London: Weidenfeld and Nicholson, 1987); Francis, *Ideas and Policies under Labour*, pp.120–3.
245 LHA, Labour Party, *A Guide to Post-War Housing Policy* (1948), p.8.
246 LHA, LP/362.5/318, George Woodcock, *Homes or Hovels: The Housing Problem and Its Solution* (1944), p.6. Woodcock was the editor of the political periodical *Now* and a contemporary of George Orwell.
247 LHA, LP/362.5/318, Birmingham Borough Labour Party, *Homes for the People! Labour's Policy for Birmingham's Need* (1943), p.17.
248 Lawrence, 'Class, Affluence and the Study of Everyday Life', 276.
249 LHA, Labour Party, *A Guide to Post-War Housing Policy* (1948), p.19.
250 LHA, Labour Party, *Challenge to Britain* (1953), p.28.
251 LHA, LP/362.5/319, James MacColl, *Policy for Housing* (1954), p.13.
252 WCML, Allaun Papers, *Labour's Northern Voice* (January 1953), p.8.
253 *Ibid.*, p.8.
254 LSEA, MacColl Papers, MACCOLL/256, Letter from Local Government Officer to W.T. Rodgers, 24 July 1957, p.3.
255 LHA, LP/362.5/318, Victory for Socialism, *A Roof over Your Head? Socialist Policy for Housing and Rents* (1958), p.5.
256 LSEA, MacColl Papers, MACCOLL/266, Harry Dickens, *Whose Home?* (1958), p.17.
257 LHA, LP/362.5/319, James MacColl, *Policy for Housing* (1954), p.14.
258 LHA, LP/362.5/318, D. L. Munby, *Home Ownership* (1957), p.23.
259 Herbert Tout, *The Standard of Living in Bristol: A Preliminary Report of the Work of the University of Bristol Social Survey* (Bristol: Arrowsmith, 1938), p.29.
260 Dennis, *People and Planning*, pp.145–8.

261 Orwell, *Coming Up for Air*, p.11.
262 LHA, LP/362.52/319, David Eversley, *Rents and Social Policy* (1955), p.16.
263 LHA, LP/362.5/318, D. L. Munby, *Home Ownership* (1957), p.23.
264 LHA, Labour Party, *Homes for the Future* (1956), p.45.
265 LHA, LP/362.5/319, Labour Party, *100 Questions Asked and Answered on Labour's Housing Policy* (1958), pp.12–13.
266 LHA, LP/362.5/319, James MacColl, *Policy for Housing* (1954), p.17.
267 LHA, LP/362.5/318, Victory for Socialism, *A Roof over Your Head? Socialist Policy for Housing and Rents* (1958), pp.8–9.
268 *Tribune* (17 February 1956), p.4.
269 Eric Shaw, *Discipline and Discord in the Labour Party: The Politics of Managerial Control in the Labour Party, 1951–87* (Manchester: Manchester University Press, 1988), pp.53–5.
270 LHA, LP/362.5/318, Victory for Socialism, *A Roof over Your Head? Socialist Policy for Housing and Rents* (1958), pp.8–9.
271 *Tribune* (3 July 1955), p.5.
272 *Tribune* (17 February 1956), p.10.
273 Davies, '"Right to Buy"', 425.
274 *Ibid.*, 429.
275 LHA, *Talking Points* (15 December 1951), p.118.
276 LHA, LP/362.5/318, Labour Party, *Facts on Housing, Labour Party* (March 1965), p.6.
277 Jones, 'Slum Clearance, Privatization and Residualization', 531.
278 Davies, '"Right to Buy"', 429.
279 *LPACR* (1967), p.152.
280 LHA, *Talking Points* (1967), p.8.
281 WCML, Allaun Papers, *Labour's Northern Voice* (December 1969), p.3.
282 BCA, 329.94249, Birmingham Borough Labour Party, 'The Housing Diary' (1967).
283 Davies, '"Right to Buy"', 434.
284 *Tribune* (20 December 1968), p.5.
285 Crosland, *The Conservative Enemy*, p.39.
286 Jackson, 'Revisionism Reconsidered', 425.
287 LHA, LP/GS/1, Labour Party, *Signposts for the Sixties* (1961), pp.9–10.
288 LHA, *Labour Woman* (October 1961), p.4.
289 *Ibid.*, p.6.
290 LHA, *Socialist Commentary* (August 1963), p.9.
291 LHA, *Socialist Commentary* (May 1964), p.24.
292 Donnison, *The Government of Housing*, p.263.
293 LHA, *Socialist Commentary* (May 1964), p.25.

294 Malpass, *Housing and the Welfare State*, p.96.
295 LHA, Labour Party Research Department Re/448, Housing Policy Study Group 'Housing: Report of the Housing Policy Study Group', August 1969, p.7.
296 Glendinning and Muthesius, *Tower Block*, p.183.
297 LHA, Labour Party Research Department Re/124, 'Housing Policies: A Review', April 1967.
298 LHA, Labour Party Research Department Re/400, 'Comments on Re.369, by W.S. Hilton MP', January 1969.
299 *Ibid.*
300 Martin Daunton, *Just Taxes: The Politics of Taxation in Britain, 1914–1979* (Cambridge: Cambridge University Press, 2002), p.262.
301 LHA, *Talking Points* (31 July 1970), p.5.
302 *Tribune* (4 September 1970), p.12.
303 *Tribune* (11 September 1970), p.11.
304 *Ibid.*, p.12.
305 LHA, Labour Party Research Department Rd/208, Housing Finance Working Group, A. Crosland, 'Towards a Labour Housing Policy', December 1971.
306 Bevan, *In Place of Fear*, p.118.
307 LHA, LP/GS/8, *Town Crier* (4 February 1950), p.10.
308 David Edgerton, *The Rise and Fall of the British Nation: A Twentieth Century History* (St Ives: Allen Lane, 2018), p.455.
309 *London Review of Books*, 36:1 (9 January 2014), 7–16 at 10.
310 Department for Communities and Local Government, *English Housing Survey 2013–4* (10 July 2013), p.25, https://www.gov.uk/government/uploads/system/uploads/attachment_data/file/461439/EHS_Households_2013-14.pdf (accessed 25 April 2016).
311 LHA, LP/362.5/319, James MacColl, *Plan for Rented Houses* (1957), p.31.
312 Department for Communities and Local Government, *English Housing Survey 2013–14*, p.25.
313 Crosland, *The Conservative Enemy*, p.195.
314 LHA, LP/GS/8, *Town Crier* (27 October 1945), p.2.
315 Crosland, *The Conservative Enemy*, p.195.
316 LSEA, MacColl Papers, MACCOLL/266, Harry Dickens, *Whose Home?* (1958), p.18.
317 LHA, Labour Party Research Department Rd/203, North Kensington Labour Party, 'Conclusions of a Study Group on Housing', January 1962.
318 LHA, *Socialist Commentary* (November 1960), p.25.
319 Meek, 'Where Will We Live', 7–16.
320 LHA, LP/GS/1, Labour Party, *Signposts for the Sixties* (1961), p.8.

Chapter 4

1. LHA, *Socialist Commentary* (June 1955), p.168. An 'Ascot' was a gas-powered water heater, with gas heating a novelty to those who had previously used coal fires.
2. Jones, *The Working Class*, p.82.
3. Jon Lawrence, *Me, Me, Me? The Search for Community in Post-War England* (Oxford: Oxford University Press, 2019); Lise Butler, *Michael Young, Social Science, and the British Left, 1945–1970* (Oxford: Oxford University Press, 2020).
4. Dominic Sandbrook offers an interesting example of this, critiquing Young and Willmott's attack on suburbia and implying that 'affluent' suburbia was regarded more positively than 'traditional' working-class communities in his history of 1950s Britain: Sandbrook, *Never Had It So Good*, pp.124–5. He went on to suggest that the end of the 'traditional' working-class community was a tragedy in his history of Britain in the early 1970s, taking on later sociological work heavily critical of council estates: Dominic Sandbrook, *State of Emergency: The Way We Were: Britain 1970–1974* (London: Allen Lane, 2011), pp.358–9.
5. Hatherley, *New Kind of Bleak*, xxiii. Joe Moran has also examined this 'Arcadia' in: Joe Moran, 'The Strange Birth of Middle England', *Political Quarterly*, 76:2 (April 2005), 159–313.
6. Burnett, *Social History of Housing*, pp.218–20.
7. LHA, LP/362.5/318, John Wheatley, *Eight-Pound Cottages for Glasgow Citizens* (1913), p.6 and p.13.
8. Peter Clark and Jussi S. Jauhiainen, 'Introduction', in Peter Clark (ed.), *The European City and Green Space: London, Stockholm, Helsinki and St Petersburg 1850–2000* (Aldershot: Ashgate, 2006), p.24.
9. Francis, *Ideas and Policies under Labour*, p.130.
10. Glendinning and Muthesius, *Tower Block*, p.154.
11. LHA, LP/362.5/318, Birmingham Borough Labour Party, *Homes for the People! Labour's Policy for Birmingham's Need* (1943), p.9.
12. LHA, LP/362.5/319, Ted Bramley, *Lights on London: The Battle for Homes* (1945), pp.46–8.
13. Ravetz, 'From Working Class Tenement to Modern Flat', p.138.
14. Brooke, 'Slumming in Swinging London', 431–6.
15. See: Jones, *The Working Class*, p.77; Langhamer, 'Meanings of Home'; Lawrence, *Me, Me Me?* (2019); Lawrence, 'Class, Affluence and the Study of Everyday Life'; Jon Lawrence, 'The British Sense of Class', *Journal of Contemporary History*, 35:2 (2000), 307–18 at 316; Wetherell, *Foundations*.
16. Lawrence, 'British Sense of Class', 318.

17 Jon Lawrence, 'Inventing the "Traditional Working Class": A Re-analysis of Interview Notes from Young and Willmott's *Family and Kinship in East London*', *Historical Journal*, 59:2 (2016), 567–93 at 593.
18 LHA, *Socialist Commentary* (September 1959), p.8.
19 Richard Jobson, '"Waving the Banners of a Bygone Age", Nostalgia and Labour's Clause IV Controversy, 1959–60', *Contemporary British History*, 27:2 (2013), 123–44 at 125.
20 Black, *Political Culture of the Left*, p.34.
21 Stacey, *Tradition and Change*, p.10.
22 Leo Kuper, 'Blueprint for Living Together', in Leo Kuper (ed.), *Living in Towns* (London: Cresset Press, 1953), p.170.
23 Lawrence, 'Class, Affluence and the Study of Everyday Life', 274.
24 Durant, *Watling*, ix; E. P. Thompson, *The Making of the English Working Class* (London: Vintage Books, 1980), first published 1963, p.10.
25 Durant, *Watling*, p.15; Jevons and Madge, *Housing Estates*, p.70.
26 Patricia L. Garside, 'Citizenship, Civil Society and Quality of Life: Sutton Model Dwellings Estates 1919–38', in Robert Colls and Richard Rodger (eds), *Cities of Ideas: Civil Society and Urban Governance in Britain 1800–2000* (Aldershot: Aldgate, 2004), p.261.
27 Beach and Tiratsoo, 'The Planners and the Public', p.528.
28 Linehan, *Modernism and British Socialism*, p.83.
29 LHA, Labour Party Research Department Re/55, Housing and Town Planning Sub-Committee, 'Preliminary Report', January 1942, p.5.
30 For work mostly conducted in the 1950s, see J. M. Mogey, *Family and Neighbourhood: Two Studies in Oxford* (Oxford: Oxford University Press, 1956); Michael Young and Peter Willmott, *Family and Kinship in East London* (London: Routledge and Kegan Paul, 1957); Michael Young and Peter Willmott, *Family and Class in a London Suburb* (London: Routledge and Kegan Paul, 1960); Peter Willmott, *The Evolution of a Community: A Study of Dagenham after Forty Years* (London: Routledge and Kegan Paul, 1963); Margaret Stacey, *Tradition and Change: A Study of Banbury* (Oxford: Oxford University Press, 1960); Hilda Jennings, *Societies in the Making: A Study of Development and Redevelopment Within a County Borough* (London: Routledge and Kegan Paul, 1962). For work mostly conducted in the 1960s, see Dennis, *People and Planning*; Pearl Jephcott, *Homes in High Flats: Some of the Human Problems Involved in Multi-storey Housing* (Edinburgh: Oliver and Boyd, 1971).
31 Butler, *Michael Young*, p.57.
32 Quoted in Butler, *Michael Young*, p.108.
33 Mike Savage, *Identities and Social Change since 1945: The Politics of Method* (Oxford: Oxford University Press, 2010), p.158.

34 *Ibid.*, p.118.
35 LHA, LP/362.5/318, Douglas Brown, *An Englishman's Home* (1945), p.26.
36 George Orwell, *The Road to Wigan Pier* (London: Penguin, 2001), first published 1937, pp.65–7.
37 Harloe, *The People's Home*, p.15. For a recent narrative that leans towards this sort of teleology, see Dorling, *All That Is Solid*.
38 Goss, *Local Labour and Local Government*, p.58.
39 Mort, 'Fantasies of Metropolitan Life', 150.
40 Lawrence, 'Class, Affluence and the Study of Everyday Life', 289.
41 Turner, 'A Land Fit for Tories to Live In', 203.
42 LHA, LP/362.5/320, Anthony Crosland, *Towards a Labour Housing Policy* (1971), p.3.
43 *Ibid.*, p.17.
44 For a discussion on the lack of consultation with residents due to be rehoused, see Shapely, *The Politics of Housing*.
45 Jones, *The Working Class*, pp.96–7.
46 *Ibid.*, p.110.
47 Shapely, *The Politics of Housing*, p.29.
48 Harloe, *The People's Home*, p.184.
49 LHA, LP/362.5/319, Labour Party, *A Guide to Post-War Housing Policy* (1948), p.22.
50 Francis, *Ideas and Policies under Labour*, p.130.
51 LSEA, Fabian Society, FABIAN/291, Kingsley Martin, *Socialism and the Welfare State* (1951), p.1. Martin's lecture was part of the Fabian Society's Autumn Lecture series of that year.
52 LHA, LP/362.5/319, Tom Braddock, *Houses, Rents and the Building Trade* (1953), p.21.
53 LSEA, Fabian Society, FABIAN/291, Kingsley Martin, *Socialism and the Welfare State* (1951), p.10.
54 McKibbin, *Parties and People*, p.175.
55 Dunleavy, *The Politics of Mass Housing in Britain*, p.35.
56 Noel Whiteside, 'Creating the Welfare State in Britain, 1945–1960', *Journal of Social Policy*, 25 (1996), 83–103 at 94.
57 LHA, LP/362.5/319, James MacColl, *Policy for Housing* (1954), p.20.
58 LHA, *Socialist Commentary* (January 1954), p.7.
59 *Ibid.*, p.8.
60 Jackson, 'Revisionism Reconsidered', 438.
61 LHA, LP/362.5/318, D. L. Munby, *Home Ownership* (1957), pp.25–6.
62 Lawrence, *Me, Me Me?*, p.111.
63 Young and Willmott, *Family and Class*, p.122.
64 Todd, 'Affluence, Class and Crown Street', 503.

65 Hanley, *Estates*, p.81.
66 Crosland, *The Future of Socialism*, p.144.
67 Malpass, *Housing and the Welfare State*, p.25.
68 Mogey, *Family and Neighbourhood*, p.140.
69 Rogaly and Taylor, *Moving Histories of Class and Community*, p.69.
70 Norbert Elias and John L. Scotson, *The Established and the Outsiders: A Sociological Enquiry into Community Problems* (London: Sage, 1994), First published 1965, p.16.
71 LHA, *Socialist Commentary* (April 1959), p.12.
72 Black, *Political Culture of the Left*, p.152.
73 Lawrence, 'Class, Affluence and the Study of Everyday Life', 284.
74 R. H. S. Crossman, *Planning for Freedom* (London: Hamish Hamilton, 1965), p.100.
75 Black, *Political Culture of the Left*, p.126.
76 Lawrence, 'Class, Affluence and the Study of Everyday Life', 284.
77 Black, *Political Culture of the Left*, p.175.
78 LHA, *Socialist Commentary* (August 1960), p.5.
79 *Ibid.*, p.6.
80 *Ibid.*
81 LHA, Labour Party Research Department Rd/87, Home Policy Sub-Committee, 'A Note on Dr Abrams' Survey', September 1960, p.3.
82 Lawrence, *Me, Me Me?* (2019), p.89.
83 John Goldthorpe, David Lockwood, Frank Bechofer and Jennifer Platt, *The Affluent Worker in the Class Structure* (London: Cambridge University Press, 1968), p.177.
84 Lawrence, *Me, Me Me?* (2019), p.106.
85 Lawrence Black, 'The Impression of Affluence: Political Culture in the 1950s and 1960s', in Lawrence Black and Hugh Pemberton (eds), *An Affluent Society? Britain's Post-War 'Golden Age' Revisited* (Aldershot: Aldgate, 2004), p.86.
86 LHA, *Socialist Commentary* (November 1954), p.310.
87 Todd, 'Affluence, Class and Crown Street', 505.
88 Ian Gazeley, *Poverty in Britain 1900–1965* (Basingstoke: Palgrave Macmillan, 2003), p.185.
89 LSEA, Fabian Society, FABIAN/353, Brian Abel-Smith, *Freedom in the Welfare State* (1963), p.9.
90 LHA, *Labour Woman* (February 1960), p.19.
91 LHA, *Labour Woman* (April 1960), pp.42–4.
92 LHA, *Socialist Commentary* (November 1964), p.23.
93 LSEA, Fabian Society, FABIAN/371, Peter Townsend, *Poverty, Socialism and Labour in Power* (January 1967), p.6.
94 *Ibid.*, p.18.
95 LHA, LPRD Re/296, Social Services Sub-Committee, Professor Peter Townsend, 'A Government Department of Social Planning: A Review of Some Ways of Satisfying Needs and Obtaining Best Value for Money in Social Planning', April 1968, p.4.

96 Szreter, 'Health, Class, Place and Politics', 48–50.
97 Carter, 'Building the Divided City', 173.
98 *Ibid.*, 162. Building upon this work, the social anthropologist Gillian Evans has observed that following their 1983 victory in the Bermondsey by-election and across the council wards, the Liberals (and then the Liberal Democrats) replicated a clientelist relationship between councillors and the white working classes through the distribution of housing and other public goods. Gillian Evans, '"The Aboriginal People of England": The Culture of Class Politics in Contemporary Britain', *Focaal*, 62 (2012), 17–29 at 26.
99 Dennis Dean, 'The Race Relations Policy of the First Wilson Government', *Twentieth Century British History*, 11:3 (2000), 259–83 at 266.
100 Dean, 'Race Relations Policy', 268.
101 LHA, Labour Party Research Department, *Partnership* (October 1965), p.1.
102 Sutcliffe and Smith, *History of Birmingham*, p.239.
103 LHA, LP/GS/1, Labour Party, *Now Britain's Strong Let's Make It Great to Live In* (1970), p.4.
104 Hansard, Debates, Commons, vol.725, col.522 (23 February 1966), http://hansard.millbanksystems.com/commons/1966/feb/23/welfare-state (accessed 14 June 2016).
105 Ferdynand Zweig, *The British Worker* (London: Penguin, 1952), p.21.
106 *Ibid.*, pp.205–7.
107 Giles, *Parlour and the Suburb*, p.50.
108 Beach and Tiratsoo, 'The Planners and the Public', p.528.
109 Blackwell and Seabrook, *A World Still to Win*, p.109.
110 Tom Forester, *The Labour Party and the Working Class* (London: Heinemann, 1976), p.101.
111 Ravetz, 'From Working Class Tenement to Modern Flat', p.133.
112 *Ibid.*, p.146.
113 *Ibid.*, p.126.
114 Durant, *Watling*, p.34 and p.117.
115 Jevons and Madge, *Housing Estates*, p.54.
116 LHA, LP/GS/8, *People's Pictorial*, 1:3 (1952), pp.2–3.
117 *Ibid.*, p.3.
118 *Ibid.*, pp.4–5.
119 Lawrence, *Me, Me Me*, p.2.
120 Butler, 'Michael Young', p.206.
121 Kuper, 'Blueprint for Living Together', pp.7–13.
122 *Ibid.*, pp.15–16.
123 *Ibid.*, p.22.
124 *Ibid.*, p.28.
125 Mogey, *Family and Neighbourhood*, p.12.
126 *Ibid.*, p.87.

127 *Ibid.*, pp.73–4.
128 *Ibid.*, p.92.
129 *Ibid.*, p.124.
130 LHA, *Socialist Commentary* (September 1954), p.252.
131 *Ibid.*
132 Butler, 'Michael Young', 205.
133 LHA, *Socialist Commentary* (July 1956), p.17.
134 Young and Willmott, *Family and Kinship*, p.35 and p.147.
135 Lawrence, *Me, Me, Me*, pp.51–2.
136 *Ibid.*, p.43.
137 Young and Willmott, *Family and Kinship*, p.122.
138 *Ibid.* p.169.
139 LHA, *Socialist Commentary* (May 1957), p.24.
140 *Ibid.*, pp.24–7.
141 Young and Willmott, *Family and Class*, p.3.
142 *Ibid.*, p.6.
143 *Ibid.*, p.103.
144 LHA, *Socialist Commentary* (January 1961), p.22.
145 LHA, *Labour Woman* (January 1961), p.15.
146 *Tribune* (2 December 1960), p.8.
147 LHA, *Socialist Commentary* (August 1958), p.16.
148 LHA, LHA, LP/362.5/319, Co-operative Party, *Housing: A Co-Operative Approach* (1959), p.20.
149 LHA, LP/362.5/319, James MacColl, *Policy for Housing* (1954), pp.23–4.
150 LHA, *Socialist Commentary* (March 1959), p.12.
151 LHA, *Socialist Commentary* (April 1959), p.13.
152 *Ibid.*
153 Glendinning and Muthesius, *Tower Block*, p.113.
154 LHA, *Socialist Commentary* (May 1962), p.19. Gavron worked on the lives of lonely mothers, her work being published posthumously after her 1965 suicide as *The Captive Wife*.
155 *Ibid.*
156 LHA, *Socialist Commentary* (May 1962), p.19.
157 Lawrence, 'Inventing the "Traditional Working Class"', 592.
158 *Ibid.*
159 Charles Vereker, John Barron Mays, Elizabeth Gittus and Maurice Broady, *Urban Redevelopment and Social Change: A Study of Social Conditions in Central Liverpool 1955–56* (Liverpool: Liverpool University Press, 1961), p.94.
160 *Ibid.*
161 Todd, 'Affluence, Class and Crown Street', 510.
162 Willmott, *Evolution of a Community*, p.19.

163 *Ibid.*, p.110.
164 Clapson, 'The Suburban Aspiration', 167.
165 Shapely, *The Politics of Housing*, p.118.
166 Langhamer, 'Meanings of Home', 355.
167 LHA, *Socialist Commentary* (April 1959), p.13.
168 Young and Willmott, *Family and Class*, p.95.
169 Zweig, *The British Worker*, p.138.
170 Kuper, 'Blueprint for Living Together', p.123.
171 Hollow, 'Governmentality on the Park Hill Estate', 128.
172 Jennings, *Societies in the Making*, p.191.
173 *Ibid.*, p.198.
174 *Ibid.*, p.240.
175 Dennis, *People and Planning*, pp.264–5.
176 Jephcott, *Homes in High Flats*, pp.29–30.
177 *Ibid.*, pp.48–9.
178 *Ibid.*, p.116.
179 Quoted in Kearns, 'Slum Clearance and Relocation', 201–25 at 214.
180 *Ibid.*, p.216.
181 Raymond Williams, *The Long Revolution* (London: Chatto and Windus, 1961), p.359.
182 Jones, *The Working Class*, pp.146–7.
183 Hoggart, *Uses of Literacy*, p.58.
184 Vereker, Mays, Gittus and Broady, *Urban Redevelopment and Social Change*, pp.119–20.
185 Crosland, *The Future of Socialism*, p.522.
186 Langhamer, 'Meanings of Home', 347.
187 Finnimore, *Houses from the Factory*, p.45.
188 Samuel, *Theatres of Memory*, p.51.
189 E. W. Cooney, 'High Flats in Local Authority Housing in England and Wales since 1945', in Anthony Sutcliffe (ed.), *Multi-Storey Living: The British Working-Class Experience* (London: Croom Helm, 1974), p.156.
190 Anthony Sutcliffe 'Introduction', in Anthony Sutcliffe (ed.), *Multi-Storey Living: The British Working-Class Experience* (London: Croom Helm, 1974), p.2.
191 Glendinning and Muthesius, *Tower Block*, p.25.
192 Quoted in Gold, *Practice of Modernism*, p.11.
193 Ruth Oldenziel and Karin Zachmann, 'Kitchens as Technology and Politics: An Introduction', in Ruth Oldenziel and Karin Zachmann (eds), *Cold War Kitchen: Americanization, Technology and European Users* (Cambridge MA: MIT Press, 2009), p.10.
194 Ravetz, 'From Working Class Tenement to Modern Flat', p.130.

195 LHA, LP/362.5/318, Birmingham Borough Labour Party, *Homes for the People! Labour's Policy for Birmingham's Need* (1943), p.9.
196 *Ibid.*, p.11.
197 LHA, LP/362.5/318, W. E. Fox, *Housing: The True Solution* (1944), p.3.
198 LHA, LP/362.5/318, Communist Party of Great Britain, *Memorandum on Housing* (1944), p.22.
199 *Ibid.*
200 LHA, LP/362.5/318, Douglas Brown, *An Englishman's Home* (1945), p.24.
201 *Ibid.*
202 Charlotte Wildman, 'A City Speaks: The Projection of Civic Identity in Manchester', *Twentieth Century British History*, 23:1 (2012), 80–99 at 93.
203 LHA, *Labour Woman* (April 1950), p.54.
204 *Ibid.*
205 LHA, *Labour Woman* (November 1950), p.227.
206 Susan E. Reid, '"Our Kitchen Is Just as Good": Soviet Responses to the American Kitchen', in Ruth Oldenziel and Karin Zachmann (eds), *Cold War Kitchen: Americanization, Technology and European Users* (Cambridge MT: MIT Press, 2009), p.85.
207 LHA, LP/GS/8, *Forward* (January, 1953), p.8.
208 *Ibid.*
209 *Ibid.*
210 LHA, LP/380.3, British Workers' Delegation, *What We Saw In Russia* (1952), p.8.
211 Jephcott, *Homes in High Flats*, p.5.
212 Becky E. Conekin, '*The Autobiography of a Nation*': *The 1951 Festival of Britain* (Manchester: Manchester University Press, 2003), p.72.
213 LHA, LP/GS/8, Labour Party, *Festival* (1951), p.6.
214 LHA, *Labour Woman* (July 1950), p.131.
215 *Ibid.*
216 LHA, *Labour Woman* (January 1956), p.41.
217 LHA, *Labour Woman* (October 1952), p.48.
218 LHA, *Labour Woman* (April 1956), p.53.
219 *Ibid.*
220 Glendinning and Muthesius, *Tower Block*, 66–7.
221 LHA, *Labour Woman* (January 1956), 8.
222 LSEA, *Tribune* (18 May 1956), 7.
223 LHA, *Labour Woman* (May 1956), 71.
224 *Ibid.*
225 Finnimore, *Houses from the Factory*, p.212 and p.217.
226 Saumarez Smith, 'Central Government and Town-Centre Redevelopment', 220.
227 Glendinning and Muthesius, *Tower Block*, pp.14–6.
228 LHA, LP/GS/8, *West Ham South Citizen* (September 1962).

229 *Ibid.*
230 *Ibid.*
231 *Ibid.*
232 Jephcott, *Homes in High Flats*, p.5.
233 Sutcliffe and Smith, *History of Birmingham*, p.432.
234 LHA, Labour Party Research Department Rd/748, 'The Quality of Living', May 1964, p.3.
235 *Ibid.*
236 Saumarez Smith, 'Central Government and Town-Centre Redevelopment', 243.
237 Gunn, 'Rise and Fall of British Urban Modernism', 850.
238 Jephcott, *Homes in High Flats*, p.49.
239 LHA, *Labour Woman* (July 1961), p.10.
240 *Ibid.*
241 LSEA, Women's Library Pamphlet Collection, Joan Maizels, *Two to Five in High Flats: An Enquiry into Play Provision for Children Aged Two to Five Years Living in High Flats* (1961), p.11.
242 LHA, *Labour Woman* (July 1961), p.10.
243 LHA, *Labour Woman* (September 1965), p.145.
244 *Ibid.*
245 Jephcott, *Homes in High Flats*, p.94.
246 Lynn Abrams, Linda Fleming, Barry Hazley, Valerie Wright and Ade Kearns, 'Isolated and Dependent: Women and Children in High-Rise Social Housing in Post-War Glasgow', *Women's History Review*, 28:5 (2019), 794–513 at 807.
247 Jephcott, *Homes in High Flats*, p.8; Matthew Hollow, 'Governmentality on the Park Hill Estate', 130.
248 LHA, *Socialist Commentary* (November 1970), p.22.
249 *Ibid.*, p.23.
250 LHA, LP/GS/1, Labour Party, *Now Britain's Strong Let's Make It Great to Live In* (1970), p.15.
251 Dunleavy, *The Politics of Mass Housing*, p.59.
252 Burnett, *Social History of Housing*, p.313.
253 *Ibid.*
254 Richard Rodger, 'Slums and Suburbs: The Persistence of Residential Apartheid', in Philip Waller (ed.), *The English Urban Landscape* (Oxford: Oxford University Press, 2000), pp.233–68 at p.263.
255 Samuel, *Theatres of Memory*, p.75.
256 LHA, LP/GS/8, Labour Party, *Festival* (1951), p.7.
257 Goss, *Local Labour and Local Government*, p.80.
258 Hoggart, *Uses of Literacy*, p.63.
259 Kenneth O. Morgan, *The People's Peace: British History 1945–1990* (Oxford: Oxford University Press, 1990), p.194.

Afterword

1. Tony Benn, *Years of Hope: Diaries 1940–1962* (London: Hutchinson, 1994), p.289. Barton House was at the centre of the redeveloped Barton Hill area of east Bristol, and Hilda Jennings' study of the new estate is discussed extensively in the fourth chapter.
2. LHA, *Labour Woman* (November 1950), p.218.
3. Benn, *Years of Hope*, p.289.
4. WCML, Allaun Papers, *Labour's Northern Voice* (May 1970), p.1.
5. Drucker, *Doctrine and Ethos*, p.25.
6. LHA, *Town Crier* (27 October 1945), p.2.
7. *Ibid.*
8. LHA, *Socialist Commentary*, October 1970, p.1.
9. *Tribune* (26 June 1970), p.1.
10. Gold, *The Practice of Modernism*, p.284.
11. Saumarez Smith, *Boom Cities*, p.172.
12. Derisive attitudes towards post-war council estates are effectively encapsulated within contemporary moves to demolish and redevelop those estates. One recent example is the Ladywood estate in Birmingham, part of the post-war masterplan, https://www.birminghammail.co.uk/news/midlands-news/life-love-death-ladywood-place-16495240 (accessed 9 August 2023).
13. Crosland, *The Conservative Enemy*, p.241.
14. Berman, *All That Is Solid*, p.324.
15. *London Review of Books*, 38:6 (17 March 2016), p.26.
16. Daunton, *Property-Owning Democracy*, p.40.
17. Greg Beales, 'Big Changes Coming in Housing', Shelter Blog (21 November 2019), https://blog.shelter.org.uk/2019/11/general-election-2019-big-changes-coming-in-housing/ (accessed 10 August 2023). See also: Phil Child, 'Labour's Radical Renting History' (8 July 2020), *Tribune*, https://tribunemag.co.uk/2020/07/labours-radical-renting-history (accessed 10 August 2023).
18. See in particular: Rebecca Searle, *A History of the Housing Crisis* (Lanham, MD: Rowman and Littlefield, 2022); Vicky Spratt, *Tenants: The People on the Frontline of Britain's Housing Emergency* (London: Profile Books, 2022).
19. See Peter Apps, *Show Me the Bodies: How We Let Grenfell Happen* (London: Oneworld Publications, 2022).

Select Bibliography

This bibliography does not include specific references to archival records, newspaper articles or other media – these are in the endnotes.

Abel-Smith, Brian and Townsend, Peter, *The Poor and the Poorest: A New Analysis of the Ministry of Labour's Family Expenditure Surveys of 1953–54 and 1960* (Andover: Chapel River Press, 1969), First published 1965.
Abercrombie, Patrick and Forshaw, J. H., *County of London Plan* (London: Macmillan, 1943).
Abernethy, Simon T., 'Opening Up the Suburbs: Workmen's Trains in London 1860–1914', *Urban History*, 42:1 (2015), 70–88.
Abrams, Lynn, Fleming, Linda, Hazley, Barry, Wright, Valerie and Kearns, Ade, 'Isolated and Dependent: Women and Children in High-rise Social Housing in Post-War Glasgow', *Women's History Review*, 28:5 (2019), 794–813.
Allaun, Frank, *No Place Like Home: Britain's Housing Tragedy* (London: Andre Deutsch, 1972).
Andreae, Sophie, 'From Comprehensive Development to Conservation Areas', in Michael Hunter (ed.), *Preserving the Past: The Rise of Heritage in Modern Britain* (Stroud: Alan Sutton, 1996), pp.135–55.
Bagwell, Philip and Lyth, Peter, *Transport in Britain: From Canal Lock to Gridlock* (London: Hambledon, 2002).
Baldwin, Peter, *The Politics of Social Solidarity: Class Bases of the European Welfare State 1875–1975* (Cambridge: Cambridge University Press, 1990).
Beach, Abigail and Tiratsoo, Nick, 'The Planners and the Public', in Martin Daunton (ed.), *The Cambridge Urban History of Britain. Vol. 3, 1840–1950* (Cambridge: Cambridge University Press, 2000), pp.525–50.
Beanland, Christopher, *Concrete Concept: Brutalist Buildings around the World* (London: Frances Lincoln, 2016).
Benn, Tony (edited by Ruth Winstone), *Years of Hope: Diaries, Letters and Papers 1940–1962* (London: Hutchinson, 1994).
Berman, Marshall, *All That Is Solid Melts into Air: The Experience of Modernity* (London: Verso, 1983), First published 1982.
Bevan, Aneurin, *In Place of Fear* (London: William Heinemann, 1952).
Black, Lawrence, 'Social Democracy as a Way of Life: Fellowship and the Socialist Union, 1951–9', *Twentieth Century British History*, 10:4 (1999), 499–539.

Black, Lawrence, 'The Impression of Affluence: Political Culture in the 1950s and 1960s', in Lawrence Black and Hugh Pemberton (eds), *An Affluent Society? Britain's Post-War 'Golden Age' Revisited* (Aldershot: Aldgate, 2004), pp.85–106.

Black, Lawrence, *The Political Culture of the Left in Affluent Britain, 1951–64: Old Labour, New Britain?* (Basingstoke: Palgrave Macmillan, 2003).

Black, Lawrence and Pemberton, Hugh (eds), *An Affluent Society? Britain's Post-War 'Golden Age' Revisited* (Aldershot: Aldgate, 2004).

Blackwell, Trevor and Seabrook, Jeremy, *A World Still to Win: The Reconstruction of the Post-War Working Class* (London: Faber and Faber, 1985).

Blau, Eve, 'From Red Superblock to Green Megastructure: Municipal Socialism as a Model and Challenge', in Mark Swenarton, Tom Avermaete and Dirk van den Heuvel (eds), *Architecture and the Welfare State* (Abingdon: Routledge, 2015), pp.27–50.

Boughton, John, *Municipal Dreams: The Rise and Fall of Council Housing* (London: Verso, 2018).

Bourke, Joanna, *Working-Class Cultures in Britain 1890–1960: Gender, Class and Ethnicity* (London: Routledge, 1994).

Brooke, Stephen, *Labour's War: The Labour Party during the Second World War* (Oxford: Oxford University Press, 1992).

Brooke, Stephen, '"Slumming in Swinging London?" Class, Gender and the Post-War City in Nell Dunn's *Up the Junction* (1963)', *Cultural and Social History*, 9:3 (2012), 429–49.

Buettner, Elizabeth, 'This Is Staffordshire Not Alabama: Racial Geographies of Commonwealth Immigration in Early 1960s Britain', *The Journal of Imperial and Commonwealth History*, 42:4 (2014), 710–40.

Bullock, Nicholas, 'West Ham and the Welfare State 1945–70: A Suitable Case for Treatment?', in Mark Swenarton, Tom Avermaete and Dirk van den Heuvel (eds), *Architecture and the Welfare State* (Abingdon: Routledge, 2015), pp.93–110.

Burnett, John, *A Social History of Housing 1815–1970* (Newton Abbot: David Charles, 1978).

Butler, Lise, 'Michael Young, the Institute of Community Studies, and the Politics of Kinship', *Twentieth Century British History*, 26:2 (2015), 203–24.

Butler, Lise, *Michael Young, Social Science, and the British Left, 1945–1970* (Oxford: Oxford University Press, 2020).

Campbell, John, *Nye Bevan and the Mirage of British Socialism* (London: Weidenfeld and Nicholson, 1987).

Carter, Harold, 'Building the Divided City: Race, Class and Social Housing in Southwark 1945–1995', *The London Journal*, 33:2 (July 2008), 155–85.

Child, Phil, 'Landlordism, Rent Regulation and the Labour Party in Mid-Twentieth Century Britain, 1950–64', *Twentieth Century British History*, 29:1 (2018), 79–103.

Child, Phil, 'Slum Clearance and Attitudes towards Social Housing in Cambridge, 1950-75', unpublished dissertation, University of Cambridge (2012).

Clapson, Mark, *Invincible Green Suburbs, Brave New Towns: Social Change and Urban Dispersal in Postwar England* (Manchester: Manchester University Press, 1998).

Clapson, Mark, 'Working-class Women's Experiences of Moving to New Housing Estates in England since 1919', *Twentieth Century British History*, 10:3 (1999), 345-65.

Clark, Peter (ed.), *The European City and Green Space: London, Stockholm, Helsinki and St Petersburg 1850-2000* (Aldershot: Aldgate, 2006).

Clark, Peter and Jauhiainen, Jussi S., 'Introduction', in Peter Clark (ed.), *The European City and Green Space: London, Stockholm, Helsinki and St Petersburg 1850-2000* (Aldershot: Ashgate, 2006), pp.1-29.

Coates, Ken and Silburn, Richard, *Poverty: The Forgotten Englishmen* (Harmondsworth: Penguin, 1976), First published 1970.

Collins, Marcus, 'Pride and Prejudice: West Indian Men in Mid-Twentieth Century Britain', *Journal of British Studies*, 40:3 (2001), 391-418.

Colls, Robert and Rodger, Richard (eds), *Cities of Ideas: Civil Society and Urban Governance in Britain 1800-2000* (Aldershot: Ashgate, 2004).

Conekin, Becky E., *'The Autobiography of a Nation': The 1951 Festival of Britain* (Manchester: Manchester, 2003).

Conekin, Becky, Mort, Frank and Waters, Chris (eds), *Moments of Modernity: Reconstructing Britain, 1945-1964* (London: Rivers Oram, 1999).

Cooney, E. W., 'High Flats in Local Authority Housing in England and Wales since 1945', in Anthony Sutcliffe (ed.), *Multi-Storey Living: The British Working-Class Experience* (London: Croom Helm, 1974), pp.151-80.

Cragoe, Matthew and Readman, Paul (eds), *The Land Question in Britain, 1750-1950* (Basingstoke: Palgrave Macmillan, 2010).

Cragoe, Matthew and Readman, Paul, 'Introduction', in Matthew Cragoe and Paul Readman (eds), *The Land Question in Britain* (Basingstoke: Palgrave Macmillan, 2010), pp.1-18.

Crook, Tony and Kemp, Peter A., *Transforming Private Landlords: Housing, Markets and Public Policy* (Oxford: Oxford University Press, 2011).

Crosland, C. A. R., *The Conservative Enemy: A Programme of Radical Reform for the 1960s* (London: Jonathan Cape, 1962).

Crosland, C. A. R., *The Future of Socialism* (New York: Schocken, 1967), First published 1956.

Crossman, Richard, *Diaries of a Cabinet Minister: Volume One: Minister of Housing 1964-66* (Worcester: Ebenezer Baylis, 1977), First published 1975.

Crossman, Richard, *The Backbench Diaries of Richard Crossman* (London: Hamish Hamilton, 1981).

Crossman, R. H. S., *Planning for Freedom* (London: Hamish Hamilton, 1965).

Cupers, Kenny, *The Social Project: Housing Postwar France* (Minneapolis: University of Minnesota Press, 2014).

Daunton, Martin, *A Property-Owning Democracy? Housing in Britain* (London: Faber, 1987).

Daunton, Martin, *Just Taxes: The Politics of Taxation in Britain, 1914–1979* (Cambridge: Cambridge University Press, 2002).

Daunton, Martin (ed.), *The Cambridge Urban History of Britain. Vol. 3, 1840–1950* (Cambridge: Cambridge University Press, 2000).

Daunton, Martin and Rieger, Bernard (eds), *Meanings of Modernity: Britain from the Late-Victorian Era to World War II* (Oxford: Oxford University Press, 2001).

Daunton, Martin and Rieger, Bernard, 'Introduction', in Martin Daunton and Bernard Rieger (eds), *Meanings of Modernity: Britain from the Late-Victorian Era to World War II* (Oxford: Oxford University Press, 2001), pp.1–24.

Davies, Aled, '"Right to Buy": The Development of a Conservative Housing Policy, 1945–1980', *Contemporary British History*, 27:4 (2013), 421–44.

Davis, John, 'Macmillan's Martyr: The Pilgrim Case, the "land grab" and the Tory Housing Drive, 1951–9', *Planning Perspectives*, 23:2 (2006), 125–46.

Davis, John, 'Rents and Race in 1960s London: New Light on Rachmanism', *Twentieth Century British History*, 12:1 (2001), 69–92.

Dean, Dennis, 'The Race Relations Policy of the First Wilson Government', *Twentieth Century British History*, 11:3 (2000), 259–83.

Delaney, Enda, *The Irish in Post-War Britain* (Oxford: Oxford University Press, 2007).

Dennis, Norman, *People and Planning: The Sociology of Housing in Sunderland* (London: Faber, 1970).

Department for Communities and Local Government, *English Housing Survey 2013–14* (10 July 2013).

Donnison, David, *The Government of Housing* (London: Penguin, 1967).

Dorling, Danny, *All That Is Solid: The Great Housing Disaster* (London: Allen Lane, 2014).

Douglas, Roy, *Land, People and Politics: A History of the Land Question in the United Kingdom 1878–1952* (London: Allison and Busby, 1976).

Doye, Zoe, 'The Labour Party and Public Housing, 1951–64: An Examination of National Policy and Its Implementation in London' (PhD thesis, Birkbeck University of London, 2004).

Drucker, H. M., *Doctrine and Ethos in the Labour Party* (London: Allen and Unwin 1979).

Duff, Peggy, *Left, Left, Left: A Personal Account of Six Protest Campaigns, 1945–65* (London: Allison and Busby, 1971).

Dunleavy, Patrick, *The Politics of Mass Housing in Britain, 1945–75: A Study of Corporate Power and Professional Influence in the Welfare State* (Oxford: Clarendon, 1981).

Durant, Ruth, *Watling: A Social Survey* (London: P.S. King, 1939).

Edgerton, David, *The Rise and Fall of the British Nation: A Twentieth Century History* (St Ives: Allen Lane, 2018).
Elias, Norbert and Scotson, John L., *The Established and the Outsiders: A Sociological Enquiry into Community Problems* (London: Sage, 1994), First published 1965.
Ellis, David John, 'Pavement Politics: Community Action in Leeds, c. 1960–1990' (PhD thesis, University of York, 2015).
English, John, Madigan, Ruth and Norman, Peter, *Slum Clearance: The Social and Administrative Context in England and Wales* (London: Croom Helm, 1976).
Esher, Lionel, *A Broken Wave: The Rebuilding of England, 1940–1980* (London: Viking/Allen Lane, 1981).
Esping-Andersen, Gøsta, *The Three Worlds of Welfare Capitalism* (Princeton: Princeton University Press, 1990).
Evans, Gillian, '"The Aboriginal People of England": The Culture of Class Politics in Contemporary Britain', *Focaal*, 62 (2012), 17–29.
Fielding, Steven and Tanner, Duncan, 'The "Rise of the Left Revisited": Labour Party Culture in Post-War Manchester and Salford', *Labour History Review*, 71:3 (2006), 211–33.
Finnimore, Brian, *Houses from the Factory: System Building and the Welfare State 1942–74* (London: Rivers Oram, 1989).
Flinn, Catherine, *Rebuilding Britain's Blitzed Cities: Hopeful Dreams, Stark Realities* (London: Bloomsbury, 2019).
Forester, Tom, *The Labour Party and the Working Class* (London: Heinemann, 1976).
Francis, Martin, *Ideas and Policies under Labour, 1945–51: Building a New Britain* (Manchester: Manchester University Press, 1997).
Garside, Patricia L., 'Citizenship, Civil Society and Quality of Life: Sutton Model Dwellings Estates 1919–38', in Robert Colls and Richard Rodger (eds), *Cities of Ideas: Civil Society and Urban Governance in Britain 1800–2000* (Aldershot: Aldgate, 2004), pp.258–82.
Garside, Patricia L., 'Politics, Ideology and the Issue of Open Space in London, 1939–2000', in Peter Clark (ed.), *The European City and Green Space: London, Stockholm, Helsinki and St Petersburg 1850–2000* (Aldershot: Aldgate, 2006), pp.68–98.
Gazeley, Ian, *Poverty in Britain 1900–1965* (Basingstoke: Palgrave Macmillan, 2003).
Geddes, Patrick, *Cities in Evolution* (London: Williams and Norgate, 1949), First published 1915.
Giles, Judy, *The Parlour and the Suburb: Domestic Identities, Class, Femininity and Modernity* (Oxford: Berg, 2004).
Gilroy, Paul, *Ain't No Black in the Union Jack: The Cultural Politics of Race and Nation* (London: Routledge, 1992), First published 1987.
Glass, Ruth, *London: Aspects of Change* (London: Cox and Wyman, 1964).
Glendinning, Miles and Muthesius, Stefan, *Tower Block: Modern Public Housing in England, Scotland, Wales and Northern Ireland* (New Haven: Yale University Press, 1994).

Gold, John R., *The Experience of Modernism* (Oxford: Routledge, 1997).
Gold, John R., *The Practice of Modernism* (Oxford: Routledge, 2007).
Goldthorpe, John, Lockwood, David, Bechhofer, Frank and Platt, Jennifer, *The Affluent Worker in the Class Structure* (Cambridge: Cambridge University Press, 1968).
Gosling, Ray, 'St Ann's, Nottingham', in Anne Lapping (ed.), *Community Action* (London: Fabian Society, 1970).
Goss, Sue, *Local Labour and Local Government: A Study of Changing Interests, Politics and Policy in Southwark from 1919 to 1982* (Edinburgh: Edinburgh University Press, 1988).
Greenhalgh, James, *Reconstructing Modernity: Space, Power and Governance in Mid-Twentieth Century British Cities* (Manchester: Manchester University Press, 2018).
Greenwood, Walter, *Love on the Dole* (London: Vintage, 1993), First published 1933.
Griffiths, Clare, 'Socialism and the Land Question: Public Ownership and Control in Labour Party Policy, 1918–1950s', in Matthew Cragoe and Paul Readman (eds), *The Land Question in Britain, 1750–1950* (Basingstoke: Palgrave Macmillan, 2010), pp.237–56.
Griffiths, Clare V. J., 'History and the Labour Party', in Clare V. J. Griffiths, James J. Nott and William Whyte (eds), *Classes, Cultures and Politics: Essays on British History for Ross McKibbin* (Oxford: Oxford University Press, 2011), pp.282–301.
Griffiths, Clare V. J., Nott, James J. and Whyte, William (eds), *Classes, Cultures and Politics: Essays on British History for Ross McKibbin* (Oxford: Oxford University Press, 2011).
Grindrod, John, *Concretopia* (London: Old Street, 2014).
Gunn, Simon, 'The Buchanan Report, Environment and the Problem of Traffic in 1960s Britain', *Twentieth Century British History*, 22:4 (2011), 521–42.
Gunn, Simon, 'The Rise and Fall of British Urban Modernism: Planning Bradford, circa 1945–1970', *The Journal of British Studies*, 49:4 (2010), 849–69.
Gyford, John, *The Politics of Local Socialism* (London: Allen and Unwin, 1985).
Hall, Peter, *Cities of Tomorrow: An Intellectual History of Urban Planning and Design in the Twentieth Century* (Oxford: Blackwell, 1988).
Hamnett, Chris, 'Gentrification and the Middle-Class Remaking of Inner London, 1961–2001', *Urban Studies*, 40:12 (2003), 2401–26.
Hanley, Lynsey, *Estates: An Intimate History* (London: Granta, 2007).
Hanna, Erika, *Modern Dublin, Urban Change and the Irish Past* (Oxford: Oxford University Press, 2013).
Hardy, Dennis, *Utopian England: Community Experiments 1900–1945* (London: Routledge, 2000).
Harloe, Michael, *The People's Home? Social Rented Housing in Europe and America* (Oxford: Oxford University Press, 1995).
Hatherley, Owen, *A Guide to the New Ruins of Great Britain* (London: Verso, 2010).
Hatherley, Owen, *A New Kind of Bleak: Journeys through Urban Britain* (London: Verso, 2012).

Hatherley, Owen, *Militant Modernism* (London: Zero, 2009).
Hatherley, Owen, *Red Metropolis: Socialism and the Government of London* (London: Verso, 2020)
Hennessey, Peter, *Having It So Good: Britain in the Fifties* (London: Penguin, 2006).
Hirsch, Shirin, *In the Shadow of Enoch Powell: Race, Locality and Resistance* (Manchester: Manchester University Press, 2018).
Hoggart, Richard, *The Uses of Literacy* (London: Penguin, 1992), First published 1957.
Hollow, Matthew, 'Governmentality on the Park Hill Estate: The Rationality of Public Housing', *Urban History*, 37:1 (2010), 117–35.
Hunter, Michael (ed.), *Preserving the Past: The Rise of Heritage in Modern Britain* (Stroud: Alan Sutton, 1996).
Jackson, Ben, *Equality and the British Left* (Manchester: Manchester University Press, 2007).
Jackson, Ben, 'Revisionism Reconsidered: "Property-owning Democracy" and Egalitarian Strategy in Post-War Britain', *Twentieth Century British History*, 16:4 (2005), 416–40.
Jacobs, Jane, *The Death and Life of Great American Cities* (London: Jonathan Cape, 1962).
Jennings, Hilda, *Societies in the Making: A Study of Development and Redevelopment within a County Borough* (London: Routledge and Kegan Paul, 1962).
Jephcott, Pearl, *Homes in High Flats: Some of the Human Problems Involved in Multi-Storey Housing* (Edinburgh: Oliver and Boyd, 1971).
Jevons, Rosamond and Madge, John, *Housing Estates: A Study of Bristol Corporation Policy and Practice between the Wars* (Bristol: Arrowsmith, 1946).
Jobson, Richard, '"Waving the Banners of a Bygone age", Nostalgia and Labour's Clause IV Controversy, 1959–60', *Contemporary British History*, 27:2 (2013), 123–44.
Jobson, Richard, *Nostalgia and the Post-War Labour Party: Prisoners of the Past* (Manchester: Manchester University Press, 2018).
Jones, Ben, 'Slum Clearance, Privatization and Residualization: The Practices and Politics of Council Housing in Mid-Twentieth Century England', *Twentieth Century British History*, 21:4 (2010), 510–39.
Jones, Ben, *The Working Class in Mid-twentieth-century England: Community, Identity and Social Memory* (Manchester: Manchester University Press, 2012).
Jones, Ben and Schofield, Camilla, '"Whatever Community Is, This Is Not It": Notting Hill and the Reconstruction of "Race" in Britain after 1958', *Journal of British Studies*, 58 (2019), 142–73.
Jones, Owen, *Chavs: The Demonization of the Working Class* (London: Verso, 2011).
Kearns, Ade, Wright, Valerie, Abrams, Lynn and Hazley, Barry, 'Slum Clearance and Relocation: A Reassessment of Social Outcomes Combining Short-Term and Long-Term Perspectives', *Housing Studies*, 34:2 (2017), 201–25.
Kefford, Alistair, 'Housing the Citizen-Consumer in Post-war Britain: The Parker Morris Report, Affluence and the Even Briefer Life of Social Democracy', *Twentieth Century British History*, 29:2 (2017), 225–8.

Klemek, Christopher, *The Transatlantic Collapse of Urban Renewal: Postwar Urbanism from New York to Berlin* (Chicago: University of Chicago Press, 2012).
Kuper, Leo, 'Blueprint for Living Together', in Leo Kuper (ed.), *Living in Towns* (London: Cresset Press, 1953), pp.1–22.
Kuper, Leo (ed.), *Living in Towns* (London: Cresset Press, 1953).
Kynaston, David, *Austerity Britain, 1945–51* (London: Bloomsbury, 2007).
Kynaston, David, *Family Britain, 1951–57* (London: Bloomsbury, 2010).
Kynaston, David, *Modernity Britain: Opening the Box 1957–59* (London: Bloomsbury, 2013).
Kynaston, David, *Modernity Britain: A Shake of the Dice 1959–62* (London: Bloomsbury, 2015).
Langhamer, Claire, 'The Meanings of Home in Postwar Britain', *Journal of Contemporary History*, 40:2 (2005), 341–62.
Latour, Bruno (translated by Catherine Porter), *We Have Never Been Modern* (Cambridge, MA: Harvard University Press, 1993).
Lawrence, Jon, 'The British Sense of Class', *Journal of Contemporary History*, 35:2 (2000), 307–18.
Lawrence, Jon, 'Class, Affluence and the Study of Everyday Life in Britain, c.1930–64', *Cultural and Social History*, 10:2 (2013), 273–99.
Lawrence, Jon, *Electing Our Masters: The Hustings in British Politics from Hogarth to Blair* (Oxford: Oxford University Press, 2009).
Lawrence, Jon, 'Inventing the "Traditional Working Class": A Re-analysis of Interview Notes from Young and Willmott's Family and Kinship in East London', *Historical Journal*, 59:2 (2016), 567–93.
Lawrence, Jon, *Me, Me, Me? The Search for Community in Post-War England* (Oxford: Oxford University Press, 2019).
Linehan, Thomas, *Modernism and British Socialism* (Basingstoke: Palgrave Macmillan, 2012).
Lowe, Rodney, *The Welfare State in Britain since 1945* (Basingstoke: Palgrave Macmillan, 1993).
Malpass, Peter, *Housing and the Welfare State: The Development of Housing Policy in Britain* (Basingstoke: Palgrave Macmillan, 2005).
Malpass, Peter, 'The Wobbly Pillar? Housing and the British Postwar Welfare State', *Journal of Social Policy*, 32:4 (2003), 589–606.
Mandler, Peter, 'New Towns for Old', in Becky Conekin, Frank Mort and Chris Waters (eds), *Moments of Modernity: Reconstructing Britain, 1945–1964* (London: Rivers Oram Press, 1999), pp.208–27.
Mass, Sarah, 'Commercial Heritage as Democratic Action: Historicizing the "Save the Market" Campaigns in Bradford and Chesterfield, 1969–76', *Twentieth Century British History*, 29:3 (2017), 459–84.
Meredith, Jesse, 'Decolonizing the New Town: Roy Gazzard and the Making of Killingworth Township', *Journal of British Studies*, 57 (2018), 333–62.

Merett, Stephen, *State Housing in Britain* (London: Routledge and Kegan Paul, 1979).
McGuire, Charlie, Clarke, Linda and Wall, Christine, '"Through Trade Unionism You Felt a Belonging – You Belonged": Collectivism and the Self-Representation of Building Workers in Stevenage New Town', *Labour History Review*, 81:3 (2016), 211–36.
McKibbin, Ross, *Classes and Cultures: England, 1918–51* (Oxford: Oxford University Press, 1998).
McKibbin, Ross, *Parties and People: England 1914–1951* (Oxford: Oxford University Press, 2010).
McKibbin, Ross, 'A Brief Supremacy: The Fragmentation of the Two-Party System in British Politics, c.1950–2015', *Twentieth Century British History*, 27:3 (2016), 450–69.
Middleton, Stuart, '"Affluence" and the Left in Britain, c.1958–1974', *English Historical Review*, 129 (2014), 107–38.
Miliband, Ralph, *Parliamentary Socialism: Study in the Politics of Labour*, 2nd edition (London: Merlin Press, 1975), First published 1961.
Mogey, J. M., *Family and Neighbourhood: Two Studies in Oxford* (Oxford: Oxford University Press, 1956).
Moran, Joe, 'Early Cultures of Gentrification in London, 1955–1980', *Urban History*, 34 (2007), 101–22.
Moran, Joe, 'The Strange Birth of Middle England', *Political Quarterly*, 76:2 (April 2005), 159–313.
Morgan, Kevin O., *The People's Peace: British History 1945–1990* (Oxford: Oxford University Press, 1990).
Mort, Frank, 'Fantasies of Metropolitan Life: Planning London in the 1940s', *The Journal of British Studies*, 43:1 (2004), 120–51.
Mumford, Lewis, *The Culture of Cities* (London: Secker and Warburg, 1940).
Muthesius, Stefan, *The English Terraced House* (New Haven: Yale University Press, 1982).
Nuttall, Jeremy, 'Pluralism, the People, and Time in Labour Party History, 1931–1964', *The Historical Journal*, 56:3 (2013), 729–56.
Nuttall, Jeremy, *Psychological Socialism: The Labour Party and Qualities of Mind and Character, 1931 to the Present* (Manchester: Manchester University Press, 2006).
Office for National Statistics, 'UK House Building: Permanent Dwellings Started and Completed', March 2021, https://www.ons.gov.uk/peoplepopulationandcommunity/housing/datasets/ukhousebuildingpermanentdwellingsstartedandcompleted (accessed 25 March 2022).
O'Hara, Glen, *Governing Post-War Britain: The Paradoxes of Progress, 1951–73* (Basingstoke: Palgrave Macmillan, 2012).
Oldenziel, Ruth and Zachman, Karin (eds), *Cold War Kitchen: Americanization, Technology and European Users* (Cambridge, MA: MIT Press, 2009).

Oldenziel, Ruth and Zachmann, Karin, 'Kitchens as Technology and Politics: An Introduction', in Ruth Oldenziel and Karin Zachmann (eds), *Cold War Kitchen: Americanization, Technology and European Users* (Cambridge, MA: MIT Press, 2009), pp.1–29.

Olechnowicz, Andrzej, *Working-Class Housing in England between the Wars: The Becontree Estate* (Oxford: Oxford University Press, 1997).

Ortalano, Guy, 'Planning the Urban Future in 1960s Britain', *The Historical Journal*, 54 (2011), 477–507.

Ortalano, Guy, *Thatcher's Progress: From Social Democracy to Market Liberalism through an English New Town* (Cambridge: Cambridge University Press, 2019).

Orwell, George, *Coming Up for Air* (London: Penguin, 1990), First published 1939.

Orwell, George, *Essays* (London: Penguin, 2000), First published 1941.

Orwell, George, 'The Lion and the Unicorn: Socialism and the English Genius', in George Orwell (ed.), *Essays* (London: Penguin, 2000).

Orwell, George, *The Road to Wigan Pier* (London: Penguin, 2001), First published 1937.

Parker, Simon, 'From the Slums to the Suburbs: Labour Party Policy, the LCC and the Woodberry Down Estate, Stoke Newington 1934–1961', *London Journal*, 24:2 (1999), 51–69.

Perry, Kennetta Hammond, *London Is the Place for Me: Black Britons, Citizenship and the Politics of Race* (Oxford: Oxford University Press, 2016).

Pooley, Colin G. and Turnbull, Jean, 'Commuting, Transport and Urban Form: Manchester and Glasgow in the Mid-Twentieth Century', *Urban History*, 27:3 (2000), 360–83.

Pooley, Colin G., Turnbull, Jean and Adams, Mags, *A Mobile Century: Changes in Everyday Mobility in Britain in the Twentieth Century* (Aldershot: Aldgate, 2005).

Powers, Alan, *Britain: Modern Architectures in History* (London: Reaktion, 2007).

Priestley, J. B., *English Journey* (London: Great Northern Books, 2009), First published 1934.

Ravetz, Alison, *Council Housing and Culture: The History of a Social Experiment* (London: Routledge, 2001).

Ravetz, Alison, 'From Working Class Tenement to Modern Flat: Local Authorities and Multi-storey Housing between the Wars', in Anthony Sutcliffe (ed.), *Multi-Storey Living: The British Working-Class Experience* (London: Croom Helm, 1974), pp.122–50.

Ravetz, Alison, *The Government of Space: Town Planning in Modern Society* (London: Faber, 1986).

Ravetz, Alison, 'Housing the People', in Jim Fyrth (ed.), *Labour's Promised Land: Culture and Society in Labour Britain 1945–51* (London: Lawrence and Wishart, 1995).

Reid, Susan E., '"Our Kitchen Is Just as Good": Soviet Responses to the American Kitchen', in Ruth Oldenziel and Karin Zachmann (eds), *Cold War Kitchen: Americanization, Technology and European Users* (Cambridge, MA: MIT Press, 2009), pp.83–112.

Richmond, Anthony E., *Migration and Race Relations in an English City: A Study in Bristol* (London: Oxford University Press for the Institute of Race Relations, 1973).

Rodger, Richard, 'Slums and Suburbs: The Persistence of Residential Apartheid', in Philip Waller (ed.), *The English Urban Landscape* (Oxford: Oxford University Press, 2000), pp.233–68.

Rogaly, Ben and Taylor, Becky, *Moving Histories of Class and Community: Identity, Place and Belonging in Contemporary England* (Basingstoke: Palgrave Macmillan, 2009).

Samuel, Raphael, *Theatres of Memory Volume 1: Past and Present in Contemporary Culture* (London: Verso, 1994).

Sandbrook, Dominic, *Never Had It So Good: A History of Britain from Suez to the Beatles* (London: Abacus 2006).

Sandbrook, Dominic, *State of Emergency: The Way We Were: Britain 1970–1974* (London: Abacus, 2011).

Sandbrook, Dominic, *White Heat: A History of Britain in the Swinging Sixties* (London: Abacus, 2006).

Saumarez Smith, Otto, *Boom Cities: Architect Planners and the Politics of Radical Urban Renewal in 1960s Britain* (Oxford: Oxford University Press, 2019).

Saumarez Smith, Otto, 'Central Government and Town-Centre Redevelopment in Britain, 1959–1966', *The Historical Journal*, 58:1 (2015), 217–44.

Saumarez Smith, Otto, 'Graeme Shankland: A Sixties Architect-Planner and the Political Culture of the British Left', *Architectural History*, 57 (2014), 393–422.

Savage, Mike, *Identities and Social Change since 1945: The Politics of Method* (Oxford: Oxford University Press, 2010).

Schaffer, Gavin and Nasar, Saima, 'The White Essential Subject: Race, Ethnicity, and the Irish in Post-war Britain', *Contemporary British History*, 32:2 (2018), 209–30.

Schofield, Camilla, *Enoch Powell and the Making of Postcolonial Britain* (Cambridge: Cambridge University Press, 2013).

Scott, James C., *Seeing Like a State: How Certain Schemes to Improve the Human Condition Have Failed* (New Haven: Yale University Press, 1998).

Scott, Peter, *The Making of the Modern British Home: The Suburban Semi and Family Life between the Wars* (Oxford: Oxford University Press, 2013).

Shapely, Peter, 'The Entrepreneurial City: The Role of Local Government and City-Centre Redevelopment in Post-War Industrial English Cities', *Twentieth Century British History*, 22:4 (2011), 498–520.

Shapely, Peter, *The Politics of Housing: Power, Consumers and Urban Culture* (Manchester: Manchester University Press, 2007).

Shapely, Peter, Tanner, Duncan and Walling, Andrew, 'Civic Culture and Housing Policy in Manchester 1945–79', *Twentieth Century British History*, 15:4 (2004), 410–34.

Shaw, Eric, *Discipline and Discord in the Labour Party: The Politics of Managerial Control, 1951–87* (Manchester: Manchester University Press, 1988).

Simon, Gunn, 'People and the Car: The Expansion of Automobility in Urban Britain, c.1955–70', *Social History*, 38:2 (2013), 220–37.

Simmonds, Alan G. V., 'Conservative Governments and the New Town Housing Question in the 1950s', *Urban History*, 28:1 (2001), 65–83.
Simmonds, Alan G. V., 'Raising Rachman: The Origins of the Rent Act, 1957', *The Historical Journal*, 45:4 (2002), 843–68.
Smith, Roger, 'Multi-Dwelling Building in Scotland 1750–1970: A Study based on Housing in the Clyde Valley', in Anthony Sutcliffe (ed.), *Multi-storey Living: The British Working-class Experience* (London: Croom Helm, 1974), pp.207–38.
Smyth, J. J., *Labour in Glasgow, 1896–1936: Socialism, Suffrage, Sectarianism* (East Linton: Tuckwell Press, 2000).
Stacey, Margaret, *Tradition and Change: A Study of Banbury* (Oxford: Oxford University Press, 1960).
Sutcliffe, Anthony (ed.), *Multi-Storey Living: The British Working-Class Experience* (London: Croom Helm, 1974).
Sutcliffe, Anthony, 'Introduction', in Anthony Sutcliffe (ed.), *Multi-Storey Living: The British Working-Class Experience* (London: Croom Helm, 1974), pp.1–18.
Sutcliffe, Anthony and Smith, Roger, *History of Birmingham, Volume III: Birmingham 1939–1970* (London: Oxford University Press, 1974).
Swenarton, Mark, 'Developing a New Format for Urban Housing: Neave Brown and the Design of Camden's Fleet Road Estate', *The Journal of Architecture*, 17:6 (2012), 973–1007.
Swenarton, Mark, Avermaete, Tom and van den Heuvel, Dirk (eds), *Architecture and the Welfare State* (Abingdon: Routledge, 2015).
Szreter, Simon, 'Health, Class, Place and Politics: Social Capital and Collective Provision in Britain', *Contemporary British History*, 16:3 (2002), 27–57.
Thomas-Symonds, Nicklaus, *Nye: The Political Life of Aneurin Bevan* (London: I.B. Tauris, 2016).
Thompson, E. P., *The Making of the English Working Class* (London, 1980), First published 1963.
Tichelar, Michael, 'The Conflict Over Property Rights during the Second World War: The Labour Party's Abandonment of Land Nationalization', *Twentieth Century British History*, 14:2 (2003), 165–88.
Tichelar, Michael, 'The Labour Party and Land Reform in the Inter-War Period', *Rural History*, 13:1 (2002), 85–101.
Tiratsoo, Nick, *Reconstruction, Affluence and Labour Politics: Coventry 1945–60* (London: Routledge, 1990).
Todd, Selina, 'Affluence, Class and Crown Street: Reinvestigating the Post-War Working Class', *Contemporary British History*, 22:4 (2008), 501–18.
Tout, Herbert, *The Standard of Living in Bristol: A Preliminary Report of the Work of the University of Bristol Social Survey* (Bristol: Arrowsmith, 1938).
Tranter, N. L., *British Population in the Twentieth Century* (Basingstoke: Palgrave Macmillan, 1996).
Turner, John, 'A Land Fit for Tories to Live In: The Political Ecology of the British Conservative Party, 1944–94', *Contemporary European History*, 4:2 (1995), 189–208.

Vereker, Charles, Mays, John Barron, Gittus, Elizabeth and Broady, Maurice, *Urban Redevelopment and Social Change: A Study of Social Conditions in Central Liverpool 1955-56* (Liverpool: Liverpool University Press, 1961).
Waller, Philip (ed.), *The English Urban Landscape* (Oxford: Oxford University Press, 2000).
Ward, Stephen V., 'Soviet Communism and the British Planning Movement: Rational Learning or Utopian Imagining?', *Planning Perspectives*, 27:4 (2012), 499-524.
Weiler, Peter, 'The Conservatives' Search for a Middle Way in Housing, 1951-64', *Twentieth Century British History*, 14:4 (2003), 360-90.
Weiler, Peter, 'Labour and the Land: From Municipalization to the Land Commission, 1951-1971', *Twentieth Century British History*, 19:3 (2008), 314-43.
Weiler, Peter, 'Labour and the Land: The Making of the Community Land Act, 1976', *Contemporary British History*, 27:4 (2013), 389-420.
Wetherell, Sam, *Foundations: How the Built Environment Made Twentieth-Century Britain* (Princeton: Princeton University Press, 2020).
Wetherell, Sam, 'Freedom Planned: Enterprise Zones and Urban Non-Planning in Post-War Britain', *Twentieth Century British History*, 27:2 (2016), 266-89.
Whiteside, Noel, 'Creating the Welfare State in Britain, 1945-1960', *Journal of Social Policy*, 25 (1996), 83-103.
Wildman, Charlotte, 'A City Speaks: The Projection of Civic Identity in Manchester', *Twentieth Century British History*, 23:1 (2012), 80-99.
Williams, Raymond, *The Long Revolution* (London: Chatto and Windus, 1961).
Willmott, Peter, *The Evolution of a Community: A Study of Dagenham after Forty Years* (London: Routledge and Kegan Paul, 1963).
Woolf, Myra, *The Housing Survey 1964 in England and Wales* (London: Her Majesty's Stationery Office, 1967).
Wright, Patrick, *On Living in an Old Country: The National Past in Contemporary Britain* (Oxford: Oxford University Press, 2009), First published 1985.
Yelling, Jim, 'The Incidence of Slum Clearance in England and Wales, 1955-85', *Urban History*, 27:2 (2000), 234-54.
Yelling, Jim, 'Public Policy, Urban Renewal and Property Ownership, 1945-55', *Urban History*, 22:1 (1995), 48-62.
Yemm, Rachel, 'Immigration, Race and Local Media: Smethwick and the 1964 General Election', *Contemporary British History*, 33:1 (2019), 98-122.
Young, Michael and Willmott, Peter, *Family and Class in a London Suburb* (London: Routledge and Kegan Paul, 1960).
Young, Michael and Willmott, Peter, *Family and Kinship in East London* (London: Routledge and Kegan Paul, 1957).
Zweig, Ferdynand, *The British Worker* (London: Penguin, 1952).

Index

Abel-Smith, Brian, *The Poor and the Poorest: A New Analysis of the Ministry of Labour's Family Expenditure Surveys of 1953–54 and 1960* 33–4, 128
Abercrombie, Patrick 39, 45, 53
   County of London Plan 44
Abrams, Mark 126–7
Addison Act of 1919 123
aesthetic(s) 13, 21–2, 24, 35, 37, 118, 141, 143, 148, 150, 155, 161 n.52
affluence/affluent 23, 30, 87, 117, 119–20, 122–31, 189 n.4
agricultural land 63–6
Allaun, Frank 18, 29–30, 34–5, 57, 67, 84, 86, 103–4, 110, 151
Amalgamated Society of Woodworkers 58
amenities 8, 19, 26, 41, 47, 49, 94, 104, 117, 146–7, 149
   modern 108, 119, 141, 143–5, 148, 150
anti-municipalization 74, 97
anti-racism/anti-racist 26–9. *See also* race/racism
anti-suburban 138
architectural modernism 4, 117, 140–9, 153
ascot 117, 189 n.1
Association of Land and Property Owners (ALPO) 91, 97
Attlee, Clement, government of 17, 19, 43, 65, 109, 124

back-to-back houses/housing 6, 18, 20
Baldwin, Peter, statutory generosity 82, 87
Ballard, J. G., *High Rise* 161 n.52
Barham, Harry 56
Barnett, M. J. 99
Barons Court Citizen 22
Barton Hill, Bristol 23, 139, 151, 198 n.1
Barton, Oxford 133–4
Basildon 46–7, 61
Beaconsfield Buildings, Islington 24

Becontree estate, Dagenham 137
Bennett, Thomas 49
Benn, Tony 151
   Years of Hope: Diaries 1940–1962 198 n.1
Berman, Marshall 3–4, 41, 153–4
Bermondsey 57, 135, 193 n.98
Bethnal Green 121, 134–8, 154
Bevan, Aneurin 56, 65, 73, 78, 107, 109
   In Place of Fear 2–3
Bevan House 118
Beveridge, William 15, 45
   Beveridge Report 2, 18
The Bill TV series 161 n.52
Birmingham 3, 6, 29, 45, 47, 51, 104, 130
   Birmingham Borough Labour Party 45, 53–4, 74, 107, 119, 142, 146, 152
      recruitment leaflet by (1955) 74, 76
   Birmingham City Council 26, 90–1, 110
   Birmingham Trades Council 54
   cost of average council flat in 67
   Irish immigrants in 26
   Ladywood estate 198 n.12
Black immigrants 26
Black, Lawrence 5, 120
Blatchford, Robert 43
Bonnesen, Kathë 145
bourgeois 35–6, 43, 82, 118–20, 134
Brack, Harry 35–6
Braddock, Tom 18, 39, 43, 78, 112, 124
Bradford 29, 47, 51, 146
Bramley, Ted 44, 48, 119
Braydon Road 133
Bristol 16–17, 22–3, 26, 47–8, 110, 132, 151
   Bristol City Council 54
British-Soviet Friendship Society (BSFS) 55, 80, 144
Brooke, Stephen 44, 119
Brown, Douglas 15, 18, 65, 122, 142

Buchanan, Colin
    Buchanan Report 51
    Traffic In Towns 51
Buettner, Elizabeth 28
Building Research Station 55
built environment 2, 8, 13, 72, 116, 127, 155
Bunton, Sam, Jr 57
Butler, Lise 118

Cabinet Housing Committee 59
Calder, Ritchie, *Science and Socialism* 6–7, 55
Cambridge 35
Camden Borough Council 54
Campaign against Racial Discrimination (CARD) 28
Canonbury 35–6
Carter, Harold, 'Building the Divided City' 164 n.76
Caruth, Florence 21–2
Casson, Hugh 152
Castlemilk estate 139
Cathy Come Home television play 34
Central Land Board 65
Challenge to Britain policy statement 65, 92, 107
Chambers, R. 102
Chartist movement of 1840s 63
Chartist settlement of Dodford in Worcestershire 42
Chesworth, Donald 27, 29
citizenship, British 25, 133
A City Speaks film 143
Civic Amenities Act of 1967 36
Clapham Labour Party 142
Clapson, Mark 46, 138
class 7, 13, 21, 35–6, 76–7, 82, 85, 95, 112–13, 117–20, 122–31, 134–6, 149. *See also* working-class
collectivism 9, 58
Commonwealth Immigrants Act (1962) 27
Communist Party of Great Britain 53, 142
communitarian/communitarianism 37, 42, 119, 133, 135–6, 140
community 13, 43, 118, 120–1, 131, 135–7, 140, 149
    artificial community 120
    community action 36, 61

community spirit 132–4, 136, 138
    failed community 123
    political communities 131
Community Development Projects 34, 36, 61
Community Land Act of 1976 70
comprehensive redevelopment programmes 2, 34–5, 64, 153
Conservative Research Department 122
Conservatives/Conservatism 3, 6–7, 10–11, 17, 19–20, 24, 27–8, 31–2, 50, 52–3, 56, 58–9, 62, 66, 70, 73, 75, 77–9, 81, 84–5, 88, 91, 94–5, 100–1, 105–6, 110, 112, 123–4, 127, 149, 153, 155
Copeland, Jean 73
Copenhagen 144, 147
Coppock, Richard 56–7
Corbyn, Jeremy 10, 114
cottages 12, 15, 23, 36, 48, 108, 133
    cottage estates 43, 53–4, 132, 147–8
    workers' cottages 117–18, 155
council estates/housing 6–8, 10, 19–20, 26–7, 29–30, 35, 39, 42–3, 46–7, 49, 58, 69, 73–4, 93–4, 101, 107, 110, 112–15, 119–20, 123–7, 128–31, 134–6, 150
    failed community 123
    paternalistic 123
    rents/rental system 77–88
Council of Industrial Design 143
council tenants 13, 61, 82, 84–7, 100, 109, 112. *See also* tenants
Coventry 43, 51, 59, 67, 120, 133, 138, 142
Covid-19 pandemic 155
Crane, Peggy 79–80, 83–4
Crawley 46–7, 49
    Crawley Development Corporation 49
Crosland, Anthony 6, 82, 119, 123
    The Future of Socialism 5, 95, 125, 140–1, 157 n.27
Crosland, C. A. R., *The Conservative Enemy: A Programme of Radical Reform for the 1960s* 63, 68
Crosland, Tony 37, 75, 89, 111, 114–15, 153
    Conservative priorities 115
Crossman, Richard 31–2, 34–5, 58–9, 69, 85–6, 103–5, 126
cul-de-sac design 133
Cullingworth, Barry 49, 96, 111

Dallas, George 65–6
Dalton, Hugh 78
Daunton, Martin 4, 74, 103, 154
Davies, Aled, sales activism 110
Davies, J. G. 100–1
Davis, John 65, 95, 106
Debden 121, 135
Dell, Edmund 20–1, 82–3, 87
Denington Committee (1966) 32
Dennis, Norman 23, 108, 139
  study on Sunderland Cottages 20
deprivation 79, 115, 129, 148, 150
Devanny, Patrick 55
developmental social politics 8–9
Development Corporation of Basildon New Town 61
Development Corporations 12, 46–7, 49, 57, 61, 136
Dickens, Harry 97, 108, 115
  Whose Home? 88
dilapidated houses/properties 1, 21, 26, 88, 91, 95, 98
direct labour 56–9
dispersal of population 44–5
Donnison, David 84–5, 111
  The Government of Housing 32
Dorling, Danny 11, 74
Drucker, Henry 4, 71–2, 151
Duff, Peggy 33, 83–4
Dunleavy, Patrick 31
  The Politics of Mass Housing in Britain, 1945-75: A Study of Corporate Power and Professional Influence in the Welfare State 2

economic crisis 59–60
economic rents 80, 82, 84–7
The Economist 98
Edmonton Borough Council 57
egalitarian 4–5, 25, 111, 130
Elvin, George 55
embourgeoisement 122, 126
employment 28, 36, 46, 49–50, 56–7, 66, 74, 120, 124
England 4, 9, 16, 19, 32, 41, 44, 48–9, 77, 89, 118
An Englishman's Home pamphlet 143
English Sovereign Land Trust 70
Esping-Andersen, Gøsta 8

Evans, Gillian, The Aboriginal People of England": The Culture of Class Politics in Contemporary Britain' 193 n.98
Eversley, David 81–2, 93–4, 100, 105, 108
  grand-parental system of finance 108
Exchequer 46, 78–80, 112

Fabian 7, 37, 50, 56, 128–9
Facts on Housing pamphlet 32
Finnimore, Brian 2, 59–60, 141
First World War 16, 43, 91. *See also* Second World War
Firth, Raymond 135, 137
Flinn, Catherine, *Rebuilding Britain's Blitzed Cities: Hopeful Dreams, Stark Realities* 160 n.43
Foley, Maurice 26
Forshaw, John, *County of London Plan* 44
Forward 65–6, 92, 143
Fox, W. E. 66
Francis, Martin 5, 107
free market 92, 95, 113–14

Gaitskell, Hugh 5, 62, 69
Garden City Movement 42–3, 45, 64, 118, 121, 131
gardens 6, 42–3, 54, 118–19, 132–4, 142, 148
Gavron, Hannah 137, 194 n.154
Geddes, Patrick 43
gender 7, 143
general elections, Labour and 10, 19, 21, 27, 31, 37, 58, 91, 94, 99, 106, 112, 120, 126, 130, 155
Generation Rent 10, 114, 116
gentrification 35–6, 154
Georgian villa 155
ghettoes 130
Gibson, Geoffrey 126, 136, 138
Gilroy, W. J. 81
ginger group 97
Glasgow 3, 15, 43, 45, 57, 90, 139
  Glasgow Rent Strike (1915) 90
Glass, Ruth 35, 120–1, 132
Glendinning, Miles 35, 40, 43, 136, 141
  subsidy manipulations 60
  Tower Block: Modern Public Housing in England, Scotland, Wales and Northern Ireland 2, 9

Goff, T. H., 'The Housewife in Labour Sweden' 144
Goldberg, Jack 22
Gold, John 4, 40, 59, 142
Gordon Walker, Patrick 27
Goss, Sue 24, 122, 149
Greater London 32–3, 101
Greater London Council (GLC) film 1–2, 156 n.1
great landowners 63, 65
Greenhalgh, James, *Reconstructing Modernity: Space, Power and Governance in Mid-Twentieth Century British Cities* 8
Greenwood Act. *See* Housing Act (1930)
Greenwood, Anthony 59, 70, 94, 104, 110
Greenwood, Walter
  birthplace being bulldozed in Salford 34
  Love on the Dole 16
Gregory, Bob 57
Greve, John 23, 96
Griffiths, Clare 62, 64, 165 n.90
Griffiths, Peter 27–8
grimy houses 15–16
Grindrod, John 11
guerrilla war 65
Guide to Post-War Housing Policy (1948) 19, 107
Gyford, John 61

Hall, Crosbie M. 55
Hanley, Lynsey 11, 125
Harloe, Michael 58
Harlow 47–8
Harry Brown film 161 n.52
Hatherley, Owen 11, 37, 118
Heffer, Eric 58
Hennessy, Peter 10
high-rise flats/housing 1–2, 7, 10, 12, 31, 34, 52–61, 122, 138–40, 145–6, 150–1. *See also* low-rise flats
Hilton, William 86, 112
Hoggart, Richard 39, 49, 121, 137, 140
  reference to Hunslet 39, 140, 168 n.3
  The Uses of Literacy 168 n.3
Hoggartsville 137, 140
Holland, Milner 34, 101
Holmans, A. E., *Historical Statistics of Housing in Britain* 178 n.5

Homes for the Future policy statement 21, 54, 94, 108
Hook, Hampshire 50
Hough, Eddie 100
Houghton, Sowerby Douglas 23, 25
house building 10, 17, 19–20, 30–1, 35, 37, 44, 48, 54, 59–60, 66, 79, 81, 90–1, 129
House Condition Survey 32
Housing Act (1930) 17
Housing Act (1935) 17, 80, 124
Housing Act (1936) 22, 109
Housing Act (1946) 19, 78
Housing Act (1949) 19, 79, 91
Housing Act (1952) 79
Housing Act (1954) 79, 92–4
Housing Act (1956) 21
Housing Act (1957) 95
Housing Act (1980) 87, 113
Housing and Planning after the War policy statement 45
Housing and Planning Sub-Committee, NEC 64, 121
housing as social services 77–88, 105, 110
  failure of 113–16
housing crisis 9–10
housing estates 1–2, 10, 13, 46–8, 120–1, 134, 140, 146, 161 n.52
Housing Finance Act of 1972 87
housing improvements 21–2, 24, 34, 89–92, 94, 98–102, 104, 118, 121–2, 125, 148
  1964–70 30–7
Housing Policy Study Group of NEC 35, 60, 68–70, 86, 94, 104, 112
Housing Repairs and Rents Act (1954) 20
Housing Revenue Account 84
housing stock 16–17, 54, 58, 88, 91, 95, 104, 106, 108, 115
Howard, Ebenezer, *To-Morrow: A Peaceful Path To Real Reform* 42–3
100 Questions Asked and Answered on Labour's Housing Policy policy pamphlet 98–9

ideal environments 71–2
Immediate Programme (1937) 64
immigrants 26–9, 33, 129–30
improvement grant system 19, 33, 35. *See also* housing improvements

inadequate housing 5, 15, 18–19, 44, 53, 100
Indian Workers' Association 28
individualism 118, 133
Industrial England 16, 41, 71
industrialised building technique 31, 56–8
Industrial Revolution 15, 18, 21, 39, 42, 89, 152
industrial slums 16
Ireland/Irish 25–6, 118
Islington 35–6
   Beaconsfield Buildings 24
   Victorian Packington Estate, redevelopment of 35

Jackson, Ben 5, 76, 106
Jackson, Rose 30
Jacobs, Jane 43, 50–1, 153–4
   against urban motorway construction 51
Jay, Peggy 135
Jenkins, Roy 28
Jennings, Hilda 23, 139, 198 n.1
Jephcott, Pearl, *Homes in High Flats* 139–40, 146–7
Jevons, Rosamund 48, 121, 132
Jones, Ben 27, 110, 119, 123, 140
Jones, Mervyn 49, 96
Jones, Owen, *Chavs: The Demonization of the Working Class* 76
Jones, Price 82–3
Jones, Silvan 115
Joseph Rowntree Trust 147
Jupp, James 29

Karl-Marx Hof estate, Red Vienna 53, 132
Kearns, Ade 139–40
Kebbell, E. 146
Khrushchyovka 55
Killick, A., 'participation' 61
Kuper, Leo 120, 138
   privacy 133

Labour Organiser 96
Labour Party Research Department (LPRD) 24, 121, 127, 146
Labour's Immediate Programme policy statement (1937) 62

Labour's Northern Voice 20, 22, 34, 69, 82, 85, 92, 98, 100, 107, 110, 115, 151
Labour's Plan for Old Houses 25, 101, 146
Labour's Voice 29, 57, 66
Labour Woman 18, 21, 23, 25, 49, 58, 80–2, 102, 128, 136, 143–8, 151
Lambeth 61, 80
land acquisition, compensation for 62, 64–5
The Land and the National Planning of Agriculture document 63–4
Land Commission 62–3, 67–70
land control, politics of 40, 62–71
landlords 10, 13, 16, 18, 21–4, 26, 31, 33, 35, 62, 65–6, 75, 151. *See also* tenants
   bucket-shop landlord 93–4
   business as landlords 96
   private landlord/landlordism 10, 16, 21, 23–4, 33, 66, 74–6, 88–105, 114–15, 155, 178 n.9
   public landlord 87, 98
   registration for 101, 104
   slum landlords 18, 26, 88, 90, 92, 98, 101, 114
land nationalisation 62–6, 70. *See also* nationalisation
landowners 64–5, 67–70
   great landowners 63, 65
land question 63
Langhamer, Clare 119, 138, 141
Lansbury Estate, Poplar 142, 144
Latour, Bruno 4, 6
Lawrence, Jon 107, 118–19, 125, 133, 135
Lears, Jackson 154
Leeds 15, 24, 31–2, 34, 80
   Hunslet 39
   Leeds City Council 24, 31, 53
legislation 17, 20, 22, 28, 33, 62, 90
Leisure for Living policy statement 40–1
Let Us Face the Future manifesto (1945) 62, 121
Liberal Party 63
   Liberals 19, 27, 63, 65, 193 n.8
Lindgren, George 46
Linehan, Thomas 4
Ling, Arthur 142
Liverpool 32, 50, 128, 137

local authorities 1, 6, 17, 19–21, 30–1, 41, 48–9, 52, 56–7, 59–62, 64–7, 70, 73, 78, 80, 83, 85, 89, 92–6, 100–1, 108–10, 123–4, 129, 134, 156 n.6
Local Government Sub-Committee of NEC 83, 99
Lodder, H. W. 84
London 1, 3, 16, 22–3, 25–6, 35, 43–4, 48–50, 53, 55, 57, 59–60, 67, 80, 88, 104, 120–1, 124, 135, 154, 156 n.1
London County Council (LCC) 32, 41, 43–4, 48, 50, 53, 131–2, 146, 156 n.1, 172 n.114
London Passenger Transport Board (LPTB) 48
low-rise flats 1, 12, 42, 54, 60, 133. *See also* high-rise flats/housing
Lowry, Ernest 27
Labour Party Research Department 23, 51, 54, 68–9, 80, 84, 98, 100–2, 104, 107, 112
Lubetkin, Berthold 12, 119, 161 n.58
Luton 125, 127

MacColl, James 35, 81, 86, 93, 95, 98, 107–9, 111, 125, 136, 147
Macmillan, Harold 79
  'Grand Design for Housing' 19–20
Madge, John 48, 121, 132
Malcolm X 28
Malpass, Peter 90, 106
  moderated market rents 103
Manchester 3, 8, 31, 43, 46, 162 n.8
Marsh, Arthur 20, 82, 125
Martin, Kingsley 124
Marxism-Leninism 5
Mass-Observation 54
material modernity 117
McKibbin, Ross 5, 77, 124
McMillan, T. C. 146
Meades, Jonathan 10
Meadows, J. S. 6
Meek, James 113–14, 116
migrants/migration 15, 25–7, 29, 129
Mikardo, Ian 99, 109
Miliband, Ralph, *Parliamentary Socialism* 5
Millfield Residents Association 20

Milner Holland Committee 22, 32
Milton Keynes 8, 46, 76, 106
Mining Review cine-magazine 12
modern/modernism/modernity 2–12, 15, 18, 34, 36, 40, 46, 52–61, 71, 77, 102, 115–19, 151–4
  architectural 4, 117, 140–9, 153
  material modernity 117
  modern communities, designing 131–40
  modern housing 2, 10, 13, 40, 54, 82, 102, 115, 122–31, 133, 141, 146, 148–50, 161 n.52
  modern moment 2–4, 9, 11–13, 39–40, 42, 88–9, 113–14, 116, 142, 150, 154
  socialism/socialist 4, 105, 113
  urban 2–3, 7–8, 11–13, 28, 31, 37, 40, 71, 116, 148–9, 153–4
  welfare state modernism 40
Mogey, John 125, 133–4, 136
Moran, Joe 36, 189 n.5
Morgan, Kenneth 149–50
Morrison, Herbert 43, 48, 171 n.73
Morris, William, *News from Nowhere* 42
Mort, Frank 39
  progressive paternalism 122
mortgages 9, 74, 76, 82, 107–8, 112–13
  option mortgage 111
Moscow Trades Council 55
Moses, Robert 154
  'Lower Manhattan Expressway' 51
Mostyn, Lyn 96
motor cars 49
Mulberry Trust housing association 30
multi-storey flats 54, 119, 132, 139
Mumford, Lewis, *The Culture of Cities* 43
Munby, Denys Lawrence 92, 108, 111
municipal/municipalisation 6, 8, 18, 22, 29–30, 33–4, 41–2, 48–9, 57–9, 64, 68, 79, 84–5, 88–9, 92–4, 96–100, 102, 105, 107–8, 112, 124–5, 134, 144
municipal socialism 41
Muthesius, Stefan 22, 35, 40, 43, 60, 136, 141
  subsidy manipulations 60
  Tower Block: Modern Public Housing in England, Scotland, Wales and Northern Ireland 2, 9

Nairn, Ian, 'Subtopia' 47
National Building Agency 56, 59
National Building Corporation 56–8
National Council of Social Service 47
National Federation of Building Trades Operatives (NFBTO) 56–7, 173 n.144
National Federation of Property Owners (NFPO) 91, 97
National Health Service (NHS) 74, 78–9, 82, 114
nationalisation 5, 47, 56–7, 62, 64–6, 68, 78, 94. *See also* land nationalisation
Nationality Act of 1948 25
National Joint Committee of Working Women's Organisations 147
National Socialist Movement 27
NEC Home Policy (1960) 54
Newbold, H. E. 96
New Jerusalem 56, 142
New Left 27, 36
New Left Review 36, 126
The New Towns 12–13, 40, 45–53, 127, 138
Nicholas, Anthony 28, 33
Nichol, Muriel 143
Northern Ireland 9, 162 n.8
North Kensington Labour Party 69, 115
Notting Hill 26–7
    Notting Hill race riots (1958) 26
    Notting Hill Summer Project 29, 36
Now Britain's Strong Let's Make It Great to Live In manifesto 148
Nuttall, Jeremy 5, 7
    'Pluralism, the People, and Time in Labour Party History, 1931–1964' 158 n.36

O'Hara, Glen 63, 66, 69
old houses/housing 17–18, 21–2, 24, 31, 37, 54, 61, 101, 128
Old Houses into New Homes policy 34, 128
option mortgage 111
Ortalano, Guy 46, 106
    property-owning social democracy 76–7, 106
    Thatcher's Progress: From Social Democracy to Market Liberalism through an English New Town 8–9

orthodoxy/orthodox planning 51
Orwell, George 16, 48, 106, 108, 147
    Nineteen-Eighty-Four 133
    The Road to Wigan Pier 18, 122
Ossulston Estate, Somers Town 53
out-country suburban estates 46, 48, 131
overcrowd/overcrowding 15, 17, 19, 21–2, 26, 29, 41, 48, 52, 63, 135
overspill development 47, 49, 125, 139
owner-occupiers/occupation 13, 22–3, 39, 73–4, 76–7, 86, 88, 93, 100, 105–15, 127

Parker Morris Committee 145
Parker, Simon 172 n.114
Park Hill complex, Sheffield 122, 139, 147
paternalistic/paternalism 3, 17, 36, 61, 77, 120, 123
    fussy paternalism 136
    progressive paternalism 122
People's Pictorial 79, 132
peripheral housing estates 43, 47–9, 121
permanent dwellings 74–5
permanent ownership pooling 64
Peterlee, County Durham 12, 45, 49
Phillips, Morgan 98
Pilgrim, Edward, suicide of 69–70
Plan for Rented Houses 107
Plymouth 67
Pole committee (1944) 106
polemics 11, 16
politics of land control 40, 62–71
Pooley, Colin G., 'Commuting, Transport and Urban Form: Manchester and Glasgow in the Mid-Twentieth Century' 171 n.72
poverty 25, 29–30, 32, 124–5, 127–30
    poverty tenure 125
Powell, Enoch 87
    'Rivers of Blood' speech 28–9
pragmatic/pragmatism 2, 12, 40, 53, 63–4, 69, 94
prices, housing/land 10, 62, 65–7, 70–1, 90, 108, 114
Priestley, J. B. 44
    'industrial England' 16
    'three Englands' 41
privacy 133, 146, 149
private builders/developers 51, 57, 67, 69, 74, 79

private landlord/landlordism 10, 16, 21, 23–4, 33, 66, 74–6, 88–105, 114–15, 155, 178 n.9
private owners/ownership 19, 62, 77, 90, 92, 106, 112, 115. *See also* public owners/ownership
private property 88–106, 115
private rented housing/sector 10, 13, 16, 23, 29, 33, 35, 73–5, 79, 89, 91, 94–5, 100–1, 103–5, 114–15, 127–9, 155
'Profumo Affair,' scandal of (1963) 101
progressive design, politics of 140–8
property-owning (social) democracy 76–7, 94, 100, 105–6, 109, 111, 113, 115, 127
public housing 3, 7, 10, 13, 17, 19–21, 52, 74, 77, 79–80, 82, 85, 88, 90–1, 93, 109, 112, 114–15
public landlord 87, 98
public owners/ownership 30, 40, 62–4, 66–8, 88–105. *See also* private owners/ownership
Public Works Department 57
pubs 138

Quarry Hill Estate, Leeds City Council 53, 132

race/racism, housing and 7, 25–9, 129–30. *See also* anti-racism/anti-racist
Race Relations Act (1965) 28, 130
Race Relations Act (1968) 28, 130
Rachman, Perec 26–7
    Rachmanism 101–3
    Rachman scandal 33, 101
radicalism 5, 52, 89
rapid building methods 58
Ravetz, Alison 119
Reading Labour Party 96
reconstruction 4, 19, 44, 51–2, 62, 65, 146, 155, 160 n.43
redevelopment 2, 8, 11, 19, 36, 52, 54, 61, 67, 91, 139, 142, 153
    of Victorian Packington Estate, Islington 35
Red Road Estate, Glasgow 57, 139
Red Vienna 41, 53
rehabilitation 30–1, 35, 60–1

Rent Act (1957) 22, 26, 29, 33, 89, 93, 96–7, 99, 102–4
Rent Act (1965) 34, 93, 103
Rent Assessment Committees 103
Rented Homes Campaign 97, 100
Rent Mortgage Restrictions Act (1939) 91
rents/rental system 1, 10, 16, 22, 24, 29, 33, 74–5, 79–86, 101, 128
    council rents 85–7, 100, 111
    differential rents 80–4
    economic rents 80, 82, 84–7
    fair rent system 87, 89, 100, 103
    low rents 79, 81–2, 84, 92, 101, 115
    moderated market rents 103
    reasonable rent 84
    rebate scheme 80–6, 88
    rent controls 22, 26, 33, 74, 91–6, 101–3, 107
    rent-fixing process 104
    rent regulation 10, 34, 103–4
    socialist rent policy 80
'Repeal the Rent Act' slogan 103
Report of the Committee on Public Participation in Planning. *See* Skeffington, Arthur; Skeffington Report
residualization 87, 106, 117, 123
Revisionists 5, 67, 76, 82, 106, 111, 115, 119–21, 125–6, 135, 152, 157 n.27
Reynolds, Stanley 147–8
ribbon developments 44, 132
Richard, Ivor 103
Rieger, Bernhard 4
Right to Buy scheme 77, 109, 113
Robin Hood Gardens, Poplar 122, 172 n.97
Ronan Point block, Clever Road estate, collapse of 60, 148
Rose, Richard 126
Royal Institute of Chartered Surveyors 67
Rudling, Anna 144–5

sales activism 110
Salford 8, 16, 34, 57–8, 100
    Salford City Council 57
    Salford City Labour Party 100
Samuel, Raphael 7, 22, 36, 126–7, 148
Sandbrook, Dominic
    Never Had It So Good 189 n.4
    State of Emergency: The Way We Were: Britain 1970–1974 189 n.4

Sandys, Duncan 81
sanitary policy 19
Saumarez Smith, Otto 40, 59–60, 153
   Boom Cities: Architect Planners and the Politics of Radical Urban Renewal in 1960s Britain 8
Schneider, Frau 145
Schofield, Camilla 27
Science and Socialism pamphlet 6, 55
scientific socialism 7, 55–6
Scotland 9, 16, 118, 162 n.8
Second World War 17, 44, 62, 64, 90, 142. *See also* First World War
self-contained estates 46, 132
self-employed workers 57
self-sufficient villages 148
semi-detached houses 1, 47, 106
Shankland, Graeme 8, 17–18, 50
Shapely, Peter, *The Politics of Housing*: *The Politics of Housing: Power, Consumers and Urban Culture* 7–8
Sharp, Evelyn 35–6
Sheffield Council Housing Committee 57, 111
shortages
   of building materials 78
   of council houses 113
   housing 10, 16–19, 27, 54
Signposts for the Sixties 50, 67, 69, 111, 116
Silkin, Lewis 55, 68–9
Simmons, Jim 90–1
Skeffington, Arthur 61, 68
   Skeffington Report 61
slum clearance 1–4, 7, 10, 13, 15–17, 19–25, 28, 30–2, 37, 53–4, 57, 60, 80, 89, 95, 99–100, 119, 124–5, 129–30, 134, 146, 148, 162 n.8
slum house/housing 1, 6, 15, 17–18, 96, 99–101, 108, 114, 122, 151
   1945–64 18–25
   1964–70 30–7
   industrial slums 16
   race and squalor 25–9
   slum landlords 18, 26, 88, 90, 92, 98, 101, 114
   Victorian slums 92
Small Man, Big World pamphlet 134

Smethwick 27–8
   Smethwick Immigration Control Association 27
The Smethwick Telephone and Warley Courier 27
social cohesion 121, 131–2, 134
social democracy 8, 46, 124
Social Democratic Sweden 144
Social Democrat Party 41
social equality 82
socialism 4–7, 12, 18, 41, 44–5, 56, 82–3, 87, 116, 151–3
   communitarian 136
   modern architecture and 140–8
   municipal 41
   scientific socialism 7, 55–6
   socialist principles 45–52, 67, 82, 136
   socialist rent policy 80
Socialist Commentary 20, 23, 27, 46–7, 50, 79, 82–3, 103–5, 111, 115, 117, 121, 125–6, 128, 133–5, 147, 152
   'Face of Britain' 50–2, 62, 67–8
socialists
   modernism 4
   utopian 4, 121
social sciences, Labor and 131–40
social services 20, 29, 57, 73, 97–8, 108, 113, 125, 136
   housing as (*see* housing as social services)
Social Services Sub-Committee, NEC 65, 93, 129
Society of Labour Lawyers 105
Southampton 59, 104
South Wales 15–16
Soviet Union 41, 55
Sparks, Joseph 78
Stacey, Margaret 120
Staffordshire 27
Stark, James T. 55
St Ebbes, Oxford 125, 134
Stevenage Development Corporation 57
Stewart, Michael 69
Stoke Newington 30, 83
Stokes, Richard 65–6
St Pancras 26, 83–4
Strategic Land Use Planning Unit 70
structurally sound houses 19, 21, 23, 32–3

subsidies 17, 19, 21, 36, 59–60, 77–83,
    85–6, 91–2, 95, 100–1, 110–12,
    115, 145
suburbs/suburban housing estates 13, 26,
    41–2, 46–9, 53–4, 64, 118–19,
    121, 126–7, 131–40, 148
Sutcliffe, Anthony 119, 141
Sutherland, Mary 81, 147
Symon, Harold 97
Szreter, Simon 77

tax/taxation, land 62–3, 65–6, 69, 81–3,
    86–7, 95, 109, 112, 115
Taylor, Stephen 47
    on suburban neurosis 47
technology 7, 40, 53, 55–6, 120, 152
'Teddy Boys' gang, attacks on Black people
    26–7
tenants 2, 6, 10, 13, 18, 22–3, 26–7, 30,
    33, 35–6, 48, 69, 79, 85–6, 89,
    92–3, 95–6, 98, 101–4, 107–8,
    114–15, 129, 145, 150–1. See
    also landlords
tenements 1, 9, 15, 18, 24, 35–6, 44, 54, 88,
    118, 140–2
tenure, housing 37, 73, 77–8, 85–7, 89,
    93, 103, 105–6, 109, 114, 117,
    123–4, 129
    poverty tenure 125
terraced homes 1, 15, 22, 26, 35–6, 40, 51
Thatcher, Margaret 74, 109, 147
Thompson, E. P. 120
The Times 88, 98, 120, 152
Todd, Selina 125, 128
Tonbridge 30
Tory/Tories 19, 27–8, 47, 60, 70, 76, 78, 88,
    91–2, 94, 99–100, 105–7, 110,
    112–13, 115, 136
tower block 1, 10, 13, 52, 139, 147, 155
Town and Country Planning Act (1944)
    61–2, 64
Town and Country Planning Act (1947)
    62, 65–8
Town and Country Planning Act (1959)
    66
Town and Country Planning Act (1972)
    87
Town and Country Planning Act (1976) 70
Town and Country Planning Association
    32, 39, 45, 67

Town Crier 113, 152
Town Development Act (1952) 66
town planning. *See* urban planning
Townsend, Peter
    *The Poor and the Poorest: A New
        Analysis of the Ministry of
        Labour's Family Expenditure
        Surveys of 1953–54 and 1960*
        33–4, 128–9
    'We Cannot Have White Socialism' 29
Towns for Our Times pamphlet 40–5,
    50–1, 54, 67
trade union/unionists 29, 55–7, 80–1, 96
trams/tramway 43, 47–9, 171 n.72
transportation/transport policy 13, 47–52,
    71
Treasury 19, 60, 83, 95
Tribune 28–9, 33, 59, 61, 67, 83–4, 86,
    95–6, 102, 109, 112, 115, 145,
    152
Tudor Walters Committee (1918) 43, 131
    Tudor Walters Report 48, 118
Turnbull, Jean, 'Commuting, Transport
    and Urban Form: Manchester
    and Glasgow in the Mid-
    Twentieth Century' 171 n.72
Turner, John 123
Two to Five in High Flats survey 147

unemployment 12, 115, 124–5
unfit houses/housing 16–17, 19–23, 25, 30,
    32–3, 37, 95, 104
unified ownership of building land 67
United States, the 51
    Bronx, New York City 4
    Los Angeles 52
Unwin, Raymond 43, 118, 131
urban capitalism 44, 154
urban environment 1–8, 12–13, 21, 43–4,
    71, 77, 95, 105, 119, 153, 155
urban history 7, 12–13, 39, 154
urban modernism 2–3, 7–8, 11–13, 28, 31,
    37, 40, 71, 116, 148–9, 153–4
urban planning 8, 13, 39–45, 62, 64,
    121–2, 132, 146
USSR 55, 80, 144
Uthwatt Committee 44, 64

Vereker, Charles 137, 140
Vickers, James 23

Victorian 13, 16–17, 21, 30, 35, 37, 40, 46–7, 71, 89, 102, 115, 125, 131, 138, 148, 155
    Victorian architecture, reappraisal of 10, 35
Victorian Society 50
Victory for Socialism (VFS) campaign 108–9, 115

Wales 9, 15–16, 19, 32, 77, 89, 118, 162 n.8
Walters, Tudor 118. *See also* Tudor Walters Committee
Wardley, Stanley 51
Ward, M. J. 101
Warrington 46
wasting assets 108
Watling estate, London 120–1, 132
Weiler, Peter 19, 63, 89, 98
    'Orwellian memory hole' 70
welfare state 7–8, 15, 29–30, 40, 73–4, 77, 82, 100, 124, 127–9, 152
welfare state modernism 40
Welwyn Garden City 30, 42
West Ham 57, 59–60, 146
Wetherell, Sam 119
    Foundations: How the Built Environment Made Twentieth-Century Britain 8
Wheatley Act (1924) 56
Wheatley, John 63, 89–90, 117
    Eight-Pound Cottages for Glasgow Citizens 48, 118

White City Estate, Shepherd's Bush 53
Williams, Raymond 13, 131
Willmott, Peter 50, 93, 122, 125, 136–9
    Family and Class in a London Suburb 135–6
    Family and Kinship in East London 121, 134–5, 137
Wilson, Harold 31, 69, 102, 129, 151
'White Heat' 7, 30
Wolverhampton 28–9
Woodford 125, 135–6, 138
workers' cottages 117–18, 155
working-class 7, 13, 15–18, 21, 23, 36, 48, 51, 63, 77, 79, 82, 117–30, 134–5, 137–8, 140, 149, 154, 189 n.4. *See also* class
Wythenshawe 46

Yelling, Jim 19–20, 37, 90
Young, Michael 21, 35, 46–7, 54, 93, 117, 121, 125, 128, 131, 133–4, 136–8, 154
    community 118, 122
    Family and Class in a London Suburb 135–6
    Family and Kinship in East London 121, 134–5, 137
    and Taylor 47

Zweig, Ferdynand 130, 138

www.ingramcontent.com/pod-product-compliance
Lightning Source LLC
Chambersburg PA
CBHW052107300426
44116CB00010B/1571